KU-166-553

CLASSIC SHORT BREAKS IN EUROPE

Published by Thomas Cook Publishing
PO Box 227
Thorpe Wood
Peterborough
PE3 6PU
United Kingdom

ISBN 1 900341 36 0

Managing Editor: Deborah Parker
Copy Editor: Leyla Davies

Picture research: Image Select International
Additional picture research: Deborah Emeny
Cover and text design: Concept 5D
Layout by Concept 5D
Text typeset in Perpetua and Trajan
Repro and imagesetting by Fisherprint Ltd, Peterborough
Printed in Great Britain by Jarrolds Book Printing, Thetford

Written and researched by Jeff Evans
Additional research: Alun Evans

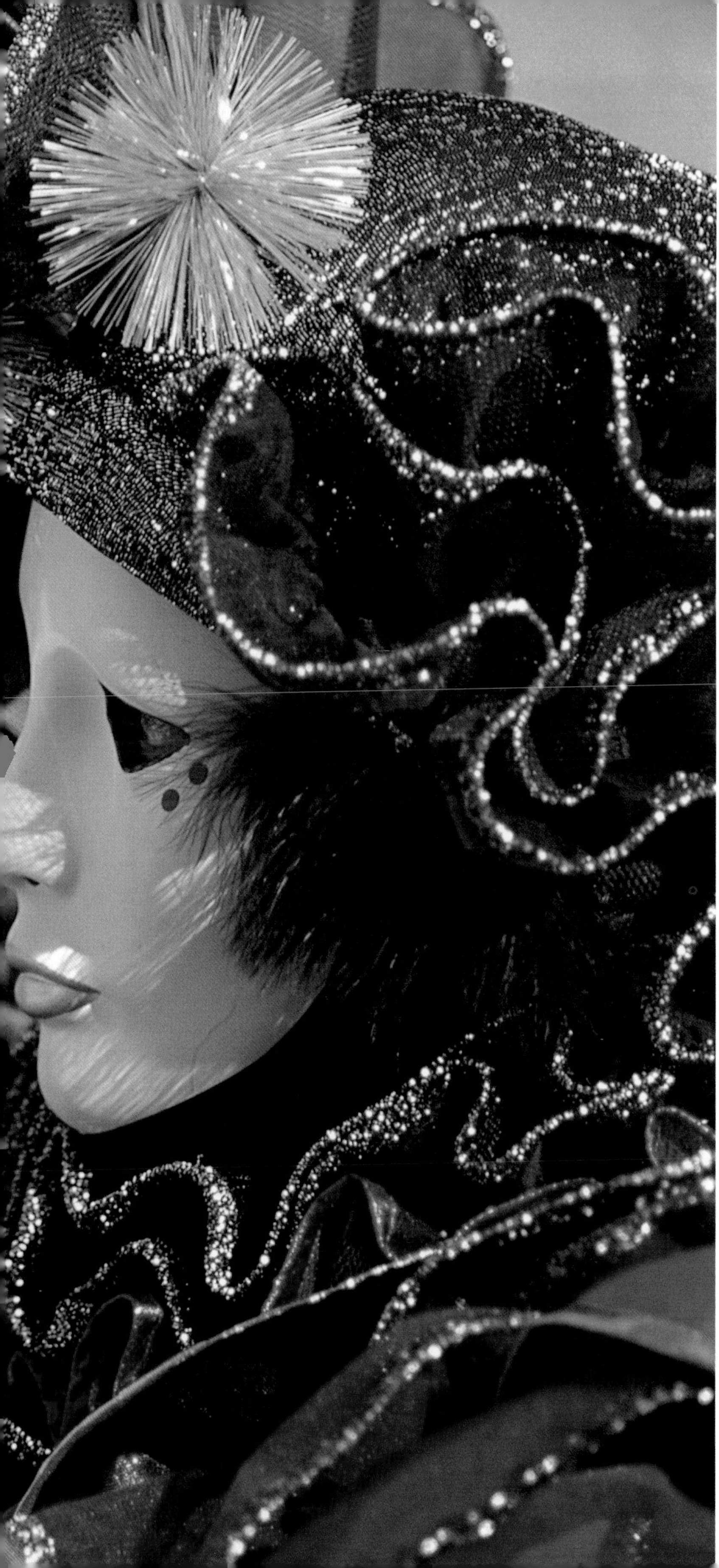

CLASSIC SHORT BREAKS IN EUROPE

JEFF EVANS

Thomas Cook Publishing

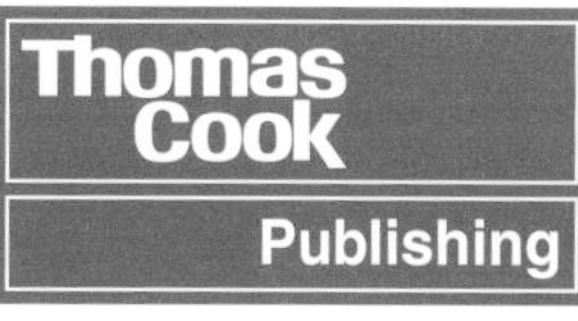

CLASSIC fM

CONTENTS

Taking a short break has become one of our most popular forms of holiday-making. A few days abroad can renew energy, rekindle romance or simply provide a convenient way of sampling places worth a longer return visit. All too often, though, the choice is limited to a few favourite cities – Paris, Amsterdam and Venice spring to mind. In reality, there are hundreds of other destinations which are suitable for that special break. *Classic Short Breaks in Europe* presents a wide selection of places to consider, mixing the deservedly well-known attractions with destinations you might not have previously considered.

I was particularly glad to see that Jeff Evans had included Granada in his selection. Ever since reading Laurie Lee's *As I Walked Out One Midsummer Morning,* I had been fascinated by Spain and, in particular, Andalucia. So when I joined Forces Radio in the early Seventies, I was delighted when they told me Gibraltar was to be my first posting. What they hadn't told me was that Franco had closed the border! Even more frustrating was that my wife and I had a flat with a beautiful view of the Iberian Peninsula. The only way to get to Spain was to take the ferry to Tangier and then another boat to Algeciras. So with a few days off we attempted this convoluted route. Our destination was Granada. It was October and the perfect time to be there, with lovely weather and very few tourists. It's a very charming historic cathedral city, easy to walk around, with a vibrant atmosphere because of the university. As an added bonus there's the backdrop of the snow-capped Sierra Nevada. But the main reason for choosing Granada was to see the Alhambra, the magnificent 13th-century palace built by the Moors to represent paradise on earth. I find that some sights are disappointing when you see them for real. Not so with the Alhambra. The magical use of space, light and water makes me think this is what the Hanging Gardens of Babylon must have been like. I can't wait to go back. Only this time I won't use two ferries to get there!

I hope that *Classic Short Breaks in Europe* inspires you. You may have always yearned to spend a few days in an historic city or a stunningly scenic region, or the descriptions and photographs within this book might prompt you to finally decide to visit that special place. And, unlike my convoluted journey to Granada, it tells you how to travel directly to your dream destination.

Nick Bailey

FOREWORD

INTRODUCTION

'You've never had it so good', were Prime Minister Macmillan's famous words some 40 years ago, words that ring true today as far as our holidays are concerned. Rising standards of living and diminishing travel costs mean that most of us are no longer content with one fortnight in the sun each year. If we don't manage a second major holiday, we do at least now look to take one or two short breaks. And with today's excellent transport connections, these short breaks do not just mean a weekend in the Lake District or the West Country, however lovely these may be.

Instead, we are looking further afield, certainly across the Channel, but increasingly to the margins of Europe – a Europe dramatically opened up by the fall of the Iron Curtain in the past decade. If we can get there in less than a day, that seems justification enough to pack our bags and go, even if only for a long weekend or a midweek break.

Having decided to take the time off and to go somewhere exotic, making the choice of destination may prove to be the hardest task. Now, in this one volume, the short break highlights of Europe have been drawn together, illustrated by words and pictures to show the vast array of destinations at our disposal and designed to whet the appetite for a new travel experience.

The following pages showcase 100 of Europe's top short break holidays. The big names everyone knows are all here – Paris, Rome, Amsterdam, Berlin and more – but you'll also find the hottest new destinations, such as Prague, Budapest, St Petersburg and the Baltic States. As well as famous cities like Madrid, Florence, Vienna and Athens, there are undiscovered gems like Dijon, Lucca, Kraków and the little Spanish city of Cáceres. Some selections are not even city-based, but centre on excellent regional options like Brittany, the Black Forest and the Peloponnese. From icy Reykjavík in the north, to baking Taormina in the south, there are holidays for every interest and for every time of the year.

The entry for each destination provides an outline of the attractions it offers, from the outstanding architecture, beautiful landscapes and fascinating museums to the quality and flavour of the local food and drink. A little background history helps put each venue into context, and there are suggestions for making the most of your visit. Major annual events are listed – fiestas, colourful medieval parades, arts and music festivals, and important sporting occasions – together with a brief indication of how to get to each destination and how to get around while you're there. There are even suggestions for hotels and restaurants that should make your visit comfortable and enjoyable. Four price categories are listed: *Very expensive* indicates a top-of-the-range, de luxe establishment; *Expensive* implies that the hotel or restaurant is first class, with all that entails; *Moderate* suggests a good, middle-range venue, while *Inexpensive* covers all hotels and restaurants priced below this level (but which very often prove to be a bargain).

All that remains now is to read on, make your choice and book your tickets. One of modern life's terrible, but immensely enjoyable, dilemmas – where to go for a Classic Short Break – has been resolved.

Jeff Evans

Austria divides holidaymakers. Very few see all the country: many make musical pilgrimages to Vienna or Salzburg; others take in the panoramas and the alpine air of the Tirol. One corner that is all too easily overlooked is the magnificent Danube Valley, which is quiet, fascinating and more than capable of giving the Rhineland a run for its money.

Some travellers may race through the valley on their way to better known attractions, but this region is worth a short holiday on its own. Rich and green, the valley's banks are strewn with vineyards and around nearly every bend sits a medieval castle or colourful abbey. Probably the best place to set up base is Linz, Austria's third largest city.

History and Culture

Linz, for all its comparative anonymity, has put down some serious historical markers. It was here, for instance, that Adolf Hitler grew up. Linz was also home to composer Anton Bruckner, who played the organ in the old cathedral. His resting place is in the stunning St Florian Monastery, 10 miles south of the city. The 17th-century astronomer Johannes Kepler was another resident. His work is commemorated in the city's planet fountain, representing all five of the planets known at the time. In recent decades, Linz has become known as an industrial city, but don't let that put you off. It is civilised and relaxing, with plenty of good hotels and restaurants. The local gourmet speciality is *Linzer Torte*, a

The highly elaborate baroque Benedictine Abbey at Melk was built in the early 18th century on the base of an 11th-century fortress. It dominates the town and appears rather at odds with the simple life of its monastic inhabitants.

DANUBE VALLEY

kind of Bakewell pudding, first produced here in the 1820s.

Sightseeing

In this distinctly baroque city, the main attractions are the Schlossmuseum, high on the hill, an exhibition of life in the region from the Middle Ages onwards. Two striking cathedrals, and the tiny, 8th-century Martinskirche – probably Austria's oldest church – provide the spiritual foundation. Another church worth a peek is the 18th-century Pöstlingberg, 1,600 feet up a hill and accessed by Europe's steepest mountain railway. At the heart of the city is the Hauptplatz, set out in the 13th century and harmoniously developed ever since. The ornate Holy Trinity Column has become one of the Linz's trademarks.

The meandering Danube takes you south-east from Linz and on into towns like Melk and Krems. The former is home to the wonderfully fanciful Benedictine Abbey, while the latter is a cobble-stoned gem of a town, with an excellent museum and some beautiful churches. Between the two are the remains of the castle at Dürnstein, where Richard the Lionheart was held captive in the 12th century.

Trains run up and down the valley, but one of the most popular ways to get around is to cycle. The Donauradweg cycleway competes with a leisurely boat cruise for the best way to take in the majestic scenery. If you decide to take to two wheels, just be careful not to be tempted into too many of the Heurigen, the wine estates which offer free tastings.

Danube Valley

Major Events

Urfahr Spring Market (early May): Austria's oldest fair, celebrating the onset of spring.
Linz Festival (May–June): festival of traditional and contemporary music and dance.
Cultural Summer (July–August): Serenade concerts at the Landhaus Courtyard and other musical and dramatic events.
Street Artists' Festival (July–August): annual international exhibition of street theatre.
International Bruckner Festival (September–October): annual homage to Linz's most celebrated son, prefaced by a laser show.
Urfahr Autumn Fair (early October): display of harvest bounty.

How to get there – and get around

By air: scheduled flights to Vienna (112 miles away) from Heathrow, Gatwick and Manchester (longest flight 2¾ hrs), then transfer by air (40 mins), or by rail (trains every hour, taking up to 2 hrs), to Linz. Free shuttle between Linz Airport and the nearest station, Hörsching. Hörsching to Linz central station then takes 11 mins.
Public Transport: Buses and trams serve Linz well and a 'Maxi' day ticket costs around ÖS36. The taxi service is adequate and fairly inexpensive.

Suggested Hotels

Hotel Schillerpark, Am Schillerpark.
Tel: (0732) 69 50 Fax: (0732) 69 509
Sumptuous city-centre hotel within easy striking distance of the railway station. Expensive.
Dom Hotel, Baumbachstrasse.
Tel: (0732) 77 84 81 Fax: (0732) 77 54 32
Well-situated hotel with the highest standards of service and facilities. Moderate.
Zur Lokomotive, Weingartshofstrasse.
Tel: (0732) 65 45 54 Fax: (0732) 65 45 55
Comfortable hotel close to the station. Moderate.
Weinerwald, Freinbergstrasse.
Tel: (0732) 77 78 81 Fax: (0732) 78 46 73
Homely small hotel just a few minutes from the city centre and the Danube. Inexpensive.

Suggested Restaurants

Kremsmünsterer Stuben, Altstadt.
Tel: (0732) 78 21 11
Winner of regular awards, renowned for its local and regional cuisine. Expensive.
La Cave, Römerstrasse.
Tel: (0732) 77 62 03
International cuisine in romantic surroundings. Moderate.
Kasper Keller, Spittelwiese.
Tel: (0732) 77 36 92
Traditional bierkeller and *wirtshaus*, offering a good range of beers and local speciality foods. Inexpensive.

INNSBRUCK

AUSTRIA

The western end of Austria is a world away from the power and grandeur of Vienna in the east. This is where the Austrian Alps take over, dividing the country from Italy to the south and Germany to the north. Between the mountains runs the River Inn, the centre-piece of a wide, flat valley. This stunning region is known as the Tirol and its capital, named after a bridge over the river, is Innsbruck.

History and Culture

The birth of Innsbruck as a holiday centre took place only fairly recently, largely thanks to its staging of the 1964 and 1976 Winter Olympic Games. But the city has a noble past. In the 16th and 17th centuries, Innsbruck was centre of the Habsburg imperial court and was endowed with architectural riches by its rulers. Before that, it was part of the main thoroughfare from Italy, picking up trade from its position just below the ancient Brenner Pass.

Innsbruck is steeped in the traditions of the Tirol, but it is also modern and cosmopolitan. Yodelling and thigh slapping are mostly confined to the tourist shows these days, but there's no getting away from the pervading alpine atmosphere in and around the city.

Sightseeing

Innsbruck is a compact city to tour. Almost everything to see is housed within the old town (Altstadt), where the focal point is without doubt the Goldenes Dachl (Golden Roof). This fancy balcony is not actually topped with gold but was covered with over 2,700 copper tiles in the 1490s. Behind it today is a museum of the Innsbruck Olympic Games. Also in the cobbled lanes of the Altstadt are the bulbous-domed Stadtturm tower, offering a wonderful view of the city, and the Hofburg Palace, an occasional royal residence with a remarkable ballroom. Across the way is the Hofkirche chapel, housing a gloriously overblown memorial to Habsburg Emperor Maximilian I. On the main street, Maria-Theresien-Strasse, two features stand out. The first is the elegant Annasäule, a memorial column to St Anne, commemorating St Anne's Day 1703, when the city was reprieved from attack by the Bavarians. The second is the Triumphpforte arch, initially planned to mark the wedding of the Empress's son, Leopold, but hastily redesigned to show gloomy funeral images on one side, after the death of her husband, Franz, during the celebrations. On this street, you can't fail to be impressed by the giant Nordkette mountain range, which looms up at its northern end. A series of cable cars can take you close to the snow-capped summit.

The Schloss Ambras, a short ride to the east on tram number 3, shouldn't be missed. This 16th-century Habsburg hunting lodge is now the area's foremost art gallery, home to works by the likes of Titian, Van Dyck, Rubens and Cranach. Excursions to the ski resorts of Kitzbuhel and Lienz, and to the mountain-top centre of Seefeld, are also easily possible, while for a more unusual attraction head south on the motorway towards Italy. You'll cross over Europe's tallest bridge, the Europabrücke, at 2,330 feet. For a better idea of the scale of this monster, come back to Innsbruck by the normal road and see the bridge tower above you.

Innsbruck has plenty of attractions and numerous artistic treasures, but it is easily covered in a day or two. With this in mind, it may pay to make your base out of the city, in one of the many small surrounding villages, like Igls, just 3 miles away. Not only are the hotels and restaurants better value, but you get a real feel for Tirolean life, and invigorating walks in the crisp alpine air. The hotels out here often dole out a guest pack with discounts for hiking and skiing.

Before you leave, one Innsbruck sight not to be missed is the Olympic ski jump, a couple of miles to the south. Climb to the top and try to imagine what was going through the minds of the Olympic jumpers, especially when at the bottom of the jump, way, way below, the only thing you can see are the gravestones of the city cemetery.

PREVIOUS PAGE: Innsbruck sits hemmed in by some dramatic mountains to the north and south. Often snow-capped, they seem to rise up from the end of the city's streets, like a giant wall of rock.

Innsbruck remains one of the best winter sports centres in Austria. Not only are the slopes good in each of the city's six skiing regions, but the views down over the city are remarkable.

Innsbruck

Major Events
International Accordion Festival (late May): gathering of accordion players from all over the world.
Austrian Alps Performing Arts Festival (June): two separate three-day festivals giving pride of place to local talent.
International Summer Dance Festival (late June–mid July): annual celebration of dance in all its forms.
Festival of Dreams and Innsbruck City Festival (early–July): musical extravaganza to celebrate the founding of the city.
Innsbruck Ancient Music Festival (July–August): early music, both sacred and profane.

How to get there – and get around
By air: there are charter flights (no scheduled) from several UK airports to Innsbruck Airport (3 miles out). Taxis into town cost around ÖS120; reasonably priced buses run every 15 mins. Otherwise, scheduled flights can be taken from Heathrow, Gatwick, Luton, Birmingham and Manchester to Munich Airport (longest flight 2¼hrs). Trains to Innsbruck from Munich Airport take 2 hrs.

Public Transport: Innsbruck has a good bus, tram and trolley-bus network (single fare around ÖS21; daily ticket ÖS45). Taxis are fairly expensive.

Suggested Hotels
Goldener Adler, Herzog Friedrichstrasse.
Tel: (0512) 57 11 11 Fax: (0512) 58 44 09
Interesting old hotel on the Inn river with an historical pedigree. Expensive.
Sailer, Adamgasse.
Tel: (0512) 53 63 Fax: (0512) 53 63 7
Popular hotel with good facilities, near the station. Moderate.
Sporthotel Igls, Hilber Strasse, Igls.
Tel: (0512) 37 72 41 Fax: (0512) 37 86 79
Attractive, alpine-style hotel with every facility. Expensive.

Suggested Restaurants
Restaurant Ottoburg, Herzog Friedrichstrasse.
Tel: (0512) 57 46 52
Traditional *'weinkeller'* serving regional and international food. Fairly expensive.
Stieglbrau, Wilhelm Greilstrasse.
Tel: (0512) 58 43 38
Quantity as much as quality when it comes to the Tirolean fare served here. Moderate.
Gasthof Sailer, Adamgasse.
Tel: (0512) 53 63
Hotel restaurant constructed from 17th-century Tirolean farmhouses. Moderate.

SALZBURG

Mozart's birthplace is probably Salzburg's most visited site. The great composer lived here for 17 years and now it is home to a Mozart museum, which features, among other items, a small violin he played as a child.

A town which gained its initial prosperity from mining salt is not a place you'd expect to be attractive to tourists. But that's exactly what Salzburg did: its very name means 'salt castle'. Apart from its beautiful, subalpine location, the city's redeeming factors for the holiday business are two-fold, and both are musical. Firstly, this is Mozart town, and you will never be able to forget that on your visit; secondly, they filmed *The Sound of Music* here. If you get carried away on a tide of Mozart melody and get your kicks from film-location spotting, Salzburg can be Heaven on Earth.

History and Culture

It's actually quite a shame that these two claims to fame overshadow the city to such a degree, for Salzburg is an atmospheric, absorbing place. The heart of the city is deeply religious, its skyline shaped by green copper church domes and sharp, piercing spires, a legacy of the Prince Archbishops who ruled the city in the 16th and 17th centuries. In the Altstadt (old town), you can hardly move for places to worship, most commissioned in an attempt to match the baroque glory of Christian Rome.

Sightseeing

Before beginning your sightseeing, indeed whilst planning your trip, consider buying a Salzburg or Salzburg Plus card. These offer deals involving all admissions, city transport, and even meals, accommodation and refreshments, for one set fee.

Salzburg is easy to explore. Most of the main sights are in the Altstadt, on the western side of the River Salzach, which carves its way through the city. Looming above the centre is the Festung Höhensalzburg. This well preserved

hill-top fortress was not designed for beauty, but rather practicality in times of turmoil. Here, the archbishops hid when the going got tough. Their weaponry and torture devices make grisly viewing. Below the fortress (a short funicular ride, if you don't fancy the walk) is its main architectural rival in the city, the Residenz, once home of the archbishops, and now including a gallery of notable artworks. Around it sit Kapitelplatz square, featuring a giant chessboard and a 17th-century horse trough fountain, the part-8th-century Franziskanerkirche, the highly ornate St Peterstift church and the beautifully proportioned Dom, Salzburg's cathedral, wonderfully restored since being bombed in World War II. It was here that Mozart was baptised and then became an organist.

The city honours its most famous son with Mozartplatz square, complete with chiming Glockenspiel clock, and three museums, one housed in his birthplace, plus, of course, many music festivals.

The Sound of Music connection goes back to the real life Von Trapp family who lived in the area. In 1964, Hollywood descended, the film was shot and Salzburg has not been the same since. Now conducted tours take visitors on a sweep of the main locations, but you can easily do them yourself, starting in the Mirabellgarten at the Schloss Mirabell, where Maria and the kids sang *Do-Re-Mi*. As part of the tour, you'll be taken out to the Schloss Hellbrunn. The Water Garden here is the main feature, but look for the gazebo where Liesl and Rolf (*16 going on 17*) began to get it together.

If all this music, makes you thirsty, take off for a coffee and an irresistible pastry, or try a local beer. Salzburg is known for its many beer gardens and there are no finer places for taking in the true atmosphere of the city. You may also want to nibble on some chocolate. The local speciality is Mozartkugeln, a filled confection, each piece graced with a portrait of the musical genius.

Salzburg

Major Events

Mozartwoche (late January): Mozart Week, featuring the Vienna Philharmonic and other orchestras.
Osterfestspiele (late March–early April): Easter classical music festival.
Pfingstfestspiele (late May): Whit Festival specialising in baroque music
Salzburger Festspiele (late July–late August): five glorious weeks of operas, concerts, chamber works and recitals - with Mozart never far from the scene.
Salzburger Marionettentheater (various times): famous puppet theatre 'productions' of opera, ballets and other stage works.

How to get there–and get around

By air: scheduled flights to Salzburg-Mozart Airport (2 1/2 miles out) from Gatwick (2 hrs). Reasonably priced buses to Salzburg centre run every 15 minutes during the day. Taxis cost around ÖS140.
Public Transport: Salzburg has convenient and cheap bus and trolleybus services (around ÖS18 flat fare, or ÖS38 for a daily ticket); taxis are fairly expensive, as are the horse carriages.

Suggested Hotels

Goldener Hirsch, Getreidegasse. Tel: (0662) 80 84 0 Fax: (0662) 84 33 49
Salzburg's premier hotel, situated in the centre. Very expensive.
Gablerbräu, Linzer Gasse. Tel: (0662) 89 9 65 Fax: (0662) 89 9 65 55
Well-appointed central hotel, close to the Mozarteum. Expensive.
Zum Hirschen, St Julienstrasse. Tel: (0662) 88 90 30 Fax: (0662) 88 90 35 8
Very comfortable, upmarket hotel, close to the railway station. Moderate.
Austria, Linzer Gasse. Tel: (0662) 87 23 13 Fax: (0662) 87 23 13 7
Value-for-money, central hotel with many facilities, but closed November–March. Inexpensive.

Suggested Restaurants

Gastof Auerhahn, Bahnhofstrasse. Tel: (0662) 45 10 52
Classy haunt of gastronomes. Expensive.
Zum Mohren, Judengasse. Tel: (0662) 84 23 87
Apparently favoured by the Mozarts, serving typical local fare. Expensive.
Der Wilde Mann, Getreidegasse. Tel: (0662) 84 17 87
Big portions are the order of the day in this meat-eater's delight. Moderate.

Music, bold buildings, coffee shops, pastries and yet more music. These are the images most people pin to the name Vienna. This famous city, once heart of a mighty empire, has grandeur written all over it – from the scale of its civic structures to the glory of its intellectual and cultural past. But Vienna is no museum piece: it is a thriving city which, while paying more than a little respect to its heritage, is not afraid to move with the times. In the State Opera House, for instance, you may just as easily hear the music of Bob Dylan as that of Beethoven.

History and Culture

From its origins as a Roman garrison town, Vienna began to prosper in the hands of the Babenberg dynasty. However, the period of greatest development and influence came with the Habsburg family, which took over the Austro-Hungarian Empire in 1278 and didn't relinquish its hold until 1918. Under the Habsburgs, Vienna became not only powerful, but fashionable too, home of musicians like Mozart, Beethoven, Schubert and Waltz King, Johann Strauss. Following the Habsburgs' demise, Vienna's fortunes changed. Hungary became a country on its own and the city was marooned to the far east of Austria. The isolation was increased after World War II, when the Iron Curtain was drawn at Vienna's back door and the city became almost a cul-de-sac of the Western world. With the demise of the Soviet bloc, however, and the relaxation of eastern borders, Vienna is once again becoming an international gateway.

Sightseeing

Vienna is an easy city to negotiate. The central area is pedestrianised and is enclosed by the cobbled Ringstrasse, a 2½ mile circuit of grandiose buildings constructed in the 19th century on the site of the old city walls. These buildings were designed by the Habsburgs to keep the restless population sweet, but, just in case the ploy didn't work, they made sure the Ringstrasse was wide enough to allow cannon to be moved quickly to the front line. The Ringstrasse is a good place to begin a tour. Here are the State Opera House, the Parliament, the City Hall, the University, and many more edifices, all monumental in scale but in differing architectural styles. Around here, too, are the excellent Natural History Museum and the Museum of Fine Arts, and the baroque Karlskirche. Within the Ringstrasse stands the Stephansdom, the city's cathedral, begun in the 13th century but finished much later. The shorter of its two towers has a lift but the views from the taller south tower – known as the Steffl – are better, providing the 343 steps don't put you off.

The Habsburgs made their home at the Hofburg, a sumptuous palace with over 2,600 rooms. Picking out highlights like the Treasury Room is the only way to do it justice. Other famous Viennese palaces are the Belvedere, now an excellent art gallery, and the Schönbrunn, a little way out to the south-west.

Back in the centre, the musically minded will not want to miss the Sunday morning service at the Hofburg Palace chapel, which features the famous Vienna Boys' Choir. Book if you want a seat; turn up about an hour before the 9.15 start if you are happy to squeeze in at the back. Equally famous are their Hofburg neighbours, the Lippanzer horses of the Spanish Riding School. These talented stallions are out of town in July and August, but you can catch their shows on weekends, and their rehearsals on Tuesday–Friday mornings, at other times of the year.

Vienna's splendid Karlskirche was the masterpiece of baroque expert Fischer von Erlach. It dates from 1713 and was commissioned by Emperor Karl IV in celebration of the city's deliverance from plague. It is dedicated to Charles Borromeo, a saint known for helping plague sufferers.

VIENNA

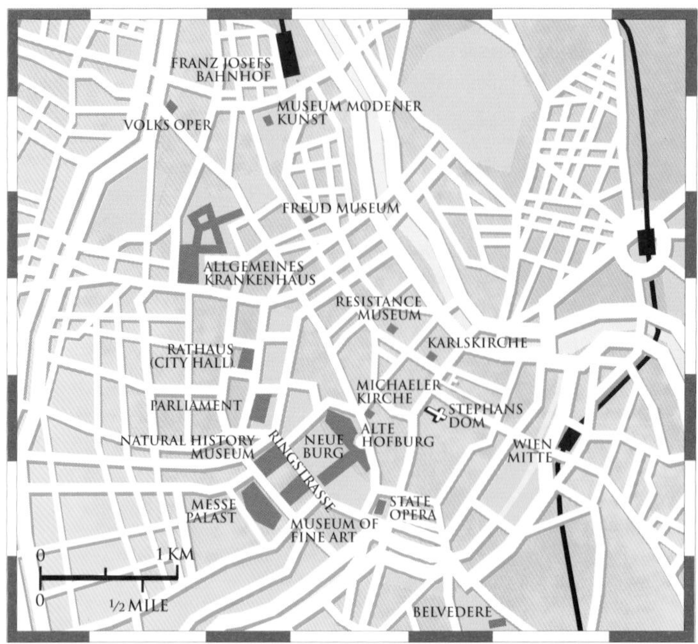

Vienna

Major Events

Viennese Dream on Ice (mid January–early March): skating on the square in front of the City Hall.

Grosser Wiener Faschingsumzug (mid February): the great Vienna Carnival procession.

OsterKlang (late March–early April): 'The Sound of Easter', classical music with top international performers.

Wiener Mozartwoche (late March–early April): Mozart Week.

Internationales Musikfest (early May–mid June): the international music festival within the Vienna Festival.

Summer Operas at Schönbrunn (mid July–late August): open-air performances of the great works.

Schubertiade (late August–early September): five nights devoted to Schubert.

How to get there – and get around

By air: scheduled flights to Vienna Airport (11 miles out) from Heathrow, Gatwick and Manchester (longest flight 2¾ hrs). Taxis to the centre, taking 20 mins, cost around ÖS350; buses, take 25 mins and cost around ÖS70; trains take 30 mins and cost around ÖS34.

Public Transport: Vienna has an extremely efficient metro (U-bahn)/tram/bus network '24-hr ticket ÖS50; 3-day ticket ÖS130'. Taxis are pricey.

Suggested Hotels

Imperial, Kärntner Ring.
Tel: (01) 515 160 Fax: (01) 515 165 50
Sumptuous hotel of the highest order – anywhere. Very expensive.

Hotel Intercontinental, Johannesgasse.
Tel: (01) 711 220 Fax: (01) 713 44 89
Modern, central hotel with all amenities, opposite the Stadpark. Expensive.

Kummer, Mariahilferstrasse.
Tel: (01) 588 95 Fax: (01) 587 81 33
Comfortable, first-class hotel near the main station (Westbanhof). Expensive.

Cima Cityhotel, Theresianumgasse.
Tel: (01) 505 16 96 Fax: (01) 504 35 52
Attractive, well-appointed hotel, near the centre. Moderate.

Suggested Restaurants

Drei Husaren, Weihburggasse.
Tel: (01) 512 10 92 10
Classic Viennese dining on a grand scale-gipsy music, too. Expensive.

Stadsbiesl, Naglergasse.
Tel: (01) 533 35 07
Bistro-style pub/restaurant with many rooms. Moderate.

Kornhäuslturm, Fleischmarkt.
Tel: (01) 535 59 36
Local and international dishes. Moderate.

RIGA

Riga's famous Freedom Monument, dates from 1935 but is now seen as a symbol for all Latvians who defied the post-war Soviet occupation. The cluster of stars above the head of the statue represents the regions of Latvia.

Riga, the capital of Latvia, is one of the great new tourism discoveries on Europe's eastern fringe. It has been variously described as a 'Little Paris' and a 1990s 'boomtown', such descriptions capturing in a nutshell the fine architecture there remains to see and the pace of change from Communism to market economy. The city knows where its future lies and welcomes visitors heartily.

History and Culture

Riga was founded in the early 13th century by a crusading German clergyman named Albert von Buxhoeveden. His town developed into an important merchant city on the Baltic, part of the Hanseatic League, but the German influence continued, even when the city fell into the hands of other powers. The Polish-Lithuanian Commonwealth, Sweden and Russia all dominated the city at various times until the end of World War I, when Latvia obtained short-lived independence. Devoured by the Soviet Union at the start of World War II, and overrun by the Nazis before the Russians returned, it took the Latvian people over 50 years to regain their sovereignty. That was in 1991 and Riga has responded strongly to the social and economic changes that have ensued.

Sightseeing

Riga has a smashing old town, hugging the bank of the River Daugava and divided in two by the street known as Kalku. All around are cobbled lanes, neat squares, old warehouses and 17th-century burgher houses with painted facades and playful sculptures. South of Kalku are the ancient St Peter's church, with a 200-foot green spire affording marvellous views over the

old town, and a museum chronicling the occupation of Latvia by the Soviets and Nazis. North of Kalku are even better sights. Riga's massive brick cathedral has walls nearly seven-foot thick and dominates an enormous cobbled square. Begun in 1211, it contains an elegant pulpit and a powerful organ with more than 6,700 pipes. Next door is the intriguing Museum of History and Navigation. On one of the town's most delightful streets, the Maza Pils, sit the three oldest houses in the country, collectively known as 'the Three Brothers'. Close to the river, Riga's castle was founded in the 14th century but has been rebuilt many times. Inside are the Latvian Foreign Art Museum (with some Flemish and German works), and the Latvian History Museum. However, the most impressive remnant of the old fortifications is the huge red brick Powder Tower, now a war museum.

Modern Riga is largely 19th-century, spacious and sedate, with wide, elegant boulevards and parks. The focal point is the 140-foot Freedom Monument. While in the new town, take the trolley-bus to the TV Tower for a wonderful view over the whole city and the wooded parklands which adorn it.

Riga is a treat for music lovers. The National Opera House has been undergoing major restoration, but both its company and the Riga Ballet, which normally performs there, are still active in other city venues, and the National Symphony Orchestra still performs at the Philharmonic Concert Hall. On the food front, there's plenty of local flavour on the menus – try bacon and onion pastries, cabbage soup, herrings, eels and other seafood, or roast suckling pig. Wash it down with the extremely popular local beer.

As you expect from this part of the world, the winter months don't make particularly good sightseeing weather. The best times to come are from May to September, and especially in June and July when you can bank on around 10 hours of sunshine a day.

RIGA

Major Events
Great Day (mid to late March): celebration of the spring equinox with lots of singing and beer-drinking.
Usini (mid April): pageant heralding the summer.
Jani (late June): John's Night, an ancient celebratory amalgam in homage to John the Baptist and the summer solstice, with fairs, feasting, bonfires and night-swimming.
Martini (November 10): festival on the eve of St Martin's Day, the patron saint of innkeepers, who shares his name day with Bacchus.
Christmas (late December): combination of Christmas and Yule (winter solstice) festivities.

How to get there – and get around
By air: scheduled flights to Riga-Lidosta Airport (5 miles out) from Heathrow and Gatwick (3fl hrs). There are also flights from Manchester, via Copenhagen or Stockholm. Buses (costing around 1 lat – approx. £1) or taxis (around 6 lati) run from the airport into Riga (15–20 mins).
Public Transport: adequate, reasonable bus/tram/trolley bus network.

Suggested Hotels
Metropole, Aspazijas.
Tel: 722 5411
Fax: 721 6140
Upmarket hotel in Riga centre. Expensive.
Rome, Kalku.
Tel: 782 0050 Fax: 782 0059
Luxurious hotel with German connections and high levels of comfort and amenities. Expensive.
Brigita, Saulkalnes.
Tel: (2) 623 000 Fax: (2) 623 190
Good, popular establishment a short trip from the city centre. Moderate.

Suggested Restaurants
Ziviju, Vagnera. Tel: 721 6713
Fairly new fish restaurant, but already with a growing reputation. Expensive.
Sena Riga, Aspazijas.
Tel: 721 6869
One of the best traditional Latvian restaurants in town. Moderate.
Andaluzijas suns, Elizabetes.
Tel: 728 9864
Popular café-bar frequented by locals. Inexpensive.

Tallinn's stunning cityscape, including the dominant Oleviste church, dedicated to King Olaf II of Norway. The church was once the place of worship for the city's Scandinavian community.

TALLINN

There's more to travelling behind the old Iron Curtain than the thrill of being somewhere that was out of bounds not so long ago. One of the other benefits is that, in some respects, time has stood still on the other side of the old political divide. It is this timelessness which makes Tallinn such an absorbing city, one you'll need at least two or three days to fully enjoy.

History and Culture

Seen from the Baltic Sea as a dark mound pierced with sharp Gothic towers, the city, upclose, emerges as a perfectly preserved Hanseatic town of the 14th–15th century. Its tangle of cobbled streets and distinctive red roof-line have barely been touched in the last century. Modernisation, as we know it in the west, has not diminished its beauty.

The Germans, the Danes, the Swedes and the Russians have all ruled over Estonia at one time or another. In 1918, the country became independent, but then the Nazis, soon followed by the Soviets, marched in. Only in 1991 did Tallinn once again find itself as capital of a free state. Forty-odd years of Soviet tradition cannot be wiped away overnight, but, strangely, Tallinn seems to have absorbed more from its earlier masters. Only 50 miles from Helsinki, the Scandinavian influence is still pronounced here. Estonia also experiences similar weather to that of its northern neighbours, so, for your visit,

remember the winters can be very cold and wet, but summer nights are long and bountiful.

On the cultural side, Tallinn is not short of opera and ballet of a high standard, and is particularly proud of its summer rock festival, but the most clearly expressed mode of relaxation here comes in the form of countless cellar cafés. Make sure you book a table if you set your heart on any particular establishment, as they are extremely popular. The cafés apart, nightlife is thin on the ground, although you could try a hotel nightclub.

Sightseeing

A meander around the Old Town (the 'Vanalinn'), is the best way to begin a tour of Tallinn's highlights. Climb the soaring Town Hall tower (the oldest building of its kind in Europe) for the finest panoramas of the city, or follow in the voyeur's footsteps at the Kiek-in-de-Kök ('Peek in the Kitchen') tower. This was so named because of its unrivalled view into everyone's homes in the 15th century. Dotted around are some marvellous churches. The Oleviste is the tallest and most striking; another, the Niguliste, houses a fragment of the *Danse Macabre* frieze by medieval artist Bernt Nothe.

The old merchant's houses reveal the comforts of everyday life 400 years ago, after which you should make your way up to the Upper Town (the 'Toompea'). Here, take a glimpse inside the ancient city cathedral, with its Scandinavian military tombs, and the Russian Orthodox Alexander Nevsky Cathedral – contrasting icons of past suppression.

The city's two levels are linked by two steep, disjointed streets: the Long Leg and the Short Leg. They have given Tallinn the nickname of the 'city which walks with a limp' – graphically accurate perhaps, but not a flattering description for a city with so much to offer.

Tallinn

Major Events

Rock Music Festival (July): week-long jamboree, offering a chance to see around 30 international bands and artists like Phil Collins and the Pogues have appeared in recent years.

How to get there and get around

By air: Scheduled flights to Tallin Airport (2 miles out) from Gatwick only (2 ¾ hrs). There are also connecting flights from Heathrow, Manchester, Newcastle, Glasgow and Edinburgh, via Stockholm, Helsinki or Vienna.Very cheap buses run regularly into the city, or take a taxi (around £5 – agree price beforehand).

Public Transport: Tallinn is easily explored on foot but has a good tram and bus network. Tallinn also has plenty of taxis and route-taxis, which travel set routes and stop on request. Tickets are sold by the driver.

Suggested Hotels

Olümpia, Liivalaia 33.
Tel: 6315 315 Fax: 6315 675
Excellent value, high-rise, 3-star hotel with satellite TVs, sauna and a choice of restaurants and bars. Ask for a room overlooking the Old Town.
Moderate–Expensive.

Palace, Vabaduse väljak 3.
Tel: 6407 300 Fax: 6407 299
Functional-looking, central, 1930s hotel, brightly decorated inside and offering a full range of services.
Moderate–Expensive.

Central, Narva mnt 7. Tel: 6339 800
Fax: 6339 900
Modern, renovated hotel, simply furnished but handy for the Old Town. Good private facilities; Italian restaurant.
Inexpensive.

Suggested Restaurants

Vanaema Juures, Ratatskevu 10/12.
Tel: 6313 928
'Grandma's Place' in English, serving homely Estonian cooking, such as Baltic herring and meatballs in sour cream. Look for the fried egg sign. Inexpensive.

Ervin's Tex-Mex Restaurant,
Tartu mnt 50. Tel: 6312 738
If the local cuisine doesn't suit, try this import which also has live music in the evenings and a children's play area.
Inexpensive.

Sanjay's, Rataskaevu 3/5.
Tel: 6440 254
Well-reputed Chinese restaurant in the Old Town. Inexpensive.

The amazing baroque interior of the Church of St Peter and St Paul in Vilnius. This exuberant place of worship dates from 1668. Italian sculptors were imported to decorate the walls, chapels and vaulted ceiling.

VILNIUS

A trip to Vilnius is a voyage of discovery. It's not the sort of destination that most of us know much, if anything, about. Shielded for so long from western eyes by the Iron Curtain, it conveys a sense of mystery. Vilnius will enthral anyone with a taste for history, its buildings testament to the struggles that have afflicted this little country for centuries. It will also entertain travellers in search of the exotic, for this is a land that is yet to fully embrace capitalism and all its familiar trappings.

History and Culture

Lithuania has been a crucible of conflict for nearly all its long life. The struggles here have been monumental: Paganism versus Christianity; Catholicism versus Protestantism; incursions from Poland and Germany; Russian domination; Nazi horrors; and Soviet brutality. Less than 10 years since it defiantly and bravely declared independence from the Soviet Union, Lithuania is only a toddler in the free world, torn between pushing ahead with painful economic reforms and backpedalling into the blinkered cosiness of communism.

Sightseeing

One of the first things that will strike you about Vilnius is the greenery. Ten big parks cover about half of the city, which was founded at the confluence of two rivers and is divided into Old and New Towns. The Old Town is full of magnificent old buildings, confirming the city's reputation as the prettiest of all three Baltic State capitals, but only one historic gateway (out of an original nine) still stands. Here, at the Gates of Dawn, you'll also find a rather unusual chapel, displaying a sacred image of the Virgin, which has long been a focus for pilgrimages. Near here is the baroque St Casimir's Church,

a place of worship for several religions since its construction in the 17th-century.

The city's spiritual heart lies in the mighty cathedral. The oldest church in the country, it was constructed in 1320 and has been a symbol of national hope in the many times of adversity. Its spacious square is dominated by a free-standing, leaning clocktower. From the cathedral, you can wander up to the tree-clad Gediminas Hill and its rather lonely tower. There were once two castles here, and the top of the tower now has a small castle museum, from which you are treated to a view of the city. You can also spy three white crosses in a nearby park. These commemorate Franciscan friars murdered by pagans in the 13th century. Not far from this shrine is the church of St Peter and St Paul, an exuberant display of baroque architecture, typified by the stunning works of 17th-century Italian sculptors.

For the best collection of art visit the Vilnius Picture Gallery, with its works from the 16th to the 19th century, or the Museum of Applied Art, displaying some fine tapestries and ceramics.

Aesthetics apart, it is the history of the people that shapes a visit to Vilnius. You must visit the KGB Museum in the New Town, where former prisoners reveal the worst secrets of the notorious undercover police force. Similarly, the State Jewish Museum and the Holocaust Museum will move you to tears with an account of how the city's Jewish population was viciously reduced from 100,000 to only 6,000 during the Nazi years. More recent troubles come to mind at the Parliament building, where the locals set up barricades to thwart Soviet tanks in 1991, and the TV Tower, which, at the same time, was stoutly, but vainly, defended against the Red Army.

Visiting these grim sites can deflate the holiday spirit but, when you see the resilience on the faces of the friendly locals, such defiant human spirit can warm the heart. The fact that this is a fun, informal city, after all the hardships, says it all. Take it at a leisurely pace. Wander through the winding backstreets. Pause for a cake and coffee at one of the many cafés. Pop into one of the burgeoning jazz clubs. Vilnius is no Disneyland, but it's beautiful and a real education.

VILNIUS

Major Events

Folk Group Festival (January): the best of Lithuanian folk music.

St Casimir Street Fair (March): traditional three-day craft fair.

Skamba, Skamba, Kankliai (late May): international festival of folklore.

International Street Festival (early August): pageants, drama, music and street fairs.

Vilnius Jazz (October): annual festival of avant-garde jazz.

How to get there – and get around

By air: scheduled flights to Vilnius Airport (3 miles out) from Heathrow and Gatwick (2 hrs 50 mins). Haggle over the taxi fare, but keep it below US$10. No. 2 bus links the airport to the city centre.

Public Transport: Most of Vilnius can be visited on foot – buses and trolleys can be unreliable and overfull, and taxis are expensive.

Suggested Hotels

Astorija Radisson SAS, Didzioji. Tel: (2) 22 01 10 Fax: (2) 22 17 62
Vilnius' premier hotel now restored under new ownership. Expensive.

Sarunas, Raitininku. Tel: (2) 72 38 88 Fax: (2) 72 43 55
Western-orientated and often busy. Expensive.

Lietuva, Ukmerges. Tel: (2) 72 60 92 Fax: (2) 72 21 30
Popular, upmarket hotel with a range of room prices. Moderate–expensive.

Karolina, Sausio. Tel: (2) 45 39 39 Fax: (2) 26 93 41
Comfortable hotel with its own Chinese restaurant. Moderate.

Suggested Restaurants

Lokys, Stikliu. Tel: (2) 62 90 46
Essential – if you fancy the Lithuanian delights of boar and elk. Expensive.

Pauksciu Takas. Tel: (2) 45 88 77
International cuisine in the TV Tower. Expensive.

Stikliai, Gaono. Tel (2) 22 23 18
French-biased food, but distinctly middle-European live folk music. Moderate.

If the stereotyped image of Belgium as a grey, boring country is imprinted on your mind, take a trip to Antwerp and be happily disabused. In its barest terms, this commercial port city on the border with Holland doesn't fire the imagination, but beyond the wharves, cranes and supertankers lies one of the liveliest and most pleasant cities in the country.

History and Culture

According to legend, the area around the city was once terrorised by a giant who cut off the hands of sailors who refused to pay tolls. The hands were then thrown away – *hand werpen,* in the local dialect – hence 'Antwerp'. The city has always taken full advantage of its position, close to the mouth of the Scheldt river (actually 55 miles inland), and has been an important harbour for centuries. In the 16th-century, it was the richest port in Europe. Despite the emergence of neighbouring Rotterdam, Antwerp's value has not diminished – this excellent access to the sea has meant that Antwerp has developed heavy, grimy industries like ship-building and petro-chemicals, but also the highly lucrative diamond trade.

Sightseeing

You can see diamonds being cut at the Provincial Diamond Museum and feast your eyes on mounds of the precious stones. Yet Antwerp's real pleasures lie elsewhere. It's a great little city, not overly attractive at first sight, especially

Antwerp's Town Hall and the Brabo Fountain, which is dedicated to the Roman Silvius Brabo. This legendary figure slayed the giant who terrorised shipping in these parts. Brabo is depicted meeting out suitable punishment, by throwing the giant's hand into the river.

around the docks area, but, once you have penetrated the Oude Stad (Old Town), and have stopped for one or two of the excellent local beers, it takes on quite a different air. The old centre is chock-full of lovely buildings, some extravagantly rich in the art nouveau style, and there's plenty to see and do.

The Grote Markt lies at the heart of the area and is home to the 19th-century Brabo Fountain, which commemorates the Roman soldier who bravely slew the giant in the legend of the founding of the city. Around the square sit well-preserved guild houses, topped by golden figures, and the Renaissance Town Hall. Next to the Grote Markt stands the wonderful Cathedral of Our Lady, completed 170 years after it was started in 1352. A veritable art gallery, it is decorated with some recently uncovered 15th-century frescos and some enormous masterpieces by Rubens, the city's native genius. The Tourist Office provides a leaflet outlining a trail to all places of Rubens interest in Antwerp, but you can have more than your fill of the artist and his greatest works by visiting the Rubenshuis, where he lived for 25 years, and particularly the Royal Museum of Fine Arts, which also contains a superb collection of other Flemish pieces from the 14th to the 17th century. The artist's tomb can be found in the city's St Jacobskerk.

A surprisingly interesting exhibit is the Plantin-Moretus Museum, dedicated to the life of printer Christopher Plantin. You can see the 17th-century print room and an intriguing old bookshop.

Antwerp has other notable galleries, churches and museums (including, as you might expect, a maritime museum), but this is a city to enjoy in other ways, too. The shopping is excellent and there's a well-respected zoo, complete with dolphinarium and planetarium. Antwerp is probably best approached by train rather than by car, as parking is less than adequate. One of the bonuses of arriving by rail is that you pitch up at the fabulous old station, a stunning period piece in marble and gold, worth a visit in its own right.

Antwerp

Major Events
Continuous Music Festival (May–September): open-air concert season
Sfinks Festival (July): open-air festival of ethnic music.
Summer of Antwerp (July and August): annual cultural festival in the city centre.
Festival of Flanders (August–October): festival of regional, national and international music.

How to get there – and get around
By air: scheduled flights to Antwerp-Deurne Airport (3 miles out) from Heathrow, Gatwick and London City (1 hr). Buses run to the centre, or there are taxis.
By car: catamaran (1¼ hrs) or ferry (4 hrs) from Ramsgate to Ostend, or ferry from Hull to Zeebrugge (13 hrs), then 1 hr by road.
By rail: Eurostar to Brussels (2 hrs 40 mins) then trains every 30 mins to Antwerp (35 mins).
Public Transport: Antwerp has efficient trams and buses and a small metro system (singles cost BEF40; 10-ticket card BEF250; 24-hour ticket BEF105). Taxis are good and reasonable.

Suggested Hotels
Hilton, Groenplaats. Tel: (03) 204 12 12 Fax: (03) 204 12 13
Exclusive and superbly-situated in historic Antwerp. Very expensive.
Alfa de Keyser, De Keyserlei. Tel: (03) 234 01 35 Fax: (03) 232 39 70
Luxury hotel close to the station. Expensive.
Prinse, Keizerstraat. Tel: (03) 226 40 50 Fax: (03) 225 11 48
Well-appointed, 16th-century establishment in the old city. Moderate.
Rubens-Grote Market, Oude Beurs. Tel: (03) 222 48 48 Fax: (03) 225 19 40
Lovely hotel in an excellent position. Moderate.

Suggested Restaurants
't Fornuis, Reyndersstraat. Tel: (03) 233 62 70 Superior gourmet restaurant, probably Antwerp's best. Very expensive.
't Vermoide Model, Lijnwaadmarkt. Tel: (03) 233 52 61 Classic restaurant famous for its Flemish dishes. Expensive.
Pottenbrug, Minderbroedersrui. Tel: (03) 231 51 47 The style may be informal, but the food is taken seriously. Moderate.

You can't say Belgium has figured prominently in the minds of British holidaymakers over the years. Recently, cities like Bruges, Ghent and Antwerp have deservedly joined Brussels on the short break map, but the southern part of the country, Wallonia – as opposed to the northern Flanders – remains somewhat overlooked. This is despite having at its heart one of Europe's great stretches of natural beauty, the Ardennes, and some wonderfully historic towns. One such settlement is Namur, easy to reach from Brussels and dutifully fulfilling its nickname of 'Gateway to the Ardennes'.

History and Culture

The university city of Namur grew up at the confluence of two rivers, the Sambre and the Meuse. The fact that its origins are steeped in ancient times is evidenced in the town's Archaeological Museum, which traces prehistoric life in the Meuse Valley, and also in the towering Citadel, which began life as a Celtic hill fort. The people here speak French, not Flemish, but are most certainly not French in character, having their own distinct traditions and way of life.

Sightseeing

The Citadel is the obvious first port of call. The structure you see today, high on a hill above the city, took shape over the 15th–19th centuries, and is indicative of the strategic importance of this part of Europe when it comes to battles. A good two or three hours can be enjoyed taking the Citadel tour, but the cable car up to the fortress is justification enough for a visit. Namur also has a beautifully-proportioned cathedral and numerous other good

Not only is the landscape breathtaking in the Ardennes, but the hospitality is good, too. Little inns like this are scattered throughout the region's towns and countryside, offering much-underrated Belgian cooking and, often, an excellent selection of the country's internationally famous beers.

ARDENNES

exhibits to complement the aforementioned Archaeological Museum. The city's craftsmen have also been honoured. There's the Guy Delforge Perfume Workshop, demonstrating the different stages of perfume production, and various expositions of the town's medieval speciality – gold and silver work: visit the Trésor d'Oignies to see the 13th-century skill of local artisan Hugh d'Oignies. Another Namur resident is commemorated at the Felicien Rops Museum. Rops was a 19th-century illustrator, particularly noted and appreciated for his brave erotic sketches and paintings.

Namur has a fine theatre, too, and some excellent shopping. However, the real reason to be in the city is to leave it again, albeit temporarily – to head out and explore the natural glory of the Ardennes. Buses criss-cross the region and allow you to home in on some terrific hiking areas, or to indulge in other outdoor pursuits like canoeing, cycling, paragliding or ballooning. The Grotte la Merveilleuse caves at Dinant, just a half-hour's train ride from Namur, reveal unusual white stalactites and underground waterfalls, and more subterranean passages can be explored in the same town's Park Mont-Fat. Down by the river, you can't help but be impressed by Dinant's dramatic cathedral.

It's worth bearing in mind, though, that, while the adrenaline rush of exercise is one of the great attractions of this area, the more contemplative traveller, perhaps taking one of the many river cruises, is just as easily overwhelmed by the untarnished beauty of the Ardennes. It's a region with something for everyone, and more than enough to keep you amused for a short break, and that's without mentioning standard Belgian treats like the wonderful cooking or the amazing beers.

Ardennes

Major Events

Namur Nocturne (April): spectacle held every Saturday in the month, focusing on the heart of old Namur.

Namur en Mai (late May–early June): open-air festival presenting some 200 performances from the world's travelling fairs.

Festival de Namur (early–mid July): classical music concerts at churches and the concert hall

Sambre et Meuse Hot-Air Balloon Championship (late August): annual ballooning contest

How to get there – and get around

By air: scheduled flights to Brussels from 12 UK airports (longest flight 2 hrs), then trains every hour (change at Brussels Nord or Midi) to Namur (journey time from airport 1½ hrs).

By car: ferries from Ramsgate to Ostend and Dunkerque (1½-4 hrs), then autoroute to Namur (2–3 hours).

By rail: Eurostar to Brussels Midi (2 hrs 40 mins), then hourly trains to Namur (journey 1 hr)

Public Transport: reasonably cheap bus services are available, but are unnecessary in central Namur. There are some train services through the Ardennes and plenty of boat trips.

Suggested Hotels

Les Tanneurs, rue de Tanneurs.
Tel: (081) 23 19 19 Fax (081) 26 14 32
Classy upmarket hotel with two distinctive restaurants. Expensive.

Château de Namur, avenue de l'Ermitage.
Tel (081) 72 99 00 Fax: (081) 72 99 99
Well-appointed hotel offering many facilities. Moderate.

Beauregard, avenue Baron de Moreau.
Tel: (081) 23 00 28 Fax: (081) 24 12 09
Popular hotel close to the centre. Moderate.

Suggested Restaurants

L'Espiglerie, rue des Tanneries.
Tel: (081) 23 19 99
Namur's highest rated restaurant. Expensive.

Les Joies Gourmands, rue des Aubépines. Tel: (081) 30 19 60
French-style menus in a popular town restaurant. Moderate.

Maison Saint-Aubin, rue des Fripiers.
Tel: (081) 23 36 11
Restaurant with a wide range of menus and prices. Inexpensive–moderate.

As short breaks go, you won't get much better than Bruges. It's so easy to get to, gives you a genuine taste of overseas culture and, with its neighbouring city of Ghent, has more than enough attractions to see you through a long weekend – even if it's raining. It's also one of the most beautiful cities you'll ever discover.

History and Culture

Bruges – Brugge to its Flemish natives – is a canal city. It was once linked to the sea by a river that has long silted up but which, in its heyday, carried boats into the city to take away the textiles that made the people prosperous. As part of the commercial alliance known as the Hanseatic League, Bruges was a genuine mercantile power in the 14th century.

Sightseeing

The older, cobbled section of town is based around two main squares, Markt and Burg, but to get an immediate feel for the shape and beauty of the city, it pays to take a canal cruise. Thereafter, because the city is as flat as a Belgian pancake, the going by foot (or by bike) is easy, except for the 366-step slog up the Belfort tower for a bird's-eye view of proceedings. Surrounded by the ornate guild houses in Markt square, this 286-foot belfry was begun in the 13th century but finished 200 years later. The buildings in Burg square are a glorious mish-mash of historical styles, with the main attraction the Basilica of the Holy Blood, partly dating from the 12th century and allegedly housing a phial of Christ's blood.

Bruges is also a treasure house of art. There aren't many places outside of Italy which can claim to own a work by Michelangelo, but Bruges is one. Its Church of Our Lady contains the master's exquisite sculpture of The Madonna and Child, transported here

Bruges & Ghent

from Italy by a Flemish trader. If you fancy a crash course in local Flemish art, the museums to take in are the Memling and the Groeninge. Such churches and galleries beckon at every turn, but Bruges also offers simpler pleasures. It is an extremely pleasant city to wander around. Stroll past the Fish Market, browse the lace and chocolate shops, stare into the so-called Lake of Love in Minnewater Park. It's what relaxation is all about.

Ghent – or Gent as the Flems prefer it – is, strictly speaking, worth a short break in itself, but, being just 20 minutes by train from Bruges, it shouldn't be overlooked if you've an extra day or two to spare. Like Bruges, Ghent is built on a series of canals and has a mercantile past. Indeed, it was the very epicentre of the Flemish cloth trade. Also like Bruges, Ghent is chock-full of absorbing museums – like the Gravensteen medieval fortress, which exhibits gruesome instruments of torture, and the excellent Folk Museum. The Sint-Baafskathedraal is almost an art gallery in itself, containing a masterpiece by Van Eyck, medieval tombs and an enormous baroque organ. It, too, has a belfry for dizzying panoramas. A tip: don't hurry away from Ghent when it gets dark; it's one of the world's most attractive cities when illuminated.

No visit to Belgium would be complete without sampling the weird and wonderful beers the country produces, and Bruges and Ghent have some of the best bars in which to try them. Some offer beer menus, featuring literally hundreds of beers. There's no better end to a tiring day's sightseeing – or beginning, for that matter.

BRUGES & GHENT

Major Events (all Bruges)
International Orchid Show (late February): annual event displaying extensive varieties.
Procession of the Holy Blood (mid May): elaborate but breathtaking parade of the holy relic every Ascension Day.
Festival van Vlaaderen (late July–early August): week-long festival of early music.
Reiefeest (late August): colourful historical pageant along the picturesque canals.
International Antiques Fair (late October–early November): annual important antiques event.

How to get there – and get around
By air: scheduled flights from numerous UK airports to Brussels (longest flight 1¼ hrs), then train connection to Bruges (1¼ hrs).
By car: catamaran or ferry from Ramsgate to Ostend, then 13 miles to Bruges by road.
By rail: Eurostar to Brussels (2 hrs 40 mins), then change for Bruges (1¼ hrs). Alternatively, take the catamaran from Ramsgate to Ostend (1½ hrs), then a train from Ostend (trains run every 30 mins and take 15 mins).
Public Transport: Bruges has a cheap bus service (around BEF110 for unlimited 24-hour usage) are available, but not generally needed.

Suggested Hotels (all Bruges)
Die Swaene, Steenhouwersdijk.
Tel: (050) 34 27 98 Fax: (050) 33 66 74
Small, but very elegant hotel in the heart of the canals area. Expensive.
De Medici, Potterieri.
Tel: (050) 33 98 33 Fax: (050) 33 07 64
Canalside hotel with much charm. Expensive.
Ter Brughe, Oost-Gistelhof.
Tel: (050) 34 03 24 Fax: (050) 33 88 73
Comfortable hotel right on the canal. Moderate.
Ensor, Speelmansrei.
Tel: (050) 34 25 89 Fax: (050) 34 20 18
Budget hotel with five-star views and no lack of facilities. Inexpensive.

Suggested Restaurants (all Bruges)
De Karmeliet, Langestraat.
Tel: (050) 33 52 89
Famous award-winning blend of French and Flemish cuisines. Expensive.
De Snippe, Nieuwe Gentweg.
Tel: (050) 33 70 70
Restaurant of the same quality as the hotel it represents. Expensive.
De Stove, Kleine St Amandsraat.
Tel: (050) 33 78 35
Small, friendly, traditional Flemish restaurant. Moderate.
Bistrot de Serre, Simon Stevinplein.
Tel: (050) 34 22 31
Modern, stylish bistro in airy surroundings. Moderate.

PREVIOUS AND OPPOSITE PAGE: Beautiful Bruges: a maze of cobbled streets constructed around placid waterways that once ferried merchant traffic in and out of the centre, but which now offer many visitors a fascinating first glimpse of the city.

MAISON DES
BRASSEURS
ANNO
1698

BRUSSELS

Brussels is quick, easy and a super place for a weekend break. The food is good, the beer even better and there are some excellent museums.

History and Culture

The one-time 'village of the marsh', as its original name of Broekzele is translated, has come a long way. So far, in fact, that Brussels is now a major international city, home of the European Union and headquarters of NATO. Its cosmopolitan attitude is not so new, however, thanks to centuries of invasion by the French, Germans and Spanish. It was once part of a United Kingdom of the Netherlands, but when Belgium broke away from Holland, Brussels became its capital city.

Sightseeing

It is in the magnificent Grand Place that you must begin. This large square is the city's focal point, combining Gothic, Renaissance and baroque in an amalgam of stunning architecture. Virtually every one of the gilded buildings which form the square could demand a chunk of your sightseeing time. A flower market is held in the Grand Place every day and, at night, the square takes on a new air. The buildings are beautifully illuminated and the pavement cafés throng with diners and drinkers.

Also in the square is the Municipal Museum, where the highlight is the collection of costumes donated from all around the world to clothe the famous statue of the Manneken-Pis. The fountain of the little boy doing what comes naturally can actually be found in the sidestreets near here.

Belgium is still a kingdom and therefore its capital has a (typically uninhabited) royal palace, which you can only visit for six weeks in the summer. But near here is the powerful St Michel cathedral, dressed in white, and the Palais de Justice, an impressive neo-classical structure with fine city views from its dome. Also close by are two complementary museums. The Museum of Ancient Art includes stacks of paintings by Rubens, Van Dyck and Breughel, while the Modern Art Museum is a treasure trove of 20th-century pieces by the likes of Magritte. Other Brussels museums include a vintage car collection and an archive devoted to comic strips, with, in pride of place, Tin-Tin, by Hergé.

A short metro ride out from the centre takes you to the Atomium science museum and other attractions such as a mini-Europe and the Océade swimming complex and some restaurants. The Atomium, built like a giant iron atom, is not as impressive as it used to be, but still warrants a few hours' exploration.

A museum of a different kind is found in the south-western suburbs. Here you can see a speciality beer being made at the Cantillon Gueuze Museum. The tart, sour *gueuze* is fermented by wild yeasts and a tour of the drafty, cobwebby brewery, followed by a free tasting, is one of the city's great idiosyncratic experiences.

Brussels has some knockout bars: one of the best being Toone, a combination of bar and puppet theatre, where you can watch a show while enjoying a brew. Toone is just off the rue des Bouchers, the gourmet centre of Brussels, a couple of blocks from the Grand Place. Even if you can't afford to eat here, it's worth a walk to see the mouthwatering displays of seafood and fresh vegetables. There are cheaper places to eat around the Grand Place area, but, inevitably, the better value establishments are away from the tourist heartland. For a quick snack, make sure you try Belgian frites, served from the street stalls.

The magnificent 18th-century guild houses, which line the famous Grand Place at the heart of Brussels, take on a different aura at night, when the square is illuminated and the bars and restaurants enjoy a roaring trade.

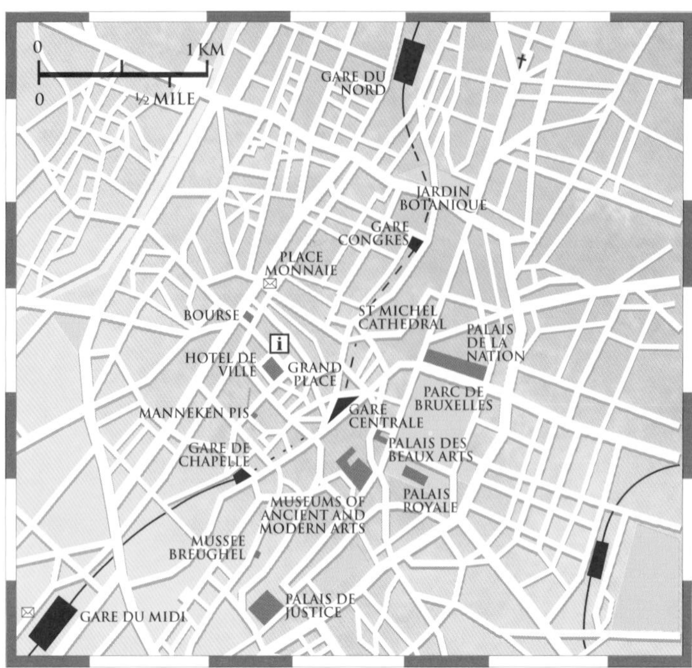

Brussels

Major Events
Ecran Total (mid June–late August): summer cinema festival ranging from the unreleased to classic oldies.
Tapis de Fleurs (mid August): 800,000 begonias laid out in a colourful carpet on the Grand Place.
Festival Bellone-Briggitines (August–September): celebration of music and dance.
Audi Jazz Festival (October–November): big international names spread over 60 or so concerts in the month-long event.

How to get there – and get around
By air: scheduled flights to Brussels Airport (8 miles out) from 12 UK destinations (flights 1–2 hrs); taxis (costing around BF1,000 and taking 20 mins), buses (BF65, 30 mins) and trains (BF85, 15 mins) run to Brussels centre.
By car: choice of cross-Channel ferries to Calais, Dunkerque, Ostend and Zeebrugge, then autoroute to Brussels (fastest crossing/road journey is via Ramsgate–Ostend catamaran or the Channel Tunnel – about 4 hrs in total).
By rail: Eurostar to Brussels Midi (2 hrs 40 mins).
Public Transport: Brussels has a good metro, bus and tram service with interchangeable ticketing (around BF50 per ticket, BF320 for 10, or BF130 per day). Reliable, if pricey, taxis.

Suggested Hotels
Métropole. place de Brouckère. Tel: (02) 217 23 00 Fax: (02) 218 02 20
Grand hotel in the heart of the shopping centre. Very expensive.
Le Dixseptième, rue de la Madeleine. Tel: (02) 502 57 44 Fax: (02) 502 64 24
A touch of the baroque, with its large rooms and bold demeanour. Expensive.
Sema, rue des Harengs. Tel: (02) 514 07 60 Fax: (02) 548 90 39
Modern, yet comfortable, hotel near the Grand Place. Moderate.
Mozart, rue de Marché aux Fromage. Tel: (02) 502 66 61 Fax: (02) 502 77 58
Friendly and surprisingly roomy, city-centre favourite. Inexpensive.

Suggested Restaurants
Comme Chez Soi, place Rouppe. Tel: (02) 512 29 21
Brussels most prestigious and fêted restaurant. Very expensive.
La Quincaillerie, rue de Page. Tel: (02) 538 35 53
French-influenced favourite of the Brussels business elite. Expensive.
Le Falstaff Gourmand, rue des Pierres. Tel: (02) 512 17 61
Well-respected traditional Belgian fare. Moderate.

Sofia & Plovdiv

Plovdiv has some remarkable ancient remains and old buildings, including a Roman stadium and amphitheatre, a stunning 14th-century mosque and some fine 19th-century houses.

Sofia is a rare find: a bargain destination with friendly hosts, some wonderful old buildings (if you look beyond the immediate Soviet structures that remind you of its past behind the iron curtain), and plenty of outdoor activity on its doorstep. Taken in conjunction with Bulgaria's second city, Plovdiv, designated a European city of culture in 1999, Sofia provides a short break that is both unusual and rewarding.

History and Culture

Sofia goes way back. It started life as a Thracian settlement 3,000 years ago, then became the Roman town called Serdica. It enjoyed strategic importance during the Byzantine era thanks to its position on the trade route from Constantinople to Belgrade. In the Middle Ages it fell into the Ottoman Empire, and was made capital of a newly independent Bulgaria in 1878.

Sightseeing

A couple of days are ample for taking in the delights of Sofia, leaving you with a day or two's excursion to Plovdiv. The name Sofia is derived from the 6th-century St Sofia's basilica, which still stands today and is worth a peek for its preserved mosaic flooring. It's not the oldest church in town. That honour goes to St George's, a Roman rotunda from the 4th century that later became a mosque. Today, it hides in the courtyard of the Sheraton Hotel.

Opposite St Sofia is the Alexander Nevsky church, a neo-Byzantine, gold-domed tribute to the Russians who died in the Russian-Turkish War of 1877–8. Take a good look at the Bulgarian icons in the crypt.

Sofia has a handful of decent museums, highlighting Bulgaria's chequered past,

although the visitor will do better to simply stroll around and take in the atmosphere of the city. There are some excellent shopping bargains to be found, and, when feet begin to ache, there are plenty of cafés from which to watch the world go by.

For your second day here, take a bus out to Mount Vitosha, a wooded mountain popular with the locals for picnics, or, in winter, skiing. A chair lift will take you up to the higher reaches, where the views are marvellous.

A third of the way towards the excellent beaches of the Black Sea Coast, Plovdiv has quite a different atmosphere. This increasingly cosmopolitan city has an excellent old town area, coarsely cobbled, cluttered with medieval houses and somewhat obscured at first sight by the grey blocks of Soviet construction. It traces its roots back to Roman times, when the city was known as Trimontium, a reference to the three hills on which the settlement was built. There is an excellent reminder of those Roman times, in the form of a 2nd-century amphitheatre (now used for plays and Verdi's operas in summer). A later era is recalled in the 14th-century mosque of Djoumaya Djamiya, which is still in use, while the National Revival Period House is not one building but a whole collection of preserved homes from the early 19th century. To see local craftsmen at work (for their own benefit, not for tourists), take a walk down Strymna alley.

In the evening, indulge yourself in a great Bulgarian pastime – leisurely dining. Bulgarian wine now has a global reputation, and, as if you needed to be reminded, it's all incredible value for money.

Sofia & Plovdiv

Major Events (all Sofia)
Arts Festival (May and June): celebration of the arts at the National Palace of Culture
Sofia Music Weeks (late May–mid June): international festival of classical music.
European Movie Festival (June): increasingly important international film festival
Modern Music Festival (June): annual forum for contemporary music
Kinomania (mid November): Sofia's homage to the cinematic arts continues

How to get there – and get around
By air: scheduled flights to Sofia International Airport (7 miles out) from Heathrow and Gatwick (2 hrs 50 mins), then by frequent bus (under US$1) or taxi (around US$8) to Sofia (15–20 mins).
Public Transport: Sofia has an adequate, very cheap bus/tram/trolley bus network. Plovdiv is easy to explore on foot, but there are cheap buses. There are plenty of trains each day from Sofia to Plovdiv, taking 2½ hrs and costing around US$1.

Suggested Hotels
Sheraton Sofia Balkan,
Sveta Nedlya Square, Sofia.
Tel: (02) 981 6541 Fax: (02) 980 6464
Luxurious hotel in the centre of Sofia. Expensive.
Kempinski Zografski,
James Bouchier Boulevard, Sofia.
Tel: (02) 62 518 Fax: (02) 681 225
Superbly-appointed central hotel. Expensive.
Novotel Europa,
Maria Louisa Boulevard, Sofia.
Tel: (02) 317 151 Fax: (02) 320 011
The usual levels of service and amenities associated with this group. Moderate.
Bulgaria, Evtimi St, Plovdiv.
Tel: (032) 225 564
One of half a dozen major hotels in Plovdiv. Moderate.

Suggested Restaurants
Shturkelovo Gnezdo
(The Stork's Nest), Panchareva, Sofia.
Tel: (02) 997 26380
Bulgarian restaurant popular with the locals. Moderate.
Merci, Dondoukov Boulevard, Sofia.
Tel: (02) 875 516
High standard of international cuisine. Moderate.
Montmartre, Hristo Smirnenski, Sofia.
Tel: (02) 665 521
Good quality French-style menu. Moderate.
Pâldin, Knyaz Tsertelev, Plovdiv.
Highly respected old town restaurant. Inexpensive.

The lovely harbour at Dubrovnik, like the rest of this beautiful old city, a great survivor. Boats from here take visitors out to shady Lokrum island, where Richard the Lionheart was once, allegedly, shipwrecked.

Dubrovnik

The horrors of war have been lifted from Croatia and it's back on the tourist map. The wonderful Dalmatian coastline was always Yugoslavia's trump card when beckoning foreign holidaymakers. It's jewel, Dubrovnik, only eight years ago subjected to a cruel bombardment, is now happily restored.

History and Culture

Dubrovnik was the ancient city of Ragusa. Founded in the 7th century by Roman refugees, it grew into a powerful maritime city state. Its merchants traded throughout the known world and brought back the prosperity that produced the beautiful city we see today. Only after a terrible earthquake in 1667 did the city begin to fail, eventually being occupied by Napoleon, before being swallowed up by the Austro-Hungarian empire and then, after World War I, becoming part of Yugoslavia. Croatia's unhappy alliance with other Yugoslav provinces is now at an end, and Dubrovnik is once again part of an independent state.

Sightseeing

The reputation of this glorious little harbour city runs before it. Scores of writers over the centuries have waxed lyrical about its stunning buildings, balmy climate and distinctive, comfortable atmosphere. The focal point is the old fortified town, the main entrance to which is the Pile Gate, dating back 500 years. From here you can tour the

historic city walls,which include over a dozen defensive towers and the giant bulk of Fort Sv Ivan, which dominates the headland. Inside the fortress, the seafaring prowess of old Ragusa is recreated in a maritime museum, and there is a fine aquarium below.

Back inside the Pile Gate, opposite the domed fountain where visitors were once required to wash before venturing into the city, stands a fine Franciscan monastery and from here the city's main street, the Placa, takes off across the centre. Like the rest of the old city, it is pedestrianised. It leads right into Luza square, the heart of the medieval town. A turn to the right brings you to the Rector's Palace and the cathedral. The former now houses the City Museum, while the latter contains a fine piece by Titian and a treasury housing religious relics and prizes.

The best way to enjoy the peaceful atmosphere of the city is to take a wander through the old streets. They contain a host of architectural treasures, like the Jesuit church of Sv Ignacija, fronting a copy of Rome's Spanish Steps leading down to the square that hosts Dubrovnik's colourful morning market. There are plenty of bars, cafés and a wealth of good restaurants around here. Local seafood features prominently – look for Croatian specialities like lobster with noodles, or the spicy fish soup called *brodet*.

Dubrovnik does have a beach, but, for a better bathing experience, head for the island of Lokrum. This wooded haven is a pleasant retreat with some good stony beaches. Boats leave the old city regularly and take just 10 minutes.

Dubrovnik is once again a safe holiday destination, so make the most of it. Explore the historic forts, stroll along the old harbour and pop into the lovely churches to say a big thank you for the city's remarkable survival.

DUBROVNIK

Major Events
Music in Dubrovnik (throughout the year): weekly performances by the Dubrovnik Symphony Orchestra and their international guests.
St Blaise Festivity (early-February): concerts, exhibitions, theatre and processions in Croatian national costume, to celebrate the patron saint.
Dubrovnik Carnival (early February): following straight on from the St Blaise celebrations, a colourful masked pageant.
Open Air Events (May, June, September, October): folklore singing and dancing in the main city square on Sundays.
International Dubrovnik Summer Festival (early July–late August): annual festival of theatre, music, ballet and folklore.

How to get there – and get around
By air: scheduled summer flights to Dubrovnik-Cilipi Airport (15 miles out) from Gatwick only (2 hrs 50 mins), otherwise there are flights to Zagreb from Heathrow and Gatwick, and transfers to Dubrovnik (total 4¼ hrs). Buses take 30 minutes to get to Dubrovnik centre (CKN100).
Public Transport: Dubrovnik's buses are frequent, with a standard cost of CKN6 per journey. The taxi service is adequate and reasonably priced.

Suggested Hotels
Excelsior, Put F Supia.
Tel: (20) 414 222 Fax: (20) 414 214
Exclusive hotel overlooking the old town. Expensive.
Villa Dubrovnik, Babin kuk.
Tel: (20) 422 933 Fax: (20) 423 465
Favourite hotel for visitors, very close to the old town. Moderate.
Villa Orsula, Put F Supia.
Tel: (20) 440 555 Fax: (20) 432 524
Popular, well-appointed and well-positioned hotel. Moderate.

Suggested Restaurants
Atlas Club Nautika, Brsalje.
Tel: (20) 442 526
Renowned for its cuisine and its atmosphere. Expensive.
Domino, Od Domina. Tel: (20) 432 832
Unusual, but highly-rated restaurant in the heart of the old town.
Konoba 'Dundo Marojo', Kovacka bb.
Tel: (20) 427 535
Excellent value-for-money restaurant in the old town. Inexpensive.

PRAGUE

Ten years ago, travellers who managed to slip behind the Iron Curtain and visit Prague were privileged and few. These days, access is easy and the secret is out. The 1989 Velvet Revolution did more than lift the veil of Communism from Czech faces. It pulled back a blanket which had been hiding one of the most majestic cities in Europe.

History and Culture

Prague's expansion began in the 14th century, when it was made a university city. In later centuries, it was part of the Austrian Habsburg empire,until the creation of the new state of Czechoslovakia in 1918. Though thankfully spared the ravages of World War II, Prague fell into the Communist bloc after the hostilities and only emerged again with the collapse of the Iron Curtain in 1989. Twenty-one years earlier, in 1968, Czech hopes of a form of political independence had been dashed by brutal Soviet intervention.

Prague, thanks to its Austrian legacy, is a musical city. Smetana was a local; Mozart made his home here. The city still has three opera houses, as well as the National Theatre, which plays host to drama and ballet, in addition to opera. Lighter entertainment is provided by puppetry. Another Prague passion is *Pivo* – or beer. The first Pilsener lager was brewed not far away, at Pilsen, and the quality of czech lager has been renowned ever since. Prague's restaurateurs, however, have gained a less welcome reputation – for cashing in on the unsuspecting tourist and topping up bills with sundry extras. Consider this when you order.

Sightseeing

Remember that Prague winters can be extremely cold, so November to March is best avoided if possible. Prague is a complex city, split into two by the river Vitava and divided into several quarters. The easiest way to organise your visit is to use these divides to break up your sightseeing.

What you'll discover is a stunning city of cobbled lanes and countless soaring spires. West of the river, trams run up to the Hradcany hilltop fortress, which dominates the city. It has stood there for 11 centuries and, today, it is an odd mixture of castle, Presidential residence and ecclesiastical centre, with, at its heart, the imposingly Gothic St Vitus Cathedral. Below the castle is the picturesque Malá Strana district of rambling streets and tiny squares. Here, is the baroque St Nicholas Church, with its boldly ornate façade, looks as if it's been transported from Rome.

Across the broad, 14th-century Charles Bridge, bustling with buskers and pavement artists, Prague stretches eastward into the Staré Mesto (Old Town) and Nové Mesto (new Town) areas. At the heart of Staré Mesto is the 15th-century Powder Tower, gateway to the time-trapped Old Town Square. The historical hub of the city, this spectacular square is ringed with medieval and baroque buildings and features a bronze monument to 15th-century religious reformer Jan Hus. Catching the eye is the glorious astronomical clock, from which figurines of the 12 apostles emerge on the hour.

Famous Wenceslas Square, in Nové Mesto, is a misnomer. Internationally known as the site of political confrontation not so long ago, the Square is actually a long avenue. At the end stand the National Museum and a moving memorial to Jan Paluch, who burned himself to death in protest against the Soviet invasion of Czechoslovakia in 1968. A happier port of call, back across the river, is the Mozart Museum. It was in this city that the Austrian composer gained his greatest success and *Don Giovanni* had its premier.

Prague has so many churches and synagogues, most endowed with fine mosaics, stained glass and other treasures, to add to its mighty towers, quaint squares, leafy parks, and notable art galleries, that you'll need at least a few days do the city justice. Otherwise, the wonderful mix of architectural styles and the real atmosphere of the streets once walked by novelist Franz Kafka will be lost to you.

PREVIOUS PAGE: Wenceslas Square – more like a boulevard in Paris than a traditional square – with the National Museum to the rear and the equestrian monument to Wenceslas, the patron saint of Bohemia, in the foreground.

The Charles Bridge is one of the focal points of Prague and bars like this, near the bridge, are one of the focal points of Prague life. The Czech Republic is the home of Pilsener lager and its fine, hoppy, golden brews are the envy of the world.

PRAGUE

Major Events

Johann Sebastian Bach Festival: (March) concert venues throughout Prague.

Musica Sacra Praga: (April, August and October) international festival of sacred music, held in concert halls and churches.

Prague Spring International Music Festival: (May–June) held at concert halls, theatres and churches for over 50 years.

Bedrich Smetana Festival: (early September) week-long celebration of this famous son of Bohemia and his music.

Mozart Festival: (October) concerts throughout the month in honour of Prague's most famous 'adopted' musical son.

How to get there – and get around

By air: scheduled flights to Prague-Ruzyne Airport from Heathrow, Stansted and Manchester (longest journey around 2½ hrs). The airport is 10 miles west of Prague and the 25-min taxi journey to Prague city centre costs around CZK400. Buses take a little longer and costs CZK40–75.

Public Transport: Prague is easy to explore on foot but is well-served by metro, trams and buses. Interchangeable tickets are available from CZK12 (short-term) and CZK70 (for 24 hours) to CZK280 (for up to 15 days).

Suggested Hotels

Savoy, Keplerova.
Tel: (02) 2430 2430 Fax: (02) 2430 2128
Opulent city-centre hotel, famous for its Sunday Jazz Brunch. Expensive.

Grand Hotel Bohemia, Kralodvorska.
Tel (02) 480 4111 Fax: (02) 232 9545
Hotel of character close to Wenceslas Square. Moderately .

Admiral, Horejsi nabrezi.
Tel: (02) 5732 1302 Fax: (02) 549 616
As an interesting alternative, one of Prague's 'botels' on the Vltava river. Inexpensive.

Suggested Restaurants

Palffy Palac, Valdstejnska.
Tel: (02) 5732 0570
Typical of the new Prague restaurant scene, serving international cuisine. Expensive.

Nebozizek, Petrinske sady.
Tel: (02) 537 902
Attractive restaurant straddling both traditional and 1990s-style cuisine. Expensive.

Pizzeria Felicita, Ricni.
Tel: (02) 533 555
Italian food, with a growing reputation for its pizzas. Inexpensive.

Copenhagen's famous Tivoli Gardens amusement park, established over 150 years but, thanks to its many cultural events – including ballet and drama – more than just an early Disneyland.

Copenhagen

Copenhagen is a city of clichés. Images of Hans Christian Andersen and choruses of *Wonderful, Wonderful Copenhagen* either stimulate you into visiting Denmark's capital, or into vowing never to set foot in the place. Whichever side you fall on, put those clichés aside, because this city is a real pleasure. Undoubtedly the pulse of Denmark, it is home to a fifth of the country's population and is a thriving, busy, at times raucous city. Yet, in some respects, it still seems like the little fishing village it began as over 1,000 years ago. It's also a beautiful city, distinguished by green parks and stylish palaces. Many of the old streets are cobbled, their little shops filled with Danish curios.

History and Culture

The modest fishing village took on a new importance in the 12th century, when a castle was built here. The town's wealth was then boosted considerably by imposing tolls on shipping passing through the narrow sound on its way into the Baltic. The settlement became known as København, or 'Merchant's Port', in the 15th century, after assuming the mantle of the most powerful harbour on the Baltic Sea. In the decades to follow, the city we see today began to take shape.

Sightseeing

Copenhagen is a city on the water, with canals cutting through the centre. You can take a canal cruise, but the city is also pedestrian-friendly and many of the sights worth seeing are huddled in one spot. The Strøget is probably the world's longest traffic-free thoroughfare and is now lined with classy shops, pretty squares and pavement cafés. Just off the Strøget, the central square known as the Radhuspladsen is home to the town hall, which, in turn, is home to a fascinating device. The world clock devised by Jens Olsen is an astronomical calendar and timepiece which accurately predicts eclipses and moon phases. Climb the Rundetårn in this area for an aerial view over the city's roofs and parks. To the south, the parliament meets in the Christiansborg Palace, but you can still visit it; to the east is the 300-year-old Nyhavn (literally 'New Harbour'), bordered by picturesque 18th-century townhouses, ships' masts and cafés.

North from the centre, the streets broaden out and become more stylish. Near here is the Rosenborg Palace. It is no longer home to the royal family, but is a museum displaying the Crown Jewels and some sumptuous furnishings. The current royal residence is the Amalienborg, a quartet of rococo palaces near the river. Watching the toy soldier-like changing of the guard is a popular tourist pastime. Further north is the Kastellet fortress, now occupied by the Danish army, and beyond it is city's most famous landmark, the diminutive statue of Hans Christian Andersen's Little Mermaid, perched at the waterside, staring out at the sea.

Copenhagen is the home of the Carlsberg brewery. Tours of the brewery are available and the company has also put its name to one of the city's best art galleries, the Ny Carlsberg Glyptotek, housing works by Rodin, Degas, Gaugin and others. For a more stereotypical Scandinavian exhibit, however, visit the National Museum, which begins with the Stone Age and leads you through the Viking era to the Denmark of today.

The city's major entertainment centre is the Tivoli Gardens. The rides have the obligatory Hans Christian Andersen theme and the park is a colourful sight at night, with its hundreds of fairy lights and occasional fireworks.

Copenhagen

Major Events
Tivoli Gardens Summer Season (May – mid September): probably the world's longest annual music festival, with serious classical concerts dotted among popular waltz and polka programmes.
Copenhagen Jazz Festival (early July): important international festival, established over 20 years.
Copenhagen International Fashion Fair (early August): annual exposition of *haute couture* at the Bella Centre.

How to get there – and get around
By air: scheduled flights to Copenhagen-Kastrup Airport from Heathrow, Stansted and nine regional UK airports. SAS runs a bus service from the airport to central Copenhagen every 10–15 min. The 25-minute journey costs DKK35. Copenhagen corporation transport is slightly less frequent, but costs only DKK15. Taxis from the Arrival Hall charge around DKK120.
Public Transport: Frequent fast train services radiate out from central Copenhagen. Tickets for these and buses are interchangeable, and are charged on a zonal basis. It is cheaper to purchase a zonal ticket than to pay for an individual fare. Taxis are commonplace and reasonably priced.

Suggested Hotels
Hotel d'Angleterre, Kongens Nytrov.
Tel: 33 12 00 95 Fax: 33 12 11 18
Copenhagen's plushest hotel, near the centre of the city. Very expensive.
Admiral Hotel, Toldbodgade.
Tel: 33 11 82 82 Fax: 33 32 55 42
Eighteenth-century hotel overlooking the Ameliehaven quayside, and now totally restored. Expensive.

Suggested Restaurants
Barock, Nyhavn.
Tel: 33 33 01 51
Celebrated waterside restaurant, influenced by both the Mediterranean and Far East. Moderate.
Restaurant Mønten, Møntergade.
Tel: 33 13 33 74
Smørgasbørd specialities in a traditional Danish restaurant close to the city centre. Inexpensive.

Helsinki's graceful Senate Square, featuring the monument to Tsar Alexander II and the splendid Upenski Cathedral. The square is so Russian in appearance it even doubles for Moscow in feature films.

Helsinki sits on the edge of the icy Baltic, with the unspoilt beauty of Finland at its back door, and offers a mixture of Western, Scandinavian and Russian civilisations. Its people are determined and hard working but this doesn't mean they don't like to party. After six months of winter darkness, the long summer evenings are employed to the full. Beer gardens fill to bursting, restaurants open till late and folk dancing and other entertainments are laid on in the parks. June, July and August are definitely the best months to visit.

History and Culture

Helsinki is a latecomer among European capitals. It was only founded in the mid 16th century. Finland, as a whole, was originally Swedish territory (hence the bilingual road signs today), and then fell into the Russian Empire. It was Tsar Alexander I who designated Helsinki as the capital of the Finnish province, and who commissioned many of the city's fine neo-classical buildings. After the Russian Revolution, Finland became an independent state and even survived the partitioning of Europe in the post-World War II years, when most of Russia's next door neighbours were subsumed into the Soviet Union. In the 1950s, splendid Modernist buildings added to the city's architectural wealth, enjoying life as a busy Baltic port and the seat of the Finnish government.

HELSINKI

Sightseeing

A solid reminder of the country's Russian past is provided by Upenski Cathedral. It still serves the Orthodox community. Another important church is the Tuomiokirkko, a domed Lutheran cathedral that sits on Senate Square. This pleasant plaza has a distinctly Russian mood and its buildings have sometimes been used by film-makers as substitutes for genuine Moscow structures. Just south of here is the City Museum, a high-tech survey of Helsinki's growth from a seaside village into the national capital.

Uncommonly among port cities, the harbour area is one of the most pleasing parts of Helsinki. Sitting at the end of a long, wide avenue called Esplanadi, which is filled with gardens, bars, restaurants and shops, the harbour features a small market, selling fresh seafood, fruit and vegetables. From here, boats take off for the islands in the bay, home to an 18th-century fortress and a World War II U-boat. The harbour waterway is kept open by ice breakers in winter.

Music lovers will want to seek out Sibelius Park, to see the striking monument to the locally born composer which resembles an elaborate organ. Also on their list will be the new white Opera House, along the street from Finlandia Hall, where many of the city's concerts are staged. Look for the wave images built into the hall's design, a contrived pun on the surname of its architect, Alvar Alto, which means 'wave'.

When you're in Finland, summon up the courage to go for a sauna. This is the great national pastime and is an exhilarating experience. Many hotels have saunas but, if you get out into the country to visit a 'natural' sauna at the edge of a lake, the experience is even more spectacular.

Dining out in Helsinki is not cheap, but the quality is generally very good. Local fish, understandably, is prominent on the menu, but you also come across such delicacies as reindeer. Alternatively you may like to take the opportunity to eat Russian – there are several good Russian restaurants in the city.

HELSINKI

Major Events

Musica Nova Helsinki (March): annual festival of contemporary music.
Helsinki Festival (late August–early September): annual celebration of the arts, with theatre, music, dance and film.
Baltic Herring Market (October): annual, traditional market where the people pay their tribute to their favourite fish.

How to get there – and get around

By air: scheduled flights to Helsinki-Vantaa Airport (12 miles out) from Heathrow, Gatwick, Stansted and Manchester (longest journey 2 hrs). Buses (taking 25 mins and costing around FIM24) and taxis (20 mins; FIM150, or FIM60 if pre-booked) run to Helsinki centre.
Public transport: Helsinki has a very good tram service and an expanding metro (single trip FIM 9, 10-trip FIM75; unlimited 1-day FIM 25, 3-day FIM50). The Helsinki Card, from the Tourist Office, provides free public transport and free or discounted museum entrance fees for one payment: 24 hrs FIM105, 72 hrs FIM165.

Suggested Hotels

Radisson SAS Hesperia, Mannerheimintie.
Tel: (09) 43101 Fax: (09) 4310995
Top-quality hotel in the centre of Helsinki. Expensive.
Vaakuna, Asema-aukio.
Tel: (09) 131181 Fax: (09) 13118234
Elegant hotel, close to the rail and bus stations. Moderate.
Helsinki, Yliopistonkatu.
Tel: (09) 131401 Fax: (09) 176014
Recently refurbished, central hotel with some 200 rooms. Moderate.

Suggested Restaurants

Alexander Nevski, Pohjoisesplanadi.
Tel: (09) 639610
Russian restaurant of the highest order. Expensive.
Havis Amanda, Unioninkatu.
Tel: (09) 666882
Finnish cooking and Baltic seafood are specialities. Expensive.
Kellarikrouvi, Pohojoinen Makasiinikatu. Tel: (09) 179021
Cellar restaurant specialising in Finnish food. Moderate.

A glimpse inside the hallowed halls of Château Lafite-Rothschild, in the comune of Pauillac, north-west of Bordeaux. The area is home to some of the greatest clarets.

Bordeaux

Let's be frank: the main reason most people visit Bordeaux is for the wine. Ever since Roman times, the local grape juice has been shipped around the world from this busy little port on the Garonne river. To fully appreciate the wines, you need to visit some of the great châteaux in the area, but don't overlook the city itself. It may not have the plethora of sights that other European cities can list, but there's more than enough to keep you amused for the days at either end of your wine tour.

History and Culture

There is only one culture here and that is wine. While it was the Romans who began exporting wine out of the harbour settlement, the reputation of the local produce was really established by the English. They occupied the area from the 12th to the 15th century and slurped vast quantities of Claret, as they called the local red wine, anglicising the French term *clairette*. Trade in later times was built on the city's position on the Atlantic coast, as routes to the New World opened up. Most of the finest buildings today date from the 18th century, a time of great prosperity and expansion for Bordeaux.

Sightseeing

If you're not a wine expert, the first port of call must be to the Maison du Vin, near the Tourist Office. Here you'll get the low-down on the grape scene, can savour some free samples and book tours and tastings. A good starting point for city sightseeing is the Grand Theatre, partly the inspiration for the Paris Opéra. Tours of this enormous 18th-century theatre explore the amazing acoustics and discuss the elaborate classical architecture. The Fine Arts Museum displays masterpieces by Titian, Rubens, Renoir, Matisse and others, while the Aquitaine Museum chronicles life in the region from the earliest days. A few fine churches, most notably the vast, Gothic St André cathedral and the St Michel basilica, provide a spiritual background, while the Girondins Monument rounds off the major sights. Topped with the statue of Liberty, this elaborate memorial honours the moderate republicans who were guillotined

during the French Revolution. A cruise along the river from the tree-lined *esplanade des Quinconces* is another pleasant diversion and allows you to appreciate the grand bankside establishments – including the splendid Palais de la Bourse – which were mostly built to hide the slum quarters which once lay behind. Today, you can still wander some old cobbled streets and contrast them with the fine wide avenues that have become a feature of the city.

Within an hour or so's drive of Bordeaux, you can cover most of the territory responsible for the region's wealth. The names of the wine districts need little introduction: Graves, Médoc, Sauternes, Entre-Deux-Mers, Pomerol and more. Make for the little town of St Emilion, east of the city, a big tourist draw for the wines which bear its name, but also a very worthwhile detour for its well-preserved walls, medieval houses and wonderful views. In addition, it has a remarkable church carved out of the side of a cliff by disciples of the town's namesake saint. Another town to seek out is St Macaire, further south, perched high on a hill with an ancient church and ramparts dating from the 13th century or before. North-west of Bordeaux is the Médoc region, where you'll find the comune of Pauillac. Here, the rows of vines are broken up by a series of wine establishments with world-famous names like Château Mouton-Rothschild, Château Lafite-Rothschild and Château Latour (though not all châteaux actually have a castle). You will need to book a few weeks in advance to visit some of the bigger estates.

It goes without saying that wine and driving don't go well together, so be prepared to hop aboard one of the buses that roam the area, or better still join one of the informative coach tours.

Bordeaux

Major Events
Bordeaux Carnival and Spring Fair (March): separate street pageants.
Bordeaux Wine Festival (June): a week-long celebration of the world's most expensive wines.
Eté Girondin (July–August): regional dance and music festivals.
International Organ Festival (July–August): important festival of sacred and secular music
Wine Harvest Festival (September): annual celebration of the gathering of the grapes.

How to get there – and get around
By air: scheduled flights to Bordeaux International Airport (8 miles out) from Gatwick only (2 hrs 25 mins), but there-many flights from the UK to Paris (see Paris), with several connections per day to Bordeaux (journey times vary). The frequent buses to Bordeaux centre take 35 mins and cost around FF35; taxis take 30 mins and cost FF100–150.
By rail: Eurostar to Paris Gare du Nord, then transfer to Gare d'Austerlitz and TGV to Bordeaux (total journey about 7 hrs). Buses take 15 mins from the station to the centre (FF7).
Public Transport: Bordeaux has a comprehensive bus network (single fare around FF7; 24-hr FF20; 72-hr FF50); taxis are reasonable and efficient.

Suggested Hotels
Burdigala, rue Georges Bonnac.
Tel: (05) 56 90 16 16 Fax: (05) 56 93 15 06
Bordeaux's most exclusive hotel, in the Mériadeck district. Very expensive.
Sofitel Aquitania, avenue Jean Gabriel Domergue.
Tel: (05) 56 69 66 66 Fax: (05) 56 69 66 00
Well-appointed, modern hotel near the Parc des Expositions. Expensive.
Grand Hotel Français, rue de Temple.
Tel: (05) 56 48 10 35 Fax: (05) 56 81 76 18
Traditional city-centre hotel close to the Garonne. Moderate.
Royal Médoc, rue de Sèze.
Tel: (05) 56 81 72 42 Fax: (05) 56 51 74 98
Cosy, central hotel, not lacking in amenities. Inexpensive.

Suggested Restaurants
Le Saint-James, place Camille-Hostein, Bouliac. Tel: (05) 57 96 06 00
Award-winning restaurant (and hotel) in a south eastern suburb. Very expensive.
Le Pavillon des Boulevards, rue Croix de Seguey. Tel: (05) 56 81 51 02
Haute-cuisine Bordeaux-style. Expensive.
Chez Dupont, rue Notre-Dame.
Tel (05) 56 81 49 59
Excellent value regional cuisine. Moderate.
Le Dégustoir, rue André Dumerq.
Tel: (05) 56 91 25 06
Popular, good quality restaurant with wine-tastings three times a week. Inexpensive.

Flower seller at the market in Rennes, just one of many colourful markets held daily or weekly in the medieval squares of Brittany's fine historic towns.

The windswept coastline of Brittany hides a land full of tradition and character. Stunning, spume-lashed beaches and hardy fishing ports to the north give way to a central area of rolling hills, woodland and hidden villages, and eventually to the milder south coast, with its valleys and sheltered white sands. Its people have defiantly preserved their ancient culture, from their language and their folksongs to their wonderful regional cuisine. Steeped in myths and legends, Brittany has something for everyone, with breathtaking landscapes and historic cities at every turn.

History and Culture

'Armorica' was the name given to the region by the Romans when they assumed control in 56 BC. The Celts who defined the culture of the area renamed it Brittany in the 5th century, after fleeing the advances of the Anglo-Saxons in Britain. In the Middle Ages, Brittany was transferred from one royal dynasty to another until it was formally integrated into France in 1532. The French banned the Breton language and tried to impose a new identity, but the resilient people have fought back and the Celtic culture of Brittany is alive and well today.

Sightseeing

It is hard to define a base for a full tour of Brittany but the capital, Rennes, despite being towards the eastern side, is as good as any. Only a flavour of what the old town looked like still exists, as Rennes was devastated by fire in 1720, but a few medieval streets came through and their crooked, half-timbered facades provide a neat contrast to the grey granite, 18th-century roads that grew up around them. The city is now a lively academic centre and has an excellent art gallery, the Musée des Beaux-Arts, featuring works by Leonardo, Veronese,

BRITTANY

Rubens, Gaugin, Picasso and other greats. Its other fine museum, the Breton Museum, provides a good introduction to the Breton way of life and the history of the region – another reason for starting your visit in this city.

Thirty miles north is the port of St Malo, heavily damaged during the war but now rebuilt and thriving. Its old cobbled streets are fun to explore, while the ramparts provide fine views. More ramparts catch the eye at medieval Dinan, which is best seen from the top of the 15th-century Tour d'Horloge. Evocatively known as the Emerald Coast, this part of the Breton coastline gives way further west to the Côte de Granit Rose, taking its name from the pink hue of the rocky shoreline. A walk along the breezy clifftops is exhilarating.

Near the westernmost tip of Brittany is the naval city of Brest, now home to a naval museum, a very fine aquarium and some good beaches. Around the corner, so to speak, on the south coast, stands the city of Quimper, allegedly the oldest in Brittany and dominated by the massive Gothic cathedral. This is one of the best places to savour the Breton atmosphere. Sample the local pancakes – *galettes* – and find out more about the famous local *faïence* pottery.

Along the coast at Carnac is one of France's major prehistoric sites. Around 2000 ancient stones are arranged in the fields around here. They probably had religious or astronomic significance, but, as with Stonehenge, no one is really quite sure these days. Rounding off the coastal circuit is the Presqu'ile de Quiberon, a peninsula which is a magnet for outdoor types.

Brittany

Major Events

Les Soirée du Thabor (June–August): free Breton entertainment involving folk music and dance at the Thabor Gardens, Rennes.

Les Tombées de la Nuit (July): the Rennes festival of contemporary Breton drama and other arts.

Festival du Clos Poulet (July): open-air international folk music performances at St Malo.

Festival du Cornouaille (July): important expression of Breton culture, through music, dance, games, tales and parades, at Quimper.

Les Jeudis du Port (July–August): open-air performances of jazz, folk and pop, on Thursdays at Brest.

How to get there – and get around

By air: scheduled flights to Rennes Airport (4 miles out) from Gatwick only (50 mins), then bus to Rennes centre (15 mins); or numerous flights to Paris-Orly Airport (see p.77), with transfers to Rennes (1 hr) and bus to the centre.

By car: ferry to St Malo from Poole, Portsmouth or Weymouth (8–9 hrs), then dual-carriageway to Rennes (1hr).

By rail: Eurostar to Paris Gare du Nord (3 hrs), then change to Paris Montparnasse for the TGV Atlantique to Rennes (1¼hrs).

Public Transport: Rennes is easily explored on foot, but buses and trains run to all parts of Brittany (including the TGV which takes just 2 hrs to reach Brest in the far west).

Suggested Hotels (all Rennes)

Lecoq-Gadby, rue d'Antrain.
Tel: (02) 99 38 05 55
Fax: (02) 99 38 53 40
Typifying the excellent value French hotels offer, this luxury hotel is very reasonably priced. Moderate.

Anne de Bretagne, rue Tronjolly.
Tel: (02) 99 31 49 49
Fax: (02) 99 30 53 48
Popular, friendly hotel, just south of the river. Moderate.

Des Lices, Place des Lices.
Tel: (02) 99 79 14 81
Fax: (02) 99 79 35 44
Homely hotel in the medieval district. Inexpensive.

Suggested Restaurants (all Rennes)

Auberge St-Saveur, rue St-Saveur.
Tel: (02) 99 79 32 56
Gastronomic *tour de force* in 15th-century surroundings. Expensive.

Le Piré, rue Maréchal Joffre.
Tel: (02) 99 79 31 41
High-class French cuisine. Expensive.

Chouin, rue d'Isly. Tel: (02) 99 30 87 86
Speciality seafood restaurant, serving all that's best from Breton waters. Moderate.

Grapes to produce the world's most famous wine are grown all around the Champagne region. The wine is produced through a process known as the *méthode champenoise*, which includes a secondary fermentation in the bottle to create the little bubbles that make the wine so distinctive and popular.

Dom Pérignon could not have realised what he was starting. When the blind Benedictine monk discovered the secret of bubbly wine in the 17th century, little did he know that the drink he had perfected would become the world's most prestigious quaff. Here, in Champagne, you can judge for yourself whether the wine is that good, or whether the hype is more powerful. There are two major centres – Reims and Epernay – but Chalons-en-Champagne is also a delightfully unspoilt little town. Not far away, technically within the Champagne region and always worth a visit, is the gorgeous city of Troyes.

History and Culture

It is tempting to simplify matters and say that there is only one culture hereabouts, and that, of course, is Champagne production. But Reims, the most logical place to stay in the region, once also had a prosperous textile trade. More than that, royalty is a tradition, with no less than 34 kings of France crowned in Reims cathedral, which, in itself, is a great survivor. The city has long been subject to occupation by foreign powers, from the English in the 14th century to the Germans during the 20th century. Much damage was caused by the two World Wars, but Reims had the last laugh by staging the simple ceremony of the Nazi surrender in May 1945.

Sightseeing

The cathedral in Reims is one of the finest in the whole country. Begun in 1211, it has somehow survived all the troubles which have afflicted the city and, thanks to careful restoration, is in good shape today. Undeniably Gothic, with its thrusting pinnacles and endless flying buttresses, it is seriously ornate on the outside, decorated with over 2,300

CHAMPAGNE

statues. Many of the cathedral's original treasures can be now viewed in the adjoining Palais du Tau, the Archbishop's Palace. Less than a mile away is Reims's second most important church, the St Remi basilica. It's older than the cathedral and benefits from being much less of a tourist draw. But the main reason most people come to Reims is to visit a Champagne house. There are many in the city, all offering free (or cheap) tours, which include films, informative guided walks and a tasting at the end. The most popular tours in Reims are Mumm, Veuve Clicquot-Ponsardin and Pommery. You can also pop over to Epernay, where you'll find the mansions of the famous Moët et Chandon and others. The tour provided by the Mercier house is the most fun: they whisk you around the chalky caves on a little electric train.

A little to the east of Epernay is Chalons-en-Champagne (formerly Chalons-sur-Marne). The least touristy of the three Champagne towns, it, too, has some well-preserved old buildings and a fine cathedral. Enclosed by the River Marne and a series of canals, it also features some attractive waterside gardens.

Forty miles to the south is Troyes, often overlooked in the tourism hinterland east of Paris and west of Germany and Switzerland. This thoroughly medieval city is a joy, with impeccably maintained, half-timbered streets, some notable museums and, of course, a number of splendid churches. Stay for dinner and try some of the local sausages *(andouillettes)*. Troyes is only an hour and a half from Paris on the train, so even if you don't make it into Champagne proper, it's a city worth bearing in mind if you ever have time to spare in the French capital.

Champagne

Major Events (all Reims)

(Les Sacres du Folklore (mid June): four days of international folklore, the biggest event of its type in northern France.

Les Fêtes Johanniques (mid June): reconstruction of Charles VII's crowning in 1429 by Joan of Arc at Reims Cathedral.

Musique et Lumière à St Remi (late-June–early October): Saturday concerts in the wonderful setting of the St Remi basilica.

Les Flâneries Musicales d'Eté (early-July–late August): 150 concerts of music from all quarters in the most unusual and prestigious venues in the city.

How to get there – and get around

By air: scheduled flights to Paris from 14 UK destinations (flights 1–2 hrs), then bus/RER/metro/taxi to Paris Est station, from where there are around 12 trains a day to Reims, some changing at Epernay (total journey 2½ hrs or less). An infrequent direct coach service runs from Paris Orly Airport to Reims (1hr 40 mins).

By car: frequent ferries from Dover to Calais, or by Channel Tunnel, then autoroute to Reims (total journey from England 3–4 hours).

By rail: Eurostar to Paris Gare du Nord (3 hrs), then transfer to Paris Est and to Reims, as above.

Public Transport: frequent buses costing around FF5 per ticket, or FF33 for 10. Taxis are fairly reasonable.

Suggested Hotels (all Reims)

Boyer Les Crayères, boulevard Henri Vasnier. Tel: (03) 26 82 80 80
Fax: (03) 36 82 65 82
Exclusive hotel, close to the St Remi basilica, renowned for its food. Very expensive.

Grand Hotel des Templiers, rue des Templiers. Tel: (03) 26 88 55 08
Fax: (03) 26 47 80 60
Small (just 11 rooms), central hotel noted for its comfort and facilities. Expensive.

L'Assiette Champenoise, avenue Paul Vaillant-Courturier.
Tel: (03) 26 84 64 64
Fax: (03) 26 04 25 69
Famous dining hotel with superb amenities, just south of the old city. Moderate.

New Hotel Europe, rue Buirelle.
Tel: (03) 26 47 39 39
Fax: (03) 26 40 14 37
Well-appointed city-centre hotel, close to the cathedral. Moderate.

Suggested Restaurants (all Reims)

Le Paysan, rue de Fismes.
Tel: (03) 26 40 25 51
Traditional regional restaurant, serving good value Champagne. Moderate.

Les Chârmes, rue Brûlart.
Tel: (03) 26 85 37 63
Cosy, champenois restaurant. Moderate.

La Coupole, place Drouet d'Erlon.
Tel: (03) 26 47 86 28
Plenty of choice on the menu, from starters to desserts. Inexpensive.

Gargoyles tease the visitor to Dijon's magnificently Gothic Notre-Dame. These grotesque human and animal figures are just one of the impressive features of this 13th-century church.

Think of Dijon and you think of mustard. Yet the spicy condiment is just the tip of the culinary iceberg in this wonderful city. The restaurants are well known for their high standards, and the wines they serve are produced just a few miles away in the heart of Burgundy. Add in the tranquillity of city life, the cleanliness of its streets and the magnificent architecture, and the recipe for a memorable short break is complete.

History and Culture

The history of Dijon is inextricably linked to the powerful Dukes of Burgundy, who dominated eastern France for 400 years, from the 11th century. It was they who took the unremarkable settlement founded by the Romans as *Divio* and endowed it with fine buildings and precious works of art. The culinary prowess of the city derives from its situation on the historic spice route – hence the classic mustard and the gingerbread the city calls its own. Here, too, the aperitif *Kir* was invented, the fruity mix of white wine and crème de cassis taking its name from one of the city's mayors.

Sightseeing

The little streets that make up the old centre nearly all have intriguing features and provide an atmospheric introduction to the city. The Dukes' own palace is imposing, but a little disappointing, and much changed since their heyday. Yet their artistic legacy lives on in its east wing, given over to the Museum of Fine Arts, where the selection of masterpieces. works by Titian, Rubens, Picasso and the Impressionists demand a visit. The old palace, here, too, and the Dukes'

mausoleum, with its gold-encrusted tombs, can also be viewed.

Dijon's Archaeological Museum is one of the best around. Based in an 11th-century Benedictine abbey, its collection of Gallo-Roman reliefs has been widely acclaimed. This and all other museums are free on Sunday. On other days, buy a modestly-priced annual ticket (around FF20) for access to all.

Magnificent churches also survive the reign of the Burgundy Dukes. The Gothic Notre-Dame has stunning 13th-century windows and, on one wall, a small brass owl sculpture, which people stroke for luck. High above the impressive gargoyles, life-size figures mark each quarter-hour on the 14th-century Jacquemart clock. Inside the church is an 800-year-old Black Virgin statue and a tapestry commemorating the 1944 liberation of the city from the Germans. Based on a 10th-century Romanesque church, the city's St-Benigne Cathedral, is also worth a visit, as is the flamboyant church of St-Michel, with its intricate facade. To savour the city's clean air (its mayor is a former Minister for the Environment), stroll through the Botanical Gardens, home to nearly 3,500 different plants.

Excursions from Dijon inevitably take you into wine country. To the south, Beaune is the obvious attraction, its ramparts, wine museum, wine market and notable clerical structures pleasing all comers, while Cluny is another magnet, thanks to its 1000-year-old abbey – once the most powerful on the Continent. If this impresses, don't miss the beautifully restored Cistercian abbey at Fontenay, north west of Dijon.

Buses will take you to all the major centres, but make sure you return to Dijon for the evening. It's a quiet city, with not a lot going on after dark, except for the civilised consumption of high quality cuisine. The food isn't cheap, but the experience is memorable.

DIJON

Major Events

Antique Fair and Flea Market (May): trading of the exquisite and old, or perhaps just the old.

Eté Musical (June): season of classical concerts featuring top-flight soloists and orchestras.

L'Estivade (end June–August): summer festival of music, ballet, theatre, jazz, folklore and cinema.

Wine and Folklore Festival (end August–September): celebration of Burgundy's wine-growing tradition.

International and Gastronomical Fair (October–mid November): inevitable exposition of the local pastime.

How to get there – and get around

By air: scheduled flights to Paris (Orly or Charles de Gaulle) from many British airports (flight time 1–2 hrs). Transfer to Paris Gare de Lyon, then TGV to Dijon (1hr 40 mins).

By rail: Eurostar to Paris Gare du Nord, then transfer to Gare de Lyon and TGV to Dijon (total journey about 5½ hrs).

Public Transport: Dijon is easy to, but there are efficient buses (around FF5 per ticket or FF23 for five) and reasonable taxis.

Suggested Hotels

Château de Gilly, Gilly-les-Citeaux – Vougeot. Tel: (03) 80 62 89 98
Fax: (03) 80 62 82 34
Gracious château 8 miles south of Dijon, surrounded by some of the best Grand Crus in Burgundy. Expensive.

Hostellerie du Chapeau Rouge, rue Michelet. Tel: (03) 80 30 28 10
Fax: (03) 80 30 33 89
Well-thought of, traditional hotel in old Dijon. Moderate.

Sofitel Dijon, place Darcy.
Tel: (03) 80 30 12 32
Fax: (03) 80 30 04 15
Comfortable, well-appointed hotel in the centre of the city.

Suggested Restaurants

Restaurant du Chapeau Rouge, rue Michelet. Tel: (03) 80 30 28 10
Hotel restaurant of the highest order. Expensive.

Restaurant Thibert, place Wilson. Tel: (03) 80 67 74 64
Not so costly, despite its numerous rosettes. Moderate.

Le Cabaret, place de la République.
Tel: (03) 80 74 05 05
Reasonably priced, centrally-situated restaurant. Inexpensive.

Dordogne

We're talking weeks, rather than days, to do full justice to this absorbing region, but if a long weekend is all you have to spare, you can still pack a lot in here, especially if you choose a sensible, convenient base like the city of Périgueux. For your entertainment, take your pick from prehistoric cave drawings, intriguing Roman remains, battle-scarred hillside fortresses, a bounteous meandering river, unrivalled panoramas and, of course, some of the best food in France.

History and Culture

Primitive sketches on cave walls prove that the area around the Dordogne river was a fruitful place for man to live many thousands of years ago. The Romans marched in and enjoyed their share of the local countryside and its rich produce, building a substantial town called Vesunna on the site of today's Périgueux. In the Middle Ages war raged across the region. Castles were erected and then destroyed. The Catholic church adorned the towns and villages with fine places of worship and, all the while, the region's culinary specialities – truffles, pork, ducks and geese – were gaining an international reputation. Today, the Dordogne is a major tourist destination, the high summer being almost unbearable in little towns like Sarlat, but with empty roads at other times of the year.

Sightseeing

Périgueux is worth a few days in itself. Begin in the La Cité area, the site of the Roman town of *Vesunna*. Here, there are still some Roman relics, including the remains of an amphitheatre. The main part of the city is dominated by its monstrous cathedral, a domed, turreted, white confection, surrounded by streets filled with market traders. Take a look at its massive baroque altar. Near here is the Périgord Museum, which chronicles the prehistoric history of the locality.

Time will be at a premium on a short break, so hire a car and make for the region's highlights. You can't miss the amazing spectacle of Rocamadour, an astonishing battlemented village, home to a basilica, other sacred sites and a château, seemingly carved out of the rock face. Pilgrims have been coming here for centuries to see the miracle-working statue of a Black Virgin in the Notre-Dame Chapel. The hilltop town of Domme affords one of the most remarkable panoramas you are ever likely to see, perched high above the lazy Dordogne river and its lush fields. Pop into Bergerac to taste the sweet wine called *Monbazillac*, and visit Sarlat, with its unspoilt medieval and Renaissance streets, constructed from distinctive golden sandstone. Step through the historic archways, cross the unspoilt squares and look for the salamander emblem marked on the walls of numerous old houses. It was the symbol of King François I. View the splendid organ in the 17th-century cathedral and make the effort to see the Lantern of the Dead, a 12th-century, beehive-shaped tower in the town's ancient cemetery. On Saturdays, Sarlat's market takes over, tempting you to buy fine, exotic cheeses, truffles, wild mushrooms, local walnuts and a variety of prized pork and poultry products, including the famous *foie gras,* duck liver pâté.

One final attraction you should not miss are the caves at Lascaux. Here, in 1940, two young boys discovered some of the world's finest palaeolithic paintings. Bulls, horses, bisons and other creatures, as viewed by prehistoric man in these parts, are sketched onto the cave walls. To prevent visitor damage, the original caves are now closed, but an excellent copy has been made, named Lascaux II, just down the hill. It may be artificial, but it took 11 years to complete and it's well worth the entrance fee.

These are the undoubted highlights of the Dordogne region, but every little village has its own tale to tell, and the outstanding natural beauty just encourages you to get out and explore the sleepy countryside. You can come back time and again – many Brits have already seen all the sights and now just return for the magnificent cuisine – so maybe the short break will provide an aperitif for the main course to follow.

The stunning landscape of the Dordogne Valley is nowhere better observed than in the area around the town of Domme. Views from the hilltop are simply magnificent.

The amazing settlement of Rocamadour was built into the cliff-face at the point where the body of St Amadour was discovered in the 12th century. It is still a place of pilgrimage today.

Dordogne

Major Events (all Périgueux)
Truffe d'Argent (July–August): amateur singing competition for the Silver Truffle.
Festival International de Mime (August): international celebration of an art form close to French hearts.
Concours de Périgueux (August): competitions for pâté-making, painting in the streets of Périgueux, and pétanque
Festival Sinfonia (September): concerts of classical music.
Semaine de la Music Traditionelle et Culture Occitane (early November): important expression of the musical and cultural traditions of the South.

How to get there – and get around
By air: scheduled flights to Bordeaux Airport from Gatwick only (2 hrs); buses run to Bordeaux centre then infrequent train or coach services to Périgueux (75 miles, 1¼–3 hrs). There are also four flights a day direct to Périgueux from Paris (1 hr).
By rail: Eurostar to Paris Gare du Nord, then transfer to Gare d'Austerlitz and TGV to Bordeaux (total journey about 7 hrs). Change for Périgueux (1½ hrs).
Public Transport: Périgueux buses cost around FF7 per ticket, or FF42 for 10. Taxis are not so visible. Trains and buses run through the region, but car hire is advised.

Suggested Hotels (all Périgueux)
Château des Reynats, Chancelade. Tel: (05) 53 03 53 59 Fax: (05) 53 03 44 84
Périgueux's most gracious and comfortable hotel: a converted château 2 miles west of centre. Expensive.
Talleyrand-Périgord, place Francheville. Tel: (05) 53 06 06 08 Fax: (05) 53 08 13 07
Peaceful hotel with every comfort, in the heart of old Périgueux. Moderate.
Bristol, rue A .Gadaud. Tel: (05) 53 08 75 90 Fax: (05) 53 07 00 49
Small, but cosy, central hotel with more than adequate facilities. Inexpensive.

Suggested Restaurants (all Périgueux)
Château des Reynats, Chancelade. Tel: (05) 53 03 53 59
One of the best restaurants in a region of gourmet delights. Expensive.
Le Rocher de l'Arsault, rue de l'Arsault. Tel: (05) 53 53 54 06
Sumptuous, central restaurant, serving local produce and fresh Biscay seafood. Expensive.
Chez Marcel, avenue Michel-Grandou. Tel: (05) 53 53 13 43
Traditional Périgord cooking in the town centre. Moderate.

There's no denying it: Annecy is without doubt one of the prettiest towns in Europe. It sits on its own, turquoise lake with, rising all around, the craggy peaks of the French Alps. Its streets twist and turn in medieval fashion, window boxes burst with floral colour and a canal runs right through the middle of the town, inevitably conjuring up the simplistic nickname 'the Venice of the Alps'. It is also well situated, making it an ideal base for exploring the beautiful french mountains.

History and Culture

The importance of Annecy was realised only in the 16th century, when the town became a bolt hole for the Bishop of Geneva, ousted during the Reformation. It has not really enjoyed any significance since, except as a marvellous staging post for travellers looking to take on the mighty Alps. In summer, it can be unbearable here: tourists simply flock in and the click of camera shutters whirrs around like crickets chirping after dark. Particularly popular is the first Saturday in August, when the fête du Lac sets the town alight with fireworks. But visit any other time, from September through to July, and you can savour the stunning scenery and magnificent old buildings in genuine peace and quiet.

Sightseeing

The most photographed of all Annecy's sights is the 12th-century Palais de l'Isle, a picturesque old prison that juts out into the Thiou canal, the waterway that winds its way through the heart of Annecy. In this part of town, some streets are arcaded, and a relaxed stroll around the jumble of buildings throws up some odd finds. Take, for example, the church of St Maurice. This one-time Dominican convent in the main square, is a confusing sight, with its

From Annecy, and the other towns around its lake, there are endless hiking possibilities, from major assaults on the grandest Alpine peaks to gentle strolls through lush lakeside meadows.

FRENCH ALPS

assymetric 15th-century walls. Opposite here is the old town hall, the Hôtel de Ville.

Away from the medieval quarter, the lakeside is the next significant port of call. You can swim from here, or take out a paddleboat, to help cool off when the summer heat is on. Don't worry about pollution: Lake Annecy – 9 miles long and 2 miles across – is reputedly the purest in Europe. High above the town stands the turreted Château, Annecy's main attraction, now home to an aquarium and a museum documenting local history through archaeological finds, early furniture and religious icons. The views from here alone merit the climb.

One side effect of being so attractive is that Annecy has also become too popular at times and consequently rather expensive. This provides all the more reason for taking advantage of the town's stunning position and heading out to explore the alpine surroundings. Little villages like Talloires, with its excellent restaurants and hotels (one housed a former Benedictine abbey), are rewarding, or pay a visit to the Fier Gorges, a glacier-carved canyon, six miles away, or call in at the Château de Montrottier, a medieval castle containing an interesting collection of furniture, china, lace and weaponry. Mont Blanc – the 15,600-foot giant of the Alps – is within striking distance, but a hike through some of the grassy meadows closer to base is just as fruitful. Excellent skiing is available within an hour's drive in winter.

The French Alps, as a region, is not short of historic little towns, placid lakes and dramatic scenery, but Annecy provides, in one complete centre, everything that is good about this evocative mountainous area.

French Alps

Major Events (all Annecy)

Festival de la Vieille Ville (early July): the old town comes alive with music and dance.

Noctibules (mid July): several days of street theatre, extending the firework celebrations of Bastille Day.

Les Choeurs de France (late July–early August): choristers in their hundreds from all over France meet for a week of song.

Fête du Lac (early August): the biggest bash of the year, with fireworks, decorated boats and music on the lake.

Plaisir de Musique (early August): five days of concerts in the ornate setting of the Imperial Palace.

How to get there – and get around

By air: scheduled flights to Geneva Airport (32 miles away) from Heathrow, Gatwick, London City and Manchester (longest flight 2½hrs). Buses run to Annecy from Geneva Airport four times a day (45 mins). Taxi fares are expensive.

By rail: Eurostar to Paris Gare du Nord, then transfer to Gare de Lyon for TGV direct to Annecy, about six times daily, (total journey around 11hrs).

Public Transport: Most of Annecy can be accessed on foot, with cheap buses only really needed from the old town to the lakeside. The taxi service is reliable and fairly inexpensive. Water taxis link the little towns along the lake (FF 67 all-day fare).

Suggested Hotels (all Annecy)

Impérial Palace, avenue d'Albigny.
Tel: (04) 50 09 30 00
Fax: (04) 50 09 33 33
Annecy's most famous hotel, situated on the lakeside. Expensive.

Splendid, quai Eustache-Chappuis.
Tel: (04) 50 45 20 00
Fax: (04) 50 52 26 23
Conveniently placed along the lake-shore, near the mouth of the Thiou river and its esplanade. Moderate.

Faisan Doré, avenue d'Albigny.
Tel: (04) 50 23 02 46
Fax: (04) 50 23 11 10
Cheaper lakeside hotel, which fills up quickly. Moderate

Suggested Restaurants (all Annecy)

Belvédère, chemin du Belvédère.
Tel: (04) 50 45 04 90
Top-class fish restaurant. Expensive.

Cordon Bleu, rue Perrière.
Tel: (04) 50 45 51 76
High quality cuisine based on local produce. Moderate.

Buffet de la Gare, place de la Gare.
Tel: (04) 50 45 42 24
Despite the railway café connotations, this restaurant specialises in savoyard cooking. Inexpensive.

The distinctive Palais de l'Isle, on the Thiou canal, in Annecy. This 12th-century structure has, at various times, been used as a prison, law court and a mint. It now hosts occasional exhibitions.

The magnificently restored medieval Cité of Carcassonne, with its battlemented ramparts and turrets that look as if they have been constructed as part of a film set. Some people believe the restoration is just too perfect.

The Languedoc region, sandwiched between Provence and Catalan Roussillon on the Spanish frontier, is a warm, easy going area, a world away from the brashness of the French Riviera. That's not to say it doesn't have its more vibrant elements. The city of Montpellier, for instance, ideal as a base for exploring the region, is youthful and lively, but Languedoc, otherwise, meets the expectation of travellers who seek plenty of sunshine, excellent cuisine and wonderful old monuments without ever feeling the need to stand on ceremony.

History and Culture

This part of France once had its own language, Occitan, and proudly preserves many old traditions to this day. Montpellier, the capital of the region, has been around for about 1,000 years and gained its early prosperity from its spice trade with the Middle East. It first made its mark on the world through its medical school, founded in 1220, and remains an important university centre, with a very young population. The countryside around is largely agricultural region, and produces much of France's table wine.

Sightseeing

There's a buzz about Montepellier, due in no short measure to the high student presence. The centre of the action is the place de la Comédie, an enormous square laid out in the 18th century. From here a wide, leafy promenade runs to the Corum, the city's ugly, modern convention centre and opera house. In contrast, the old town is a pleasure, featuring fine 17th- and 18th-century mansions and elegant court-yards. These buildings replaced parts that were destroyed during the religious wars of the 16th century. The Musée Farbre contains great artworks by French, Dutch, Italian and Spanish painters, while a collection of prehistoric objects and classical artefacts from Greece and Egypt makes intriguing viewing at Musée Languedocien.

Heading east along the coast from Montpellier brings you to the historic city of Nîmes, the birthplace of denim (originally *de Nîmes*, 'from Nîmes').

LANGUEDOC

The city's other claim to fame is its fabulously preserved Roman heritage, best showcased by the stunning 1st-century amphitheatre, back in use today for concerts and shows. Just outside Nîmes is the even more remarkable Pont du Gard. This three-storey, arched aqueduct was the highest ever built by the Romans and you can still walk along the top today, if you've a head for heights.

One of the region's other great highlights is the wonderful city of Carcassonne, to the south-west of Montpellier. Its modern streets lie at the foot of the old town, which is known as La Cité. Perched on a crag and floodlit at night, it is a convincing 19th-century reconstruction of a medieval fortified town, with 50 towers, high double walls and a population of just 200. Within its walls stands the beautiful church of St Nazaire.

Back along the River Aube valley, towards the coast, sits Narbonne, a city split in two by the Canal de la Robine, with a well-restored medieval district and a fascinating underground maze of granaries from the 1st century BC. While in the city, you can't fail to spot the massive cathedral, a glorious 14th-century edifice with fine stained glass and marvellous tower views.

Along the coast, Languedoc has plenty of fine, sandy beaches, whilst inland, the ground rises up into rugged hills, clad with the vines which produce wine for denominations like Corbières and Minervois.

Cruising the countryside, lazing on the beach, dropping by the ruins of an old fortress, stopping for a long, leisurely lunch – these are the unhurried elements that make the Languedoc so appealing to discerning travellers.

Languedoc

Major Events (all Montpellier)
Printemps des Comédiens
(mid June–early July): unusual event blending theatrical arts and tradition in open-air performances.
Festival International Montpellier Danse (late July): well-established annual festival of all kinds of dance, encouraging contemporary themes.
Festival de Radio France
(mid July–early August): some 80 annual events involving opera, concerts, recitals and jazz.
Festival de Musique Georges Aurac
(September): annual season of chamber music.
Mediterranean Film Festival
(October): yearly festival paying homage to the region as an influence in film-making.
Wine and Vine Fair (October): celebration of the harvest in the world's biggest wine-producing area.

How to get there – and get around
By air: scheduled flights to Montpellier-Mediterranean Airport (6 miles out) from Gatwick only (2 hrs). There are also connecting flights from UK airports via Lyon (see p.67; transfer to Montpellier 1¼ hr) and Paris-Orly and -Charles de Gaulle (see Paris p.74; transfer to Montpellier 1⁄hrs), and the option of taking the TGV train from Charles de Gaulle direct to Montpellier (4hr 50 mins).
Public Transport: Montpellier is easy to explore on foot, but buses are reasonable and fairly reliable. Buses and trains connect all the major towns in the region, but car hire is advised for greater flexibility.

Suggested Hotels (all Montpellier)
Le Jardin des Sens, avenue St Lazaire.
Tel: (04) 67 79 63 68
Fax: (04) 67 72 13 05
Easily the most luxurious hotel in Montpellier. Very expensive.
Sofitel Antigone, rue des Pertuisanes.
Tel: (04) 67 99 72 72
Fax: (04) 67 65 17 50
One of the best hotels in an excellent chain. Expensive.
Holiday Inn Metropole, rue de Clos René. Tel: (04) 67 58 11 22
Fax: (04) 67 92 13 02
Plenty of comfort and amenities for your money. Moderate.

Suggested Restaurants (all Montpellier)
Le Cercle des Anges, rue Collot.
Tel: (04) 67 66 35 13
Classic French Mediterranean cooking of the highest order. Expensive.
Le César, place du Nombre d'Or.
Tel: (04) 67 64 87 87
Popular restaurant specialising in Languedoc fare. Moderate.

LOIRE VALLEY

The Loire, the longest river in France, runs through a broad, lush valley as it approaches the sea. Here, French royalty set up its court in the Middle Ages. Here, Joan of Arc turfed out the English. Here, sit a series of the most magnificent châteaux to be seen in all of France. There's enough of interest in the Loire to swallow up all your summer vacation, but a long weekend can provide a good taster – especially of the gourmet restaurants and the region's renowned wines.

History and Culture

The Loire Valley we enjoy today is a product of the turbulent years of the Valois dynasty of French kings and queens. They ruled France from the 14th to the 16th century, and made the Loire their base. With the royalty came their entourage, the dukes and the counts. Consequently, the countryside bordering the river is littered with glorious palaces and châteaux. To build the new mansions, workers dug deep into the tufa banks of the Loire, leaving a honeycomb of caves throughout the region. These have spawned their own industries: their constant coolness providing the right conditions for wine storage and the cultivation of mushrooms. They even became homes for the local people.

Sightseeing

To get the most out of a short trip to the Loire, you need to be fairly central and also have your own transport. There are trains and buses, but the more out-of-the-way attractions require the flexibility of your own set of wheels. Tours makes a good base. It's an attractive city: its cobblestoned old quarter is a pleasant place to wander and there are some fine old buildings. Heading upstream, the sedate little town of Blois is chiefly famous for its dominant château, with four contrasting, but complementary, wings. South of Blois is the stunning Château de Chenonceau, elegantly spanning the River Cher.

From Tours downstream, the highlights include the turreted and moated Château d'Azay-le-Rideau, a treasure among local Renaissance structures. Inside, there's a fireplace by Rodin. At Chinon, the ruins of the hilltop castle dominate proceedings. It was here that Joan of Arc first spotted the future King Charles VII and urged him to send forces against the occupying English. Down below, old Chinon is a pleasant jumble of well-preserved medieval streets. A few miles north is the château at Ussé, used by storyteller Charles Perrault as the inspiration for his Sleeping Beauty's castle, while just south of Chinon, away from the river, is the historic abbey at Fontevraud, founded in the 12th century. Here lie the remains of Richard the Lionheart and other Plantagenet rulers.

Further west, you arrive at the little town of Saumur, noted for its cavalry academy and one of the most striking fairytale châteaux in the region. Along the riverbanks here are many of the troglodyte cave homes.

At the end of this most interesting stretch of the Loire is the city of Angers. Its powerful riverside castle is home to a magnificent 14th-century tapestry depicting the Apocalypse, while the Romanesque cathedral and the cobbled streets around are a pleasure to explore.

All along the river, you can't help but notice the countless vineyards; names like Vouvray, Muscadet, Bourgeuil and Sancerre have international resonance. To match the quality of the wines, the restaurants here pull out all the stops, concentrating on good, simple, healthy cooking.

Saumur's fairytale château, overlooking the regal River Loire. It was built in the 14th century but restyled a hundred years later. Illuminated at night, it is one of the region's most enchanting sights.

The Loire Valley is one of the most important wine-producing regions in France. Its fine reds and usually dry, but also sparkling, whites have an excellent reputation internationally.

Loire Valley

Major Events
Florilège Vocal de Tours (late May): international festival of choral singing for Whitsun.
Le Chore-Graphique (early June): celebration of contemporary dance
Aucard de Tours (late June): week-long rock festival culminating in 'la Grande Nuit de Rock'.
Au Nom de la Loire (July – August): spectacles, concerts, exhibitions in the name of France's mightiest river.
Les Sonates d'Automne (October): concerts, exhibitions and workshops throughout the Tours area.

How to get there – and get around
By air: scheduled flights to Paris (Orly or Charles de Gaulle) from many British airports, but transfers into Paris centre and alternative transport to Tours are messy and longer than alternatives.
By car: ferry to Caen or Le Havre from Portsmouth (6 hrs) then by road to Tours (a further 3–5 hrs).
By rail: Eurostar to Paris Gare du Nord, then transfer to Gare d'Austerlitz and TGV to Tours (total journey about 5 hrs).
Public Transport: reasonably priced-trains and buses connect the towns along the river but getting to individual châteaux takes time.

Suggested Hotels
L'Univers, boulevard Heurteloup. Tel: (02) 47 05 37 12 Fax: (02) 47 61 51 80
Luxurious hotel that has hosted famous statesmen, including Churchill. Expensive.
Parc Belmont, rue Groison. Tel: (02) 47 41 41 11 Fax: (02) 47 51 68 72
Tours' most exclusive hotel, with different pricing levels. Moderate–expensive.
Alliance Trois Rivières, avenue de Grammont. Tel: (02) 47 28 00 80
Fax: (02) 47 27 77 61
Large, airy hotel near the railway station, with excellent facilities. Moderate.

Suggested Restaurants
Bardet, rue Groison.
Tel: (02) 47 41 41 11
The Parc Belmont hotel's Michelin-acclaimed restaurant. Very expensive.
L'Univers, boulevard Heurteloup.
Tel: (02) 47 05 37 12
Well-respected hotel restaurant in the heart of the city. Moderate.
La Chope, avenue de Grammont.
Tel: (02) 47 20 15 15
Popular restaurant with seafood specialities. Inexpensive.

Lovely Lyon, so often overlooked by travellers. With its Roman remains, medieval covered walkways and some of the best restaurants in France, it must be one of the country's best-kept secrets.

Many travellers choose Lyon as a resting point on the way to the South of France, or as a stepping stone to the French Alps. It's a wise choice: the food is terrific and there's plenty of comfortable accommodation. Yet Lyon deserves more than a cursory one-night stand. It's a magnificent city, with its roots lodged in antiquity and reminders of its medieval prosperity all around the old centre.

History and Culture

Lyon began life as *Lugdunum*, a Roman settlement at the confluence of the Rivers Rhône and Saône that soon became capital of Roman Gaul. In the Middle Ages, Lyon blossomed into the silk capital of the world. Special covered walkways *(traboules)* were built at this time to shelter the expensive fabric as it was carried around town and they can still be followed today. With 2 million inhabitants, Lyon is now France's second city and is built over three distinct areas, separated by its two rivers. Fourvière hogs the inside curve of the Saône, to the west, and the modern city lies on the other side of the Rhône, to the east. Between the two is the Presqu'ile.

Sightseeing

Begin in Fourvière, which marks the area of the old Roman city. At the top of the hill, accessed by funicular, the Gallo-Roman museum puts the ancient history of the area into excellent perspective. Near here are two particularly well-preserved Roman amphitheatres which now host music events. Also on the hill can be seen the city's landmark Notre-Dame basilica, decorated with mosaics and turrets.

Take the *Chemin de la Rosaire* path down to see the best-preserved Renaissance mansions in France, constructed with

the wealth derived from the silk business and the banking and printing trades. At the side of the Saône stands the venerable St-Jean cathedral, begun in the 12th-century and displaying an ingenious astronomical clock from the 1300s. It shows every feast day from its construction up to the year 2000 and beyond.

Across the water is the Presqu'ile, just as historic and characterised by pedestrianised shopping streets and some fine old squares. The northern section, the Croix-Rousse, is a glorious maze of lanes and alleys, criss-crossed with *traboules*. These take you through some magnificent Renaissance courtyards.

The legacy of the silk trade is fully explored in the city's Textile Museum, but don't miss the Fine Arts Museum, either. Here you'll find the next best collection of masterpieces in France, after the Louvre. There are even Rodin statues in the courtyard. Puppetry is celebrated in the equally enjoyable Marionette Museum, while cinema history comes under the spotlight in the Lumière Museum, dedicated to the pioneering work of the local Lumière brothers.

You can, of course, plan an excursion into the French Alps from Lyon, but an easier and, in some respects more rewarding, trip is to the Beaujolais vineyards, just a short drive out. If you plan to drink take a bus tour

Back in the city, the restaurants beckon. Gourmet eating is a way of life here and the city is brim-full of top-notch establishments. Even the little, inexpensive bistros seem a cut above the average. They underline the point that Lyon is just too absorbing a city to quickly pass by.

LYON

Major Events

Pennons de Lyon (June): festival of past traditions, featuring horse racing.

Les Musicades (September): annual celebration of classical music, from chamber to opera.

Festival de Musique de Vieux Lyon (November–December): recitals, Gregorian chant and other sacred music events.

Illuminations (early December): traditional and spectacular candle celebration for Advent.

How to get there – and get around

By air: scheduled flights to Lyon-Satolas Airport (10 miles out) from Heathrow and Birmingham (longest journey 2 hrs). Frequent buses to the city centre cost around FF46 and take 40 mins); taxis cost FF200–250 and take 25 mins.

By rail: Eurostar to Paris Gare du Nord, transfer to Gare de Lyon then TGV to Lyon (total journey about 7 hrs).

Public Transport: Lyon has excellent metro, funicular and bus services (a carnet of 10 tickets costs around FF68; a 24-hr ticket costs FF24). Efficient, but fairly expensive, taxi service.

Suggested Hotels

Métropole Concord, quai Joseph Gillet. Tel: (04) 71 10 44 44 Fax: (04) 78 39 99 20 Lyon's swankiest hotel on the Croix-Rousse bank of the Saône. Very expensive.

Le Méridien Part-Dieu, rue Servient. Tel: (04) 78 63 55 00 Fax: (04) 78 63 55 20 Popular hotel near the Gare de la Part Dieu and the Pont Wilson over the Rhône. Expensive.

Carlton, rue Jussieu. Tel: (04) 78 42 56 51 Fax: (04) 78 42 10 71 Renovated, central Belle Epoque hotel, just two mins from many restaurants. Moderate.

Foch, avenue Maréchal Foch. Tel: (04) 78 89 14 01 Fax: (04) 78 93 71 69 Well-positioned, comfortable hotel across Pont Morand from the Opera House. Inexpensive.

Suggested Restaurants

Léon de Lyon, rue Pléney. Tel: (04) 78 28 11 33 Classic haute cuisine with local specialities. Expensive.

La Tour Rose, rue de Boeuf. Tel: (04) 78 37 25 90 Despite the street name, this quality restaurant specializes in salmon and lamb dishes. Expensive.

Le Gourmet de Sèze, rue de Sèze. Tel: (04) 78 24 23 42 Gourmet dishes at reasonable prices. Moderate.

Comptoir du Boeuf, place Neuve St Jean. Tel: (04) 78 92 82 35 Excellent local fare, typical of the cheaper 'bouchins' in Vieux Lyon. Moderate.

The largest city on the Riviera, and the fifth largest in France, Nice is bold and sophisticated. Yet, at the same time, it is also warm and intriguing – paradoxically, both flashy and surprisingly human. With long hours of sunshine, it's a glorious rendezvous in summer, and the mild climate makes the area a welcome retreat in winter.

To see Nice at its best, visit in June or September, when the days are still rich and sunny, but the crowds are thankfully less pervasive.

History and Culture

Founded by Greeks, colonised by Romans and a part of Italy until the last century, Nice has a truly cosmopolitan background. Visitors can follow in the footsteps of Russian princes, British royalty and the Victorian well-to-do, who left Britain's chilly shores for a life in the sun here – the very expatriates who financed the building of the city's foremost boulevard, the promenade des Anglais, in the 1830s.

Sightseeing

The promenade des Anglais is a sweeping three-mile drive of premier hotels, exclusive boutiques and swaying palm trees, arcing around the city's pebbly beach and blue bay. Behind the promenade, fine avenues stretch back into the heart of the city, where more modest accommodations, shops and eateries may be found. Here the nightlife bustles into the early hours.

Nice is sprawling, but, with the aid of public transport, the city is very manageable. Buses will ferry visitors to the various museums and galleries which add a cultural dimension – one devoted to Matisse, another focusing on Chagalle, a third displaying local Roman finds. These can be found in the fashionable Cimiez district, overlooking the city.

'The chief pleasure city on the Riviera', as it has so often been described, Nice is a vibrant combination of wide, showy avenues and atmospheric, hidden backstreets. You can splash out with the wealthy on the seafront promenade des Anglais, or enjoy the simpler pleasures on offer in the more down-to-earth heart of the city.

NEGRESCO
NEGRESCO

A stroll through the narrow streets of the Italianate Old Quarter, close to the Cathedral and beneath the ruins on the hill known as 'the Château', offers a contrast to the broad avenues of showy mansions. Here, visitors can browse flower markets, craft stalls and cheaper fashion outlets before taking a seat at one of the many outdoor tables for lunch or supper.

With more time to spare, and a car at your disposal, a stunning, cliff-hugging ride around the corniche roads to Monaco reveals even more about the area's prosperity and natural beauty. The old city centre is a pleasant place to wonder around. You can see the royal palace and the cathedral. Anyone can play for fun at Monte Carlo's famous casino, but access to the big rollers' room is more restricted. If gambling doesn't appeal, perhaps the city's opera season does. Nice, too, has its own casino and a highly-regarded opera house, as well as other venues offering anything in the way of concerts, from chamber music and ballet to rock and jazz.

With the Mediterranean at its doorstep, Nice is heaven for seafood devotees, and is also the birthplace of the *salade niçoise* (try it in a *pan-bagnat* – a large bun), and *pissaladière,* a French onion tart, flavoured with anchovies and olives. For a tasty snack, seek out *socca,* a hot, flat bread made from crushed chick peas, sold by street vendors.

Between Monte Carlo and Nice are a number of picture postcard fishing villages like Villefranche-sur-Mer, with its waterfront cafés and lively beach, and precariously perched medieval settlements like Eze, now known for its artisan workshops and exotic gardens.

Nice

Major Events

Monte Carlo Rally. (January): famous automobile event.

Carnival Roi de XXème Siècle. (mid to late February): two weeks of celebrations, including several 'battles of the flowers', a fireworks display and grand parades at Nice.

Monte Carlo Spring Arts Festival. (early April – to early May): celebration of the performing arts over five weeks, including concerts, plays, recitals, dance, workshops and master classes.

Formula One Grand Prix de Monaco. (mid May): practice, qualifying, and the greatest of all motor races, over three days

Nice Jazz Festival (mid July): week-long extravanganza which has featured big names like Tony Bennett, Chuck Berry, Joe Cocker and Phil Collins.

How to get there – and get around

By air: scheduled flights to Nice-Côte d'Azur Airport (4 miles out) from Heathrow, Gatwick, Luton and Liverpool, plus a summer service from East Midlands. Buses, costing around FF21, run every 20 mins to Nice centre and take 15 mins. Taxis are frequent but fairly expensive.

By rail: Eurostar to Paris Gare du Nord, transfer to Gare de Lyon TGV to Nice (total journey time 10 ½ hrs).

Public Transport: Buses serve Nice reasonably well and a five-ticket carnet costs FF32.50. Trains run along the eastern Côte d'Azur frequently and are the cheapest, and least busy, way of travelling between Nice and Monte Carlo.

Suggested Hotels

Négresco, promenade des Anglais. Tel: (04) 93 16 64 00 Fax: (04) 93 18 35 68
Class oozes from this splendid reminder of *la Belle Époque*, which dominates the main promenade. Very expensive.

Sofitel Nice Centre, Parvis de l'Europe. Tel: (04) 92 00 80 00
Fax: (04) 93 26 27 00
Flagship hotel for the Sofitel-Novotel-Mercure chain, suitably embellished for its location. Expensive.

Hotel Windsor, 11 rue Dalpozzo. Tel: (04) 93 88 59 35 Fax: (04) 93 88 94 57
Fifty-seven-room, simple, family-run hotel. Moderate.

Suggested Restaurants

Coco Beach, avenue Jean Lorrain. Tel: (04) 93 89 39 26
Specialist in seafood with impeccable style and service. Expensive.

Dominique Nicol, boulevard Victor Hugo. Tel: (04) 93 82 48 63
Traditional niçoise fare, with the emphasis on quality. Moderate.

Passez à Table, 30 rue Pertinax. Tel: (04) 93 85 02 16
A good option for vegetarians. Inexpensive.

Nice's palatial Négresco hotel, built for the one time violinist Henri Négresc, epitomises the glamour of the city. If you can't afford to stay there, you can at least visit the hotels public rooms. The salon is dominated by a baccarat chandelier made for a Tsar

BAR l'Albatros
CREPES
STEACK FRITES CREPES
CAEN
A VENDRE

For many British travellers, Normandy provides the first taste of France. Just a few hours' comfortable cruise across the English Channel, you disembark into a lush, green countryside of rolling hills and half-timbered old buildings. Yet Normandy can be quite ritzy, too. A stroll along the seafront at Deauville reveals that the Channel coast has long been the playground of the rich and famous. And, with truly momentous events in history commemorated in such varied places as the Bayeux Tapestry and the D-Day beaches, Normandy's fascination can easily spill over from the few days of a short break to a fully-fledged summer fortnight.

History and Culture

The most prominent early settlers were Vikings from the Nordic countries. They gave their name to the region and set it up as a base from which to launch further forays. The Norman Conquest of England is one of history's best-known tales. Nearly 900 years later, the Allied assault on Normandy's beaches in 1944, which led to the liberation of Europe, is equally well documented. For its wealth, Normandy leans on agriculture, producing some of France's finest soft cheeses, cider to wash them down and the powerful Calvados apple brandy.

Sightseeing

The trouble with Normandy is that there is too much to see, particularly over a few days. Over to the east, the region is dominated by its biggest city, Rouen, and its sparkling Gothic cathedral, but many of the best attractions are to the west, where Caen, a short hop from the ferry port at Ouistreham, makes an ideal base. Like most towns around here, Caen suffered badly during the war. However, it has somehow preserved some fine old buildings, including two abbeys and a prized 14th-century church, St-Pierre. From Caen, you can run east or west along the coast. If you go east, you pass through a series of resorts, including Cabourg, Trouville and brash Deauville, as well as the pretty harbour town of Honfleur, one of the war's remarkable survivors. If you go west, you're soon into the area now famed for its D-Day beaches, most famous of which is Arromanches. Here, the British contingent came ashore on what was dubbed Gold Beach. On the seafront is now a D-Day museum, an essential port of call to fully take in the enormity of the events of 6 June 1944. Immaculately maintained cemeteries – dedicated by nationality and including a stark German place of rest – tell in few words, but with choking images, the human tragedy that was World War II. To pay one's respect here is a moving experience.

The historic city of Bayeux will lift the spirits. The majesty of the Bayeux Tapestry, which recalls the Battle of Hastings, has not been over-exaggerated. In its special museum, with exhibitions and an informative film show, its value is obvious. The rest of the city should not be overlooked, however. At its heart stands a beautiful cathedral and the old town has some intriguing streets and squares.

Fifty miles south-west of Bayeux is one of France's most famous tourist attractions. Mont St Michel, a medieval island settlement, rises dramatically from the sea mist and is crowned with an impregnable Gothic abbey. It was once a major destination for religious pilgrims. Today, pilgrims of a different sort head for its portals. You'll be lucky to find it quiet, but it's one of the places you just have to see. Those with the energy can climb the narrow streets to the top; others can just stay below, or on the mainland, and admire the view.

Honfleur's remarkably unspoilt old harbour, dating from the 17th century and surrounded by tall, narrow buildings now houses fine restaurants and shops. Market stalls sell fish fresh from the trawler.

The seaside town of Arromanches was the site of some of the heaviest fighting during the D-Day landings. Here the famous Mulberry Harbour, a pre-fabricated floating dock, was assembled to shelter Allied craft.

Normandy

Major Events (all Caen)
Festival aspects des musiques d'aujourd'hui (March): celebration of modern music.
Foire de Pâques (early April): three-week Easter Fair.
Fêtes à Caen la Paix (mid May): peace festival in a city where memories are poignant.
Commémoration du 6 juin 1944 (early June): commemoration of the D-Day Landings with a musical fete at the Caen Peace Memorial.
Festival Caen (July–August): 'Evening of Summer' celebrations, featuring music and theatre.

How to get there – and get around
By air: scheduled flights to Caen Airport (3 miles out) from Gatwick and Biggin Hill (taking 55 mins). Taxis and infrequent buses run to Caen centre.
By car: ferry from Portsmouth to Caen (actually Ouistreham 10 miles north; 6 hrs). For foot-travellers, buses connect with sailings and run into Caen centre (20 mins).
Public Transport: Caen has a reliable bus service and plentiful taxis. Some trains and buses run throughout the region, but your own car is advised.

Suggested Hotels (all Caen)
Relais des Gourmets, rue de Geôle.
Tel: (02) 31 86 06 01 Fax: (02) 31 39 06 00
Caen's best hotel, small but elegant. Moderate.
Holiday Inn, place Foch.
Tel: (02) 31 27 57 57 Fax: (02) 31 27 57 58
Modern city-centre hotel with many amenities. Moderate.
Bristol, rue de 11 Novembre.
Tel: (02) 02 31 84 76 Fax: (02) 31 52 29 28
Cosy, small and traditional central hotel. Inexpensive.

Suggested Restaurants (all Caen)
Les Echevins, route de Trouville.
Tel: (02) 31 84 10 17
Classic Norman and international cuisine. Expensive.
Le Dauphin, rue Gémare.
Tel: (02) 31 86 22 26 Popular restaurant serving local fare. Moderate.
Chez Michel, rue Jean Romain.
Tel: (02) 31 86 16 59
Excellent value for money. Inexpensive.

PARIS

Boat trips down the Seine, giddy views from the Eiffel Tower, traffic swirling around the Arc de Triomphe and the Champs Elysées, Gothic Notre Dame – Paris is known to everyone. These attractions and more are so obvious that it would insult the reader to spell them out. If you've only two or three days to spare, of course you must concentrate on these famous sights, but if you've longer at your disposal, or you're returning to Paris for a second or third visit, it's time to branch out.

History and Culture

Paris is now over 2,000 years old. The little Roman settlement of Lutetia, built on an island in the Seine, has certainly expanded. It was made capital in the 6th century and has prospered ever since, despite falling into the hands of the English in the 15th century. The Bourbon kings beautified the city, before losing interest and heading out to Versailles. Napoleon modernised Paris, adding new bridges and monumental arches, then, later in the 19th century, the medieval heart was swept away by architect Baron Haussman, who introduced the wide leafy avenues for which Paris is now famous. Although occupied in World War II, Paris thankfully survived the conflict mostly unscathed.

It goes without saying that shopping and eating out are *de rigeur*. *Haute couture* calls Paris its home, with designer houses like Chanel, Dior, Laroche, St Laurent and Ricci all clustered together on the Right Bank. More affordable are the excellent department stores such as Galleries Lafayette and Au Printemps. Paris swarms with restaurants and bistros. Build up an appetite by skipping a sit-down lunch and just raiding one of the fabulous patisseries.

Sightseeing

So, forgoing the obvious attractions, here are some lesser known ports of call. First of all, museums and galleries. Rather than fighting through the crowds at the Louvre, you could head for the Musée d'Orsay, a converted railway station where one of the world's finest collections of Impressionist art can be found. Renoir, Manet, Toulouse-Lautrec, Van Gogh, Monet, they're all here. The Petit Palais, the Musée Marmottan and the Musée de l'Orangerie, all with yet more Impressionism, plus the Dali museum in Montmartre and the Picasso Museum, near the Bastille, are similar treats. On a different tack, the Cité des Sciences is an excellent museum of science and technology. You can fool around with hands-on exhibits, see a film on the world's largest cinema screen, and then watch a spectacular star show in the planetarium. Star gazing of a quite different kind is on offer at the Père Lachaise Cemetery. Pick up a map of famous gravesites from the cemetery office and seek out the tombs of Molière, Marcel Proust, Frédérick Chopin, Oscar Wilde, Sarah Bernhardt, Edith Piaf, Simone Signoret, Yves Montand and Jim Morrison, leader of the rock band the Doors.

You could enjoy the mostly free pleasures of the many Parisian parks. Join the locals and hire a boat in the Bois de Boulogne, watch the Wednesday puppet shows in the Jardin du Luxembourg and sniff the exotic shrubs in the Jardin des Plantes. Indeed, many of the best Parisian pleasures are free. Wander around the narrow streets of the arty Le Marais quarter, thread your way through prosperous Montmartre, browse the bookstores of St-Germain-des-Prés and the picture of Parisian life you pick up is worth the price of a ticket any day: commuters having their morning shot of coffee, old ladies parading their pampered pooches, the lazy bartender drawing on a Gauloise – the classic Parisian cameos are all there.

When evening comes, rather than falling for the clichéd can-can, why not seek out one of the many jazz clubs or take in a little African music? You could also try to get a ticket for the opera, but book in advance. Productions are now staged at the modern Opéra-Bastille. If you've set your heart on facing off the legendary phantom, don't despair: you can still, in the daytime, tour Charles Garnier's opulent old opera house, where he allegedly made his home.

PREVIOUS PAGE: Paris' many bridges offer a classic view of the city. The Pont des Arts, with the stunning backdrop of the Ile-de-la-Cité, the medieval city of romance.

Paris

Major Events

Salon de Mars (late March): major flower show.
Musicora (mid April): classical music festival.
French Open Tennis Championship (early June): Grand Slam tournament, held at Stade Roland Garros.
Festival St Denis (June–July): classical concerts, often featuring grand choral works.
Paris Quartier d'Eté (July–August): theatre, music and dance festival
Tour de France (late July): finale of the famous cycle race on the Champs-Elysées.
Jazz Festival (October): month-long events all over the city.
Prix de L'Arc de Triomphe (early October): Europe's premier horserace at Longchamps.

How to get there – and get around

By air: scheduled flights to Paris (Orly, 10 miles out or Charles de Gaulle, 16 miles out) from 20 British airports (longest flight 1½ hrs), then by rapid trains or buses (15–30 mins, costing around FF40–60) to central Paris. Taxis take 20–40 mins and cost FF150–200.
By rail: Eurostar to Paris Gare du Nord (3 hrs).
By car: Several cross-channel routes from Dover and Folkestone to Calais or Boulogne (taking 35–90 mins), then (tolled) autoroute to Paris (3 hrs).
Public Transport: Paris has a super-efficient metro and RER (regional trains) system, backed up by a comprehensive bus service. Interchangeable tickets cost from FF8 for a single to FF52 for a carnet of 10.

Suggested Hotels

Ambassador, boulevard Haussmann. Tel: (01) 42 46 92 63 Fax: (01) 40 22 08 74
Renowned for its food and attractive art deco architecture; in the Opéra quarter. Expensive.
Timhôtel Montmartre, rue Ravignan. Tel: (01) 42 55 74 79
Fax: (01) 42 55 71 01
Very decent hotel in a convenient, charismatic spot. Moderate.

Suggested Restaurants

La Cagoulle, place Constantin Brancusi. Tel: (01) 43 22 09 01
Excellent fish restaurant in the newer buildings of Montparnasse. Expensive.
L'Oeillade, rue de St-Simon. Tel: (01) 42 22 01 60
Popular restaurant close to the Eiffel Tower. Moderate.

The perfect light and the warm natural colours of this part of France attracted the great painters of the 19th century. Arles was immortalised in the works of Vincent Van Gogh and Gaugin, while Aix-en-Provence, a comfortable, if a little upmarket, base for a break, was the home town of Paul Cézanne. Provence extends from the River Rhone over to the Italian border, covering the area from the southern end of the French Alps to the Mediterranean Sea. Over on the eastern side are the ritzy resorts of Nice and Cannes; further west the tourist presence, while heavy, is not so pressing, especially if you head inland.

History and Culture

That the Romans conquered this region is never in doubt, once you have set eyes on the marvellously preserved old buildings in Arles. Aix was founded by these invaders, too, in 103 BC, and later suffered at the hands of the likes of the Visigoths and Lombards. The Franks and the Saracens pitched in, too, but better times were ahead. The city became known as a cultural centre, particularly during the 15th century, a heritage reflected in its many museums today. Avignon, on the other hand, was for a while the seat of the Papacy when the Pope and his courtiers moved here in 1377, to escape trouble in Rome. Today, Provence makes its living out of tourism, wine and agriculture.

Sightseeing

Aix is a pretty enough town with attractions for a couple of days, but, having come so far, you surely have to visit Arles and Avignon. And, if you're a nature lover, the unspoilt wilderness of the Camargue shouldn't be overlooked.

Aix has been dubbed 'the city of a thousand fountains', and its elegant streets are indeed a picture. Such pictures by the local artist were not appreciated by the townsfolk here while he was alive, but Cézanne is undoubtedly a hero now. You can visit his studio, kept in the same condition as at his death in 1906. More artworks can be admired in the cathedral, a 13th-century mix of styles, but home to some notable medieval pieces.

To the north of Aix is the rural area called the Lubéron, and west of that are the cities of Arles and Avignon. Arles is a real stunner. It's not big but it's perfectly formed, a harmonious blend of ancient, ochre-coloured buildings, with at its heart one of the finest surviving Roman amphitheatres. The town also has a remarkable Roman baths and a second Roman theatre, which now hosts the Arles Festival, a theatrical season, in summer. Don't miss the Romanesque church of St-Trophime, either, with its marvellous façade.

Arles is known as the gateway to the Camargue. Here, the delta of the River Rhône has produced an area of wetland and pasture, home to a variety of wild birds and animals, particularly the famous white horses and black bulls.

Avignon, to the north, is a powerful sight. The fortifications remain largely untarnished, the mighty Palais des Papes seeming as impregnable today as it was 700 years ago. Most of the treasures were looted during the French Revolution, but the palace is still worthy of a visit. A clutch of fine old churches and a couple of good museums ensure your day in Avignon is used to the full.

To round off your stay in Provence, you could always spice things up in metropolitan Marseille, a salty French port with all that entails, but with a number of pleasant surprises up its sleeve.

The magnificent amphitheatre at Arles. Once the seen of Roman blood sports, it is now used for concerts and, in summer, bullfighting – but the bulls are never killed, these days.

PROVENCE

Shopping at Marseille's Old Port fish market for the ingredients for *bouillabaisse* – the classic Provençal stew of fish, tomatoes, garlic, olive oil, white wine and saffron.

PROVENCE

Major Events

Grand Corso Carnavalesque (March): Aix pageant welcoming the onset of spring.
Aix Jazz Festival (June): the old town jumps on those hot summer nights.
International Dance Festival (July): ballet and contemporary dance at Aix.
Aix International Festival (July): famous open-air operas, which can be combined with those held concurrently at Orange's Roman Theatre, an hour or so up the Rhône Valley.
Avignon Festival (July): opera, theatre, ballet, music and dance throughout the city.

How to get there – and get around

By air: scheduled flights to Marseilles-Provence Airport from Gatwick only (1 hr 50 mins), with buses and taxis (15–20 mins) to Aix; otherwise there are scheduled flights from several UK airports to Nice (see Nice; longest journey 2 hrs 40 mins), then coach to Aix (2½ hrs).
By rail: Eurostar to Paris Gare du Nord (3 hrs) then transfer to Gare de Lyon for the TGV to Aix (total journey around 8½ hrs).
Public Transport: Aix centre is mostly pedestrianized, but there is a reasonable bus and taxi service. Trains connect all the main towns in Provence, but car hire is required for more rural areas.

Suggested Hotels

Villa Gallici, avenue de la Violette. Tel: (04) 42 23 29 23 Fax: (04) 42 96 30 45
Gracious villa in its own grounds in the centre of Aix. Very expensive
Mercure Roi René, boulevard du Roi-René. Tel: (04) 42 37 61 00 Fax: (04) 42 37 61 11
Traditional, central hotel now under the Mercure banner, and offering a high level of comfort. Moderate.
Cardinal, rue Cardinale. Tel: (04) 42 38 32 30 Fax: (04) 42 26 39 05
Unassuming, yet atmospheric, very popular hotel. Inexpensive.

Suggested Restaurants

Villa Gallici, avenue de la Violette. Tel: (04) 42 23 29 23
The restaurant's quality matches the hotel's. Very expensive.
Le Clos de la Violette, avenue de la Violette. Tel: (04) 42 23 30 71
Arguably Aix's most popular restaurant, with imaginative menus. Expensive.
Le Bistro Latin, rue de la Couronne. Tel: (04) 42 38 22 88
Well-priced, much-admired restaurant on two floors. Moderate.

STRASBOURG

The little rue Mercière, leading to Notre Dame cathedral in the old centre of Strasbourg, is filled with ancient houses, featuring timber façades and interesting gables.

Strasbourg is one of France's hidden gems. Because of its position on the German border, and at the heart of a rather empty tourist region, it is often neglected and passed by. But it merits further attention: two or three days should do it.

History and Culture

Strasbourg is a rather odd city, a strange mix of France and Germany. When you consider that, although it's in France today, it's been in Germany four times in the last 300 years, the architectural and cultural mix becomes understandable. From its origins as a Celtic fishing village on the Rhine, the city has always been a crossroads and its strategic position has made it a sought after property from the Roman times on.

The cross-culture influence is now growing by the day, thanks to the positioning of the European Parliament in the city, which brings in representatives and their entourage from all the member states of the European Union.

Sightseeing

Strasbourg is an island city, sitting at the heart of a ring of the River Ill. A boat trip offers excellent views of the distinctively Germanic, half-timbered houses along the banks and the medieval watchtowers over the Ponts-Couverts bridges, part of the old city fortifications. The cobbled, mostly pedestrianised old town is a collection of medieval houses and shopping arcades. The undoubted centrepiece is the Notre Dame Cathedral, a wonderfully intricate sandstone confection

begun in Romanesque style in the 11th century and continued in Gothic style until its completion in 1439. It's bigger than the Paris Notre Dame, and in fact is the second tallest church in Europe (its spire soars up 460 feet). For a small fee you can witness the daily chiming (12.30pm) of the astronomical clock, and on summer evenings the cathedral is bathed in the glow of a *son et lumière* display. The Cathedral Works Museum is also worth a visit, to see the outstanding statues and paintings which used to furnish the cathedral itself.

The city's complex past is explored in the Historical Museum, while local arts and crafts are covered by the Alsatian Museum (nothing to do with dogs – Strasbourg is the capital of the Alsace region!). Three more museums are housed in the Palais des Rohan, former residence of the powerful Rohan family, while the Old Customs House is home to a modern art museum with works by Braque and Rodin, among others.

Arguably the most picturesque area of Strasbourg is Petite France, the old tanners' quarter, which features restored old houses set among leafy locks and bridges. Wandering here is a great way to relax, as is a visit to one of the many *winstubs* or *bierstubs* (wine or beer bars). Outside the canal ring, Strasbourg also has some attractive parklands, while the ancient university has a botanical garden, open to the public. And don't miss a ride on one of the swish new city trams.

Finally, if you've ever wondered what European parliamentarians get up to, and how much gravy is really on that particular train, book a tour of the Parliament building. The MEPs seem happy to keep coming back here, and who can blame them?

STRASBOURG

Major Events
Carnaval de Strasbourg (mid March): traditional street carnival, highlighting the colourful traditions of Alsace.
International Festival of Music (June–early July): the oldest annual music festival in France.
Festival de Jazz (early July): summer jazz in the city.
Foire Européene (early–mid September): 10-day long exposition with Europe as its theme.

How to get there – and get around
By air: scheduled flights to Strasbourg-Entzheim Airport from London City Airport (2 hrs); there are many alternatives if you change at Amsterdam, Brussels, Paris or Frankfurt. Buses and taxis link the airport to the city (10 miles) and are frequent and fairly cheap. There are also flights from the UK to Basel/Mulhouse Airport (70 mins away by train).
By rail: Eurostar to Paris Gare du Nord, then transfer to Gare de l'Est for Strasbourg (total journey around 8 hours).
Public Transport: A bus and modern tram service runs through the city and from park-and-ride sites on the outskirts (a 24-hr pass costs around FF20). The taxi service is comprehensive and fairly inexpensive.

Suggested Hotels
Regent Petite France, rue des Moulins. Tel: (03) 88 76 43 43
Fax: (03) 88 76 43 76
Plush hotel in the heart of the old town and near the riverside attractions. Expensive.
Baumann, place de la Cathédrale. Tel: (03) 88 32 42 14 Fax: (03) 88 23 03 92
Traditional hotel situated near the cathedral square. Moderate.
Mercure, rue Thomann. Tel: (03) 88 75 77 88 Fax: (03) 88 32 08 66
City-centre hotel, part of the popular chain. Moderate.

Suggested Restaurants
Buerehiesel, parc de l'Orangerie.
Tel: (03) 88 45 56 65
Strasbourg's most exclusive restaurant, renowned for its exceptional cuisine. Very expensive.
Château de Pourtales, rue Mélanie.
Tel: (03) 88 31 37 40
Gastronomic restaurant with international menus. Moderate.
Le Bois Lilas, rue des Juifs.
Tel: (03) 88 36 81 19
Traditional city-centre *winstub* with Alsatian food washed down by the excellent local whites. Inexpensive.

Bamberg and Nuremberg

It's easy to overlook the northern part of Bavaria in a headlong rush to the cosmopolitan attractions of Munich or the simple lure of the Alps. Yet, here are some of Germany's great unknowns, marvellous, historic cities which barely gain a mention in the holiday brochures. The little town of Bamberg is a traveller's discovery of a lifetime. You could spend the whole short break here, but only 35 miles to the south is the almost as attractive city of Nuremberg, which makes a much more comprehensive base.

History and Culture

The golden age of Nuremberg was the 15th–16th century, when the city sat on a trading crossroads and was home to some of the finest craftsmen (particularly gold and bronze beaters) in Germany. However, Nuremberg will not want to remember the 20th century. Its blackest days came in the inter-war years, when Hitler made the city the focus of the Nazi movement. Attempting to emulate Nuremberg's former glorious relationship with the Holy Roman Empire, the Führer held his infamous rallies here. Fittingly, the Allies chose Nuremberg as the setting for the war crimes trials once the conflict had ended.

Sightseeing

You can't get away from the Nazi heritage, so perhaps it's best to mention it first and then forget about it in favour of more pleasurable attractions. On the outskirts of the city are huge open spaces known as the Reichsparteitagsgelände, where Hitler urged the crowds to follow his sinister lead. There is not much to see, except for a poignant exhibition in the Zeppelin grandstand called 'Fascination and Terror', revealing the poisonous mentality of the Nazi regime. Much more appealingly, other parts of the city look like they've been drawn from the pages of the Brothers Grimm: narrow streets and quaint little houses with 'gingerbread' façades. In winter, the main square, the Hauptmarkt, with its half-timbered houses and memorable Gothic fountain, hosts an atmospheric Christmas fair that attracts the whole region. In summer, buskers and street artists take over. Just off the square is the twin-towered St Sebald's church, the most important in the city, but the most delightful church in Nuremberg is the St Lorenzkirche on Lorenzer Platz.

Towering over the town, and offering excellent views, is the Kaiserburg castle, where the emperors once lived. Near here is the home of Albrecht Dürer, Germany's most famous Renaissance artist and sculptor. An enormous National Museum, with the biggest collection of German art in the country, the Transport Museum, containing some vintage steam engines, and a nostalgia-inducing Toy Museum round off the major attractions. Most of these wonderful buildings are not, in fact, originals, but remarkable reconstructions in the wake of World War II bombing, which lay waste to over 90 per cent of the city.

To reach Bamberg, jump on a train or a bus. It takes less than an hour and the journey is amply rewarded. Half-timbered houses, alluring little alleyways and neat cobbled streets criss-cross the town, which began life as a farming village in the 2nd century. Its cathedral is a treasure, one of the most impressive medieval structures in the whole country, commissioned by Bamberg's most famous son, Holy Roman Emperor Heinrich II. The square to the front is one of Germany's finest. Near here is the Neue Residenz, a massive Renaissance/baroque edifice, once home of the ruling classes during the Holy Roman Empire. But don't spend all your visit indoors. Give yourself time to wander around this gorgeous little town. In particular, try to find the area known as Little Venice, where colourful houses line the banks of the River Regnitz. Unlike Nuremberg, Bamberg's buildings are all genuine, and there are more jewels at every turn.

When you return to Nuremberg for the evening be sure to sample the local fare. The area is home of the *bratwurst* (sausage) and *lebkuchen* (spiced bread), while beer is a speciality of Bamberg. One particular offering, the smoked Rauchbier, will not appeal to everyone's taste, but is worth a try all the same.

PREVIOUS PAGE: Albrecht Dürer's house in Nuremberg. The highly-influential painter and master wood-engraver – the leading figure in German Renaissance art – was born in the city and lived in this building from 1509 to 1528.

The figurines on the clock at the Liebefrauenkirche in Nuremberg's Hauptmarkt emerge at midday. They represent city electors swearing allegiance to the Holy Roman Emperor in the 14th century.

Bamberg and Nuremberg

Major Events (all Nuremberg)
International Puppet Theatre Festival (May): biennial festival of marionette theatre.
International Organ Week (late-June–July): Europe's premier annual sacred music festival.
Franconian Wine Festival (late June–July): annual tasting of the vintage.
Festival of the Bards (late July–August): annual celebration of song-writing.
Old Town Festival (late September): the biggest of its type in Germany, including a 'Market of Hospitality'.
Christkindlesmarkt (late November–late December): world-famous Christmas market.

How to get there – and get around
By air: scheduled flights from Heathrow only to Nuremberg Airport (4 miles out) take 2 hrs 10 mins: otherwise there are flights to Frankfurt International Airport from Heathrow, Gatwick, Stansted, London City, Birmingham, Edinburgh, Glasgow and Manchester, with transfers to Nuremberg (total journey 3½–4 hrs). Taxis from Nuremberg Airport to the centre are frequent and cheap.
Public Transport: Good bus and metro services, costing from around DM3 individually to DM15 for 10 short journeys. The Kultur Ticket gives free local transport, along with entrance fees to museums other attractions (DM23 for 48 hrs). Reliable and reasonably priced taxi service.

Suggested Hotels (all Nuremberg)
Le Méridien Grand Hotel, Bahnhofstrasse.
Tel: (0911) 23 22 0 Fax: (0911) 23 22 44 4
Nuremberg's finest hotel, set close to all the attractions. Very expensive.
Atrium, Münchenerstrasse. Tel: (0911) 47 48 0 Fax: (0911) 47 48 42 0
Upmarket hotel, just south-east of the old town. Very expensive.
InterCity Hotel, Eilgutstrasse. Tel: (0911) 24 78 0 Fax: (0911) 24 78 99 9
City centre hotel, near the railway station. Moderate.

Suggested Restaurants (all Nuremberg)
Try the restaurants at the hotels above, or, more modestly:
Heilig Geist Spital, Spitalgasse.
Tel: (0911) 22 17 61
Classic local specialities, with a super outlook over the River Pegnitz. Moderate.
Bratwursthaüsle, Rathausplatz.
Famous sausage restaurant which gets very busy. Inexpensive.

Germany's highest mountain, the Zugspitze, towers above the other Bavarian Alps and over the twin town of Garmisch-Partenkirchen. It can be ascended from both the German and the Austrian sides.

Mention the Alps and most people will think or Switzerland or Austria. Yet if there is one region that sums up the picture-postcard image of traditional mountain life, it is the Bavarian Alps. Here, south of Munich, are the sort of villages that you thought only existed in holiday brochure hype. Wooden-framed houses, surrounded by green, grassy meadows in summer, twinkle out from beneath snow-laden roofs on winter evenings. Don't be surprised to see villagers wearing traditional costume – lederhosen are practical working clothes – and if you see Heidi bringing in the cows, she's doing it for real, not for effect.

History and Culture

Travelling among these little communities, with their painted houses and fields littered with hay barns, is a breath of fresh air, in more ways than one. The atmosphere is relaxed, unpretentious and uncomplicated and there's even more than high, snowy peaks, densely wooded hillsides and deep blue lakes to admire. The region was particularly favoured by Bavaria's royal family, most notably the 'mad' King Ludwig II, who endowed it with some dream-like castles in the 19th century. Any number of small villages can offer hospitality, but Garmisch-Partenkirchen makes the most convenient base, being well-connected and having all the facilities you're likely to need. The town was actually two separate villages – Garmisch and Partenkirchen – until they came together to stage the 1936 Winter Olympic Games. It is now Germany's most popular ski resort.

Bavarian Alps

Sightseeing

As in most holiday areas, there are certain 'musts'. If the weather is clear, you must take the cog railway and cable car up to the peak of Germany's highest mountain, the Zugspitze (9,600 feet). The views are unrivalled and, if you want to, you can descend into Austria. You must also visit at least one other alpine village. Mittenwald, on the Austrian border, is a popular choice, or you could try Oberammergau, the wood-carvers' village famous for its Passion Play, staged by the locals every 10 years in gratitude for being spared from the Black Death in 1633. If it's Play year (as it will be in the year 2000), and you haven't got a ticket, give Oberammergau a wide berth, but at other times it's not as touristy as you might think.

The final 'must' involves a trip to Ludwig's fairy-tale castles. His fantasy fortress at Neuschwanstein, near Füssen, was the model for Walt Disney's Sleeping Beauty castle and the inspiration for the plastic centrepieces of the Disney theme parks. Near here is the 12th-century Hohenschwangau fortress, where Ludwig spent his dreamy youth, and where Wagner was a guest and great influence. Fifteen miles away, the castle Ludwig built at Linderhof is a miniature Versailles, with, in its landscaped gardens, a grotto based on a set from Wagner's *Tannhäuser*.

In winter, of course, you might want to to enjoy some winter sports; in summer, the hiking is second to none. Anytime is a good time for a short break here.

Bavarian Alps

Major Events

International Wintersports Week (early January): ice-skating, ski-jumping and social events.
Alpine World Cup Races (mid February): Men's Downhill and 'Super G' world cup events.
Richard Strauss Festival (early June): tribute to the composer of the Alpine Symphony (separate Strauss events in September to celebrate the 50th anniversary of his death).
Street Festival of the Ludwigstrassler (July): the shop-owners of Partenkirchen's have their very own festival.
Garmisch Heimatwoche (late July): beer festival and other Bavarian customs.

How to get there – and get around

By air: scheduled flights to Munich Airport from Heathrow, Gatwick, Luton, Birmingham and Manchester – longest flight 2¼ hrs. Rail to Munich central station (20 mins), then trains hourly to Garmisch-Partenkirchen (1 hr 20 mins). Taxis are available for the short distances to the hotels.
Public Transport: almost non-existent and unnecessary in the two villages, although there are inter-town routes. Car hire is advised for sightseeing in the surrounding area.

Suggested Hotels

Dorint Sporthotel, Mittenwaldestrasse, Partenkirchen. Tel: (08821) 70 60
Fax: (08821) 70 66 18
Upmarket hotel in central Partenkirchen, catering for winter and summer sports-people. Expensive.
Grand Hotel Sonnenbichl, Burgstrasse, Garmisch. Tel: (08821) 70 20
Fax: (08821) 70 21 31
Stylish hotel in the more ritzy Garmisch, with every facility. Expensive.
Clausings Posthotel, Marienplatz, Garmisch. Tel: (08821) 70 90.
Fax: (08821) 70 92 05
Impressive and well-appointed hotel in central Garmisch. Moderate.
Posthotel Partenkirchen, Ludwigstrasse, Partenkirchen.
Tel: (08821) 5 10 67 Fax: (08821) 7 85 68
Ornate 14th-century building, with 20th-century amenities, in one of the main streets. Moderate.

Suggested Restaurants

Reindl's Restaurant, Banhofstrasse,Garmisch-Partenkirchen. Tel: (08821) 5 80 25
High-class hotel-restaurant with a national and international reputation. Expensive.
Clausings Posthotel, Marienplatz, Garmisch. Tel: (08821) 70 90
Popular hotel terrace restaurant, featuring rustic Bavarian or international food. Moderate.
Posthotel Partenkirchen, Ludwigstrasse. Tel: (08821) 5 10 67
Bavarian and international cuisine in lovely surroundings. Moderate.

DEM DEUTSCHEN VOLKE

In Berlin the transition from communism to capitalism can physically be seen in fragments of the monstrous Wall that until 1989 divided the city in two. All around new building works are re-emphasising the enormity of the changes that have been wreaked on the city. Reunited, Berlin is now Europe's largest city, a metropolis so full of fascination and intrigue that you will need plenty of time to explore it. Don't come for less than three whole days; if you can, stay much longer.

History and Culture

Berlin's prosperity took off in the 17th century, even though its roots date back much further. As capital of Prussia, it was Europe's most important city. In the tumultuous early years of the 20th century, Berlin became seat of the Weimar Republic. This troubled age of hyperinflation and political unrest was sealed by the arrival of the Nazis in 1933. With their demise at the end of World War II, Berlin was subdivided amongst its liberators. The Soviets took the eastern half; the Allies, through the British, the Americans and the French, held onto the West, creating an island of capitalism in a sea of communism that was the new East Germany. The exodus of thousands of unhappy East German citizens led the Soviet authorities to construct the Berlin Wall overnight in 1961, an act damned as an affront to humanity. The events of 1989, leading to and the re-unification of Germany, once again turned the city in a new direction.

Sightseeing

The obvious place to start exploring is at the Wall, or what's left of it. Checkpoint Charlie, the notorious border crossing between East and West, offers the most poignant reminders of the brutality of the communist regime. Its museum is devoted to the (mostly unsuccessful) attempts to escape across to the West. Brandenberg Gate, a Prussian triumphal arch, was stuck right on the old East-West frontier and is now open again, leading visitors into the old eastern sector, where the pick of the sights can be found today. Stroll down the beautiful Unter den Linden avenue, with its monumental buildings, then view the contrastingly ugly, concrete buildings around Alexanderplatz square. Whilst here, take a lift to the top of the Television Tower (once the East's one-finger salute to the West) for the best city views. Don't miss the Pergamonmuseum, an astonishing collection of treasures plundered from the ancient world.

The old West Berlin's strident neon and swanky modern buildings were intended, it seemed, to tease and provoke its poorer neighbour. It's still a glamorous area today, though the prosperity has begun to even out over the city as a whole. Go shopping on the Kurfürstendamm. Wander in the Tiergarten parkland, once a royal hunting ground. Visit the re-unified East and West German art collections in the new Gemäldegalerie. View the Reichstag building, once seat of the German parliament. It is soon to resume its old function, when government transfers here from Bonn.

The 17th-century Charlottenburg Palace, a zoo, an aquarium, a planetarium, churches, cathedrals and synagogues, historic memorials and monuments, canal cruises, wonderfully cosmopolitan restaurants, pulsating nightclubs, countless concerts and recitals: Berlin has it all and more besides. After all this, it may be asking a lot of the weary sightseer, but, whatever you do, make time to take the S-bahn train out to the town of Potsdam. Its baroque palaces, pavilions, sumptuous parklands and remarkably unspoilt old centre will admirably round off a marvellous break.

Berlin's Reichstag, opened in 1894, mysteriously burned down during the days of Hitler, but is soon to be restored to eminence as the new home of the unified Germany's parliament.

The famous Brandenberg Gate in winter is nothing like as cold as relations used to be between the glitzy, over-dressed West and the dour, suspicious East, in this once-again unified city.

Berlin

Major Events
Berlin Film Festival (mid February): one of the heavyweight film festivals, championing Europe's best.
Summer Opera (all summer): the Komische Oper and other venues almost daily host the repertoire of Mozart, Strauss, Verdi and Puccini.
Köpenicker Blues & Jazz Festival (August): concerts and open-air sessions on weekends.
Internationale Berlin-Biermeile (late August): Berlin's own beer festival.

How to get there – and get around
By air: scheduled flights to Berlin-Tegel Airport (5 miles out) from Heathrow, Gatwick, Birmingham and Manchester (longest flight 2½ hrs). Taxis to Berlin centre cost around DM25 and take 25 mins; buses every 10 mins cost DM3 and take 35 mins.
Public Transport: Berlin has comprehensive bus, train, tram and metro services (a 24-hr interchangeable ticket costs around DM7.5; the Berlin Welcome Card gives free local transport along with free or reduced entrance fees to museums, theatres and other attractions – DM29 for 72 hrs). Taxis are fairly expensive.

Suggested Hotels
Bristol Kempinski, Kurfürstendamm.
Tel: (030) 88 43 40
Fax: (030) 8 33 60 75
One of the world's most charismatic and elegant hotels on the famous Ku'damm. Very expensive.
Grand Hotel Esplanade.
Tel: (030) 25 47 80 Fax: (030) 2 65 11 71
Berlin's other legendary address, despite its modernity. Very expensive.
Forum, Alexanderplatz.
Tel: (030) 23 89 0 Fax: (030) 23 89 43 05
Large, modern hotel with incomparable views of the former East Berlin from its upper floors. Expensive.
Hotel California, Kurfürstendamm.
Tel: (030) 88 01 20
Fax: (030) 88 01 21 11
Small, but comfortable, hotel in one of the most-fashionable areas. Moderate.

Suggested Restaurants
Bamberger Reiter,
Regensbergerstrasse. Tel: (030) 2 18 42 42
Probably Berlin's finest, known for its outstanding international gastronomy. Expensive.
Paris Bar, Kantstrasse.
Tel: (030) 3 13 80 52
French-owned, bustling restaurant. Expensive.
Merz, Schöneberger Ufer.
Tel: (030) 2 61 38 82
Value-for-money regional food in the centre of town. Moderate.
Wilhelm Hoeck's, Wilmersdorfstrasse.
Tel: (030) 3 41 81 74
Traditional beer, meat and pickles. Inexpensive.

The Black Forest is the land of the Grimm fairy tales, of cuckoo clocks and of wood carvings. It is a region of thickly wooded hills, where conifers and oaks compete for every inch of spare countryside and the occasional lake sparkles in the midday sun. Inevitably, there is a huge tourist presence, but, if you can get off the beaten track, the wonder of the Black Forest can still be yours.

History and Culture

There are two obvious centres within the Black Forest. Baden-Baden has long been one of Germany's plushest resort and conference cities, famed for its natural springs and restorative waters that were first recognised by the Romans. The other is Freiburg, established in the 12th century, and undoubtedly the best city base in the area, thanks largely to its university, which ensures there's always something going on. Freiburg was heavily bombarded during the last war, in which it lost most of its old buildings.However, the magnificent cathedral has survived. Most of the rest of the Black Forest is rural and, thankfully, unspoilt. In the little villages, you will still find warm-hearted locals living in traditional wooden houses and speaking a dialect barely comprehensible even to other Germans.

Sightseeing

In Freiburg, the red sandstone cathedral is the big must-see. Its earliest parts are Romanesque, dating from the 12th century, while the rest of the massive structure is Gothic and took 300 years to finish. Stunning stained-glass windows throw patchy light onto the dark interior, while, up above, the 380-foot tower provides the best views for miles. There are over 300 steps to the top but it's worth the effort.

Baden-Baden, on the northern edge of the Black Forest, is an upmarket resort, known for its spa waters, which have been treating ailments for thousands of years – it is said the Roman Emperor Caracalla bathed here as a cure for his rheumatism.

BLACK FOREST

In the streets below, Freiburg has a gently happy-go-lucky air. Street artists and buskers perform for passers-by. The city's museums are free and provide a good insight into the local culture and history. Watch out, though, for the little gulleys that run through some of the city's streets. Part of an ancient drainage system, they were once used for watering livestock. Now it's tourists feet that receive irrigation.

From Freiburg, buses and trains run throughout the Black Forest, allowing you to explore its unrivalled natural beauty. And the train journeys themselves are wonderful enough to make rail buffs ecstatic. One such ride takes you southeast to lovely Titisee, a lake hemmed in by wooded hills and now used for water sports. There's a wealth of fresh air activity in the Black Forest and hiking is particularly big around the town of Triberg, north of Titisee. The town itself has a major draw in its impressive 500-foot waterfall.

To take advantage of Baden-Baden, on the northern edge of the region, you need to have a wallet full of cash. The main attractions all cost money, from the bath houses to the popular casino, an elaborate, richly decorated establishment, which has been attracting high-rollers for years. If you can't afford the stakes, take a tour and see what goes on among the big spenders. Another cheap option is to visit the ancient Roman baths, with their inventive underground heating system.

As befits a student city, Freiburg has a great choice of eating establishments, at all prices. The marvellous climate has encouraged extensive vine growth around the city, so the local wines are well worth trying, too. There are colourful daily markets in the Münsterplatz and the city also stages numerous concerts, festivals and theatre performances, so there is always likely to be plenty of entertainment at your disposal.

Black Forest

Major Events (all Freiburg)
Alemannic Fastnacht (mid February): carnival to celebrate the coming of Lent.
Freiburg Wine Festival (late June–mid July): three-week celebration of the wines of Baden-Württemberg, held in the Münsterplatz.
Concerts in the Cathedral (early July): series of organ concerts and recitals
Münstersommer (mid July): open-air concerts.
Rathaushofspiele (August): summer season of theatre and concerts.
Christmas Market
(late November–late December): colourful Advent shopping.

How to get there – and get around
By air: scheduled flights to Basel/Mulhouse Airport from Heathrow, Birmingham and Manchester (2 hrs), then bus to Freiburg (1 hr).
Public Transport: Freiburg has a bus network, but is easy to explore on foot. Trains and buses run throughout the region, but car hire is recommended for greater flexibility.

Suggested Hotels (all Freiburg)
Columbi, Am Columbipark.
Tel: (0761) 21060 Fax: (0761) 31410
Super-luxury hotel with every comfort. Very expensive.
Panorama Mercure. Am Jägerhäusle Wintererstrasse. Tel: (0761) 51030
Fax: (0761) 5103 300
Traditional, comfortable hotel. Moderate–expensive.
Victoria, Eisenbahnstrasse.
Tel: (0761) 207340
Fax: (0761) 20734 444
Popular hotel with good facilities. Moderate.

Suggested Restaurants (all Freiburg)
Columbi, Am Columbipark.
Tel: (0761) 21060
High gastronomic standards and an international menu. Expensive.
Zinnstüble, Auf der Zinnen.
Tel: (0761) 34493
Specialities of the Baden-Württemberg region. Moderate.
Rappen, Münsterplatz.
Tel: (0761) 31353
Traditional restaurant in the cathedral square. Inexpensive.

Cologne and Bonn

Cologne – Köln to its residents – has all the ingredients for a sparkling weekend break. This city, hugging the bank of the Rhine, is a useful starting point for the Rhine Gorge sights outlined elsewhere in this book, but has more than enough to keep you amused in itself.

History and Culture

Over 2000 years old, Cologne was important in Roman times – its name, originally 'Colonia', comes from the Latin term for a military settlement. By the 13th century, the city was a thriving metropolis of 40,000 people, protected by Europe's longest (four miles) city walls. The towering presence of the cathedral began to take shape in the mid-13th century, when the city was at the height of its medieval power. After a period of decline, Cologne enjoyed a revival in the 18th century, thanks partly to the concoction here of the world-famous Eau de Cologne. In World War II, Cologne was not spared by the Allied bombers. Amazingly, the cathedral came through and, with running repairs, still dominates the city today.

Sightseeing

The twin spires of the cathedral, Germany's finest Gothic church, can be seen for many a mile. The building was established to house the remains of the Magi, brought here from Milan, but took an astonishing 700 years to complete, so great were the regular interruptions for war. You can spend ages in the cathedral, admiring the marvellous stained glasswork; the 9th-century Cross of Gero; the stunning Shrine of the Magi from the 12th century; and Stefan Lochner's fabulous 15th-century triptych, *The Adoration of the Magi*. Don't forget to climb to the top of the South Tower for some fabulous views.

Very close to the cathedral, the Roman-Germanic Museum has been built to cover the ancient Dionysus Mosaic, unearthed in 1941 during the digging of an air raid shelter. This terrific piece of flooring once graced a patrician's dining room in the 3rd century and depicts the flamboyant Greek god. Near here, two more fine museums share the same, modern building. The Wallraf-Richartz and Ludwig Museums between them feature an excellent collection of masterpieces by Cologne masters from the 14th–16th centuries, plus a fascinating gathering of 20th-century pieces.

As you stroll around the city centre, you'll come across a strange combination of churches, from ancient Romanesque survivors to modern symbols of the rebuilding work that Cologne has undertaken in the post-war years. There are also other good museums to visit, but, when culture-fatigue sets in, head for the pedestrianised area, where the major shops are excellent, or pause for a glass of the local beer. Kölsch, as it is known, is a very pale, fruity ale particular to Cologne, and is served only in small, one-fifth of a litre glasses.

Along the river, the city of Bonn, although home of the German parliament (at least until it is moved to Berlin in the year 2000), has practically become a suburb of Cologne. In the Altstadt (old town), the market square features a much-photographed pink rococo town hall. Beethoven was born in Bonn and his house, now a well-organised museum, can be visited. The town also has two fine modern art museums, plus a museum which, through impressive audio-visuals, teaches you all about Germany since World War II. As small as it is, Bonn even has its own suburbs, delightful little villages like Bad Godesburg. Another village on the same bank of the river is Schwarz-Rheindorf, home of the intriguing Doppelkirche, a 12th-century church in two halves – one for the nobility, the other for the lesser folk.

Dining out is a doddle in Cologne, with a choice of beer halls, which serve cheap, hearty meals, or more refined restaurants. As befits a one-time international capital, Bonn is not short of nightlife, either. Together, these lovely cities put on quite a show for the tourist.

PREVIOUS PAGE: Ludwig van Beethoven is Bonn's most-famous son and his birthplace has been converted into a museum. Here, you can see a selection of Beethoven memorabilia, from the organ he played at the age of 10 to some of the ear-trumpets he was forced to use as his hearing diminished.

Cologne's mighty cathedral is not just impressive from the outside: the interior is magnificent, too, with, among the treasures, a remarkable set of stained-glass windows, some dating from the 13th century.

Cologne and Bonn

Major Events
Karneval (mid February): six days of pre-Lent celebrations, including processions, costume balls and a large fun fair.
Bach Festival (late March–early April): long-established, important annual festival.
German Choir Festival (late April–early May): choirs from all over Germany meet here every year.
Medieval Jousting (May–September): feudal frolics at Burg Satzvey
Musikfestwoche (mid–late August): classical musical festival at the Schloss Brühl.

How to get there – and get around
By air: scheduled flights to Cologne (Köln)-Bonn Airport (9 miles out) from Heathrow and Gatwick (2 hrs), then by bus (30 mins; DM8.20) or taxi (20 mins; DM40) to Cologne centre.
By rail: Eurostar to Brussels Midi (2 hrs 40 mins), then change for Cologne (another 2½–3 hrs).
Public Transport: Cologne has a comprehensive train/bus/tram/metro network (24-hr tickets at DM10 provide the best value). The trains, buses and trams also run to Bonn (20 mins).

Suggested Hotels
Dom, Domkloster. Tel: (0221) 2 02 40 Fax: (0221) 2 02 44 44
Famous luxury hotel adjacent to the cathedral and railway station. Very expensive.
Savoy, Turinerstrasse.
Tel: (0221) 1 62 30 Fax: (0221) 1 62 32 00
Very well-appointed city-centre hotel. Expensive.
Esser Minotel, An der Malzmühle.
Tel: (0221) 23 41 41
Fax: (0221) 23 39 43
Comfortable hotel close to the centre. Moderate.
Speer, Gladbacherstrasse.
Tel: (0221) 51 67 76 Fax: (0221) 52 49 27
Small, but cosy, central hotel. Inexpensive.

Suggested Restaurants
Dom, Domkloster. Tel: (0221) 2 02 40
Stately hotel restaurant with an outstanding pedigree. Expensive.
Scampino, Deutz-Mülheimerstrasse.
Tel: (0221) 61 85 44
High quality Mediterranean-style fish restaurant. Moderate.
Alt Köln, Trankgasse.
Tel: (0221) 13 46 78
Classic Cologne beer hall, where several of the city's brews complement the plain, but hearty, fare. Inexpensive.

The impressive Town Hall in Hamburg, as seen from the elegant shops in the Alsterarkaden arcade. Built in neo-Renaissance style in the 19th century, the Town Hall is topped by one of the city's highest towers (367 feet).

HAMBURG

Europe's third largest port, with one of the sleaziest red light districts on the continent, does not seem the obvious choice for a short holiday. Think again. Hamburg is vibrant, Hamburg is cultured and, best of all, Hamburg is easy to get to. An overnight ferry crossing from Newcastle or Harwich whisks you right into the very heart of the city.

History and Culture

Hamburg's prosperity is tied in with the Hanseatic League, the commercial union of cities in the Middle Ages. Its port, established in the 12th century, made it one of the most powerful and wealthy cities in Europe. Much of the city was destroyed by fire in 1842, and World War II bombing added further devastation, but Hamburg, phoenix-like, has risen from the ashes.

Today, it is Germany's second largest city. Like all port cities, it caters for the needs of the deprived seamen – hence the breweries, bars, clubs and seedy hot spots. But, away from the red light district and the port, Hamburg is much more refined, and the shopping is as good as it gets in Germany.

Sightseeing

Even as you step off the ferry, there are sights to be seen. The harbour area can be toured by boat, and is more interesting than it may sound. If you stay over a weekend, force yourself out of bed early on Sunday morning, for the 'fish

market'. You can buy the strangest goods here, from a case of exotic fruits to a squawking parrot. Near the harbour is the notorious Reeperbahn in the St Pauli district. Not all this area is given over to 'adult' activities, but certain parts are definitely not for the faint-hearted.

Hamburg is a surprising city, with a network of canals and more bridges than Amsterdam and Venice put together. Many of them criss-cross the Speicherstadt, just east of the docks, a district of early 20th-century, red-brick, gabled warehouses that are still in use. At the heart of the city, the neo-Renaissance Rathaus (Town Hall) is a magnificent sandstone building. Its tower is one of half a dozen which dominate the city skyline. The others belong to churches, among them St Nicholas, left ruined as a memorial to wartime bombing, and St Michael, a high baroque structure with panoramic views from its 354-ft copper spire.

Hamburg has a good range of museums, most notably the knockout collection of art in the Kunsthalle. Virtually every important artist is represented. More unusual sights include the TV Tower, with its revolving restaurant 890 feet up, the Star Club, where The Beatles played in the early 1960s, and the Holsten brewery, which offers free tours (except in August).

From Hamburg, it's easy to nip along to more relaxed cities like Lübeck, Hannover, Bremen and even down to Hamelin, of Pied Piper fame. Lübeck was once capital of the Hanseatic League, and its old town has been designated a World Heritage Site by UNESCO. Bremen, home of the Grimm Brothers' Bremen Town Musicians, is another harbour town, but with an atmospheric, cobbled heart of twisted streets and medieval homes. Hannover, reconstructed after the war, has some particularly attractive gardens and fine museums.

Hamburg

Major Events

Hamburger Kabarettfestival (late May–late June): annual festival of cabaret acts.

West Port (July): international jazz festival, the biggest in Germany

Der Hamburger Jedermann (July – August): famous 'Everyman' open-air theatre at the warehouse complex.

Schleswig-Holstein Musik Festival (July–August): international classical music festival in concert halls and churches.

International Sommertheater Festival (mid August–mid September): Germany's largest dance and theatre festival.

How to get there – and get around

By air: scheduled flights to Hamburg Airport (5 miles out) from Heathrow, Gatwick, Stansted, Birmingham, Glasgow and Manchester (longest flight 1½ hrs). Taxis to Hamburg centre cost around DM30; buses, every 15 mins, cost from DM8.

By car: ferries from Harwich (22 hrs) and Newcastle (24 hrs) directly to Hamburg.

Public Transport: a comprehensive bus/train/metro (U-bahn) service runs throughout the city. Fares can be linked to the 'Hamburg Card', which includes free access to museums, etc. (1-day around DM12.50; 3-day, DM25.50).

Suggested Hotels

Atlantic Hotel Kempinski, An der Alster. Tel: (040) 28 88 0 Fax: (040) 24 71 29. Hamburg's most famous hotel, overlooking the Aussenalster lake, built in the heyday of transatlantic sea crossings. Very expensive.

Maritim Hotel Reichshof, Kirchenallee. Tel: (040) 24 83 30 Fax: (040) 24 83 38 88
Central hotel with fine range of facilities, including an indoor pool. Expensive.

Hotel Alster-Hof, Esplanade. Tel: (040) 35 00 70 Fax: (040) 35 00 75 14
Comfortable hotel near the Elbe and the main railway station. Moderate.

Suggested Restaurants

Old Commercial Room, Englische Planke. Tel: (040) 36 63 19
Comfortable, traditional eating house, full of old world charm. Expensive.

Bavaria Blick, Bernard Nochtsrasse. Tel: (040) 31 16 31 16
Smart fish restaurant with wonderful views over the Elbe. Expensive.

Ratsweinkeller, Rathaus. Tel: (040) 36 41 53
Regional dishes are the speciality of this Hanseatic cellar restaurant beneath the Rathaus. Moderate.

HEIDELBERG

The spectacular pink ruins of the castle are never far from view in lovely Heidelberg. Begun in the 13th century, it was considerably expanded in the 16th-century, before being laid waste by the French in 1689.

Heidelberg is many people's perfect vision of a German city. In the flesh, the city does not let you down. It is beautiful, dramatic and lively, but at the same time, unfortunately, over-touristed in summer, so make this your destination for a long weekend in the spring or the autumn.

History and Culture

Heidelberg has the oldest university in Germany, founded in 1386, and this seat of learning has shaped the character of the city for centuries. The town was the major settlement in the region of the Rhineland Palatinate and its rulers ensured that the area developed into a major European centre in the 13th–16th centuries. During this period, the city's finest buildings went up, including the impressive castle. However, attacks by the French in 1689 inflicted great damage on the castle, and much of the old town was devastated by a major fire four years later. The buildings were largely reconstructed in a new baroque style.

Sightseeing

The pink sandstone castle is the obvious highlight. It towers above all else and can be reached by funicular from the city's Kornmarkt. It actually comprises a collection of buildings; inside you can see the Grosses Fass, a giant barrel, said to be the world's largest wine vat. The Gesprengter Turm, or 'Blown Up Tower', lies in ruins, part of its outer fabric now crumbled into the moat below.

Many fine old mansions are scattered

around the old town. Near the Marktplatz are the Renaissance Haus zum Ritter and the 14th-century Church of the Holy Spirit. Universitätplatz has the Lion Fountain in the centre and is the location of both the 'old' and 'new' universities, the latter added in 1930 and now mostly sited on a campus out of town. Until 1914, students who got out of hand were confined in the special Students' Prison, just around the corner. It was regarded as an honour to be locked up here, as evidenced by the self-portraits among the graffiti on the walls.

Across the Alte Brücke, the old Neckar bridge, a steep pathway zig-zags up through orchards to a scenic lane called the Philosophenweg, so-called because its marvellous views inspired deep thought.

From Heidelberg river cruises ply eastward past half-timbered villages. To the west, a short drive brings you to Speyer, on the banks of the Rhine, which has a fine Romanesque cathedral. Eight Holy Roman Emperors are buried in its crypt.

From Heidelberg, an evening tour of the pubs is part of the routine. Imagine you are one of the rowdy students and set about tackling a stein or two of the flavoursome local beer, while humming to yourself the famous *Drinking Song* from *The Student Prince*. The bars serve good, cheap food, but there are stacks of other fine restaurants in the city, some showcasing the local cuisine; others tempting you with international fare. The latter is undoubtedly encouraged by Heidelberg's heavy tourist presence, which can be a drag, but, if you time your visit right and book accommodation well in advance, the city will prove itself to be – as you probably always imagined – one of Germany's most enjoyable destination.

Heidelberg

Major Events

Heidelberger Frühling (April–May): spring festival of the arts, with music, dance and theatre.
Illumination of Heidelberg Castle (early-June, early July and early September): the castle floodlit and spectacular fireworks at the Old Bridge.
Schlossfestspiele (August): spectacular castle music festival with opera, musicals and concerts.
International Film Festival (October): important international film fair shared with Mannheim.
Christmas Market (late November–late December): romantic market on the Universitätsplatz, with church concerts.

How to get there – and get around

By air: scheduled flights to Frankfurt Main Airport (45 miles away) from Heathrow, Gatwick, Stansted, London City, Birmingham, Edinburgh, Glasgow and Manchester (longest journey 2 hrs), then reasonably-priced bus to Heidelberg (1 hr).
Public Transport: Heidelberg has a bus and tram network (single tickets DM3.80; 24-hrs DM9), but most of the major sights are close together. Considering buying a Heidelberg Card which provides free transport and entrance to the castle. Trains, buses and boats run from the city to other regional centres.

Suggested Hotels

Europa, Friedrich-Ebert-Anlage.
Tel: (06221) 5150 Fax: (06221) 515506
Heidelberg's most exclusive hotel. Expensive.
Renaissance, Vangerowstrasse.
Tel: (06221) 9080 Fax: (06221) 908698
Fine, central hotel with good facilities. Moderate.
Bayricherhof, Rohrbacherstrasse.
Tel: (06221) 184045 Fax: (06221) 184049
Comfortable hotel close to the centre. Inexpensive–moderate.

Suggested Restaurants

Simplicissimus, Ingrimstrasse.
Tel: (06221) 183336
Well-regarded restaurant serving both local and international dishes. Expensive.
Schnookeloch, Haspelgasse.
Tel: (06221) 14460
Popular, if small, eaterie, attracting locals and tourists alike. Moderate.
Zum Roten Ochsen, Hauptstrasse.
Tel: (06221) 20977
Historic students' tavern, dating back to 1703. Moderate.

The atmospheric Auerbachs Keller in Leipzig. This historic, formal restaurant was frequently enjoyed by local writer Goethe and used as a setting for part of his play *Faust*.

It was in Leipzig in autumn 1989 that the movement to bring down the Berlin Wall and tear up the Iron Curtain gathered impetus. To visit the city's beautiful Nikolaikirche, the focus for the people's protests, is almost reason enough for travelling to Leipzig, but this splendid old city and its near neighbour, Weimar, have even more to offer.

History and Culture

Leipzig has been a university town since 1409. Amongst its other claims to fame is being the site of the Battle of the Nations in 1813, at which Napoleon tasted defeat. For many years, Leipzig has been a major convention centre, giving the city, even while still officially in the East, an international flavour. Musically, Leipzig was once second only to Vienna, the home of the likes of Bach, Mendelssohn and Schumann. Their tuneful heritage lives on. Weimar, 50 miles south-west, is even more artistically rich. The European City of Culture for 1999, it numbers writers like Goethe and Schiller as past residents, along with composers Bach and Liszt. Here, too, Germany's revised constitution was drawn up after World War I, the new regime going by the handle of the Weimar Republic.

Sightseeing

A tour of Leipzig must begin in the Markt, the central square that was badly damaged in the war but has been fantastically restored to its old-fashioned beauty. Look for the Old Town Hall, in elaborate Renaissance style, with its asymetrical tower and unavoidable blue clock. The square is surrounded by small, attractive streets, which provide excellent shopping opportunities. For art lovers, the city's Museum of Visual Arts has one of the best collections of

LEIPZIG AND WEIMAR

masterpieces in all of Germany. Those who have come to be musically entertained should not miss the Bachmuseum, the city's marvellous opera house or the Thomaskirche, where Bach was choirmaster. His choir can still be heard at weekends.

Weimar is just an hour's journey from Leipzig. Again, the Markt is an obvious starting point. Dating from around 1400, it is surrounded by superb old buildings. Adjacent is the Theaterplatz, a cobbled square containing the neo-classical German National Theatre (established by Goethe) and the Bauhaus Museum, where innovative artworks can be inspected. Weimar Castle is a powerful hulk, dominating Burgplatz to the east of centre, and now home to an art gallery. Near here is the baroque Stadtkirche, with a marvellous altarpiece by Lucas Cranach. The houses of Goethe and Schiller can both be toured.

Not all 'tourist sights' are designed to give pleasure. One such destination is the Buchenwald concentration camp, four miles north of Weimar. The horrors and brutality of the regime here will always, it is hoped, shock the visitor. If you can stomach it, this is a rare chance to pay respect to the thousands who suffered and died here. Another wartime relic within easy reach of Leipzig is Colditz Castle, the supposedly impregnable prisoner of war camp for perennial escapees.

You will need cheering up after these dispiriting visits and both Leipzig and Weimar do their best to oblige. The uplifting tones of beautiful music can be heard at concerts staged throughout the year, in deference to the composers who once worked here, while there are some excellent restaurants to be visited. For a moving experience, both culturally and otherwise, these lovely cities certainly demand attention.

Leipzig and Weimar

Major Events (all Leipzig)
Gewandhaus Concerts: (October–May): season of concerts performed by one of the world's oldest orchestras.
Street Music Festival (May): annual city-centre street entertainment.
International Bach Competition (end June– mid July): annual music competition bearing the name of Leipzig's most famous son.
Classic Open (early August): classical music on a big screen, with good food, in the Market.
Christmas Market and the Christmas Oratorio (December): major Christmas market plus the Advent highlight of Bach's seasonal choral masterpiece.

How to get there – and get around
By air: scheduled flights to Leipzig-Halle Airport (12 miles out) from Heathrow only (2 hrs 10 mins). Buses (taking 30 mins) run to Leipzig centre; there are also taxis. Alternatively, there are many flights from British airports to Frankfurt (1hr 40 mins) or Hamburg (see Hamburg), then transfers to Leipzig-Halle (about 1 hr).
Public Transport: Leipzig has a comprehensive tram network. Tickets cost around DM10 for 24 hrs; DM21 for 72 hrs. Reasonably-priced trains run hourly to Weimar (1 hr 20 mins). To reach Colditz from Leipzig, change trains at Grossbothen (1 hr total).

Suggested Hotels (all Leipzig)
Inter-Continental, Gerberstrasse.
Tel: (0341) 7990 Fax: (0341) 7991229
Super-sophisticated modern hotel with every facility. Very expensive.
Hotel Stadt Leipzig, Richard-Wagner-Strasse.
Tel: (0341) 21450 Fax: (0341) 2145600
Well-appointed and positioned hotel. Expensive.
Deutscher Hof, Waldstrasse.
Tel: (0341) 2116005 Fax: (0341) 286076
Comfortable hotel close to all attractions. Moderate.

Suggested Restaurants (all Leipzig)
Auerbachs Keller, Grimmaischestrasse.
Tel: (0341) 21600
Famous as much through Goethe's *Faust* as for its excellent food. Expensive.
Thüringer Hof, Burgstrasse.
Tel: (0341) 949 99
Haunt of Martin Luther nearly 500 years ago, and still a popular eating house. Moderate.
Zill's Tunnel, Barfussegasse.
Tel: (0341) 960 2078
Beerhouse-restaurant, a cut above the standard Saxon hostelry. Moderate.

Café am Dom
H 300

GERMANY

A sense of good living pervades Munich. The citizens take pride in their city and have good reason to. It is highly civilised, great fun and full of attractions. While a winter visit is pleasant enough (especially if you also pop along and see the Alps, just an hour's drive away), summer is the best time to come to Munich. The outdoor life is then in full swing, with beer gardens and pavement restaurants doing a roaring trade.

History and Culture

Munich was founded in the 12th century and has endured a rather chequered history. Hitler found his power base here and considered Munich to be the natural home of National Socialism. Today, however, the culture is enjoyment, manifested to the extreme in the Oktoberfest, held – confusingly – every September. This orgy of beer swilling, sausage eating and oompah-band playing was first held in 1810, to celebrate the marriage of Prince Ludwig and Princess Theresa. Today, combined with a funfair it has become an international tourist convention: it's good entertainment, but very commercial. If you don't want to join in, stay away from the city because hotel rooms will be impossible to find. The rest of the year, beer drinking is merely one of the staples of life, but the beer is generally so good that you can understand why 'liquid bread' is consumed at all hours. This might lead you to consider that Müncheners are purely hedonistic and perhaps a little philistine. Not so. There are so many museums and fine artworks in the city that you'd be hard pressed to cover even half of them in a short break.

Sightseeing

Heart of the city is the Marienplatz, a pedestrianised square featuring the Glockenspiel clock, which demands attention three times a day when tiny figures emerge to dance to the chimes. The clock is part of the neo-Gothic 19th-century New Town Hall, and also on the square is the Old Town Hall, dating from the Middle Ages and now housing a small toy museum. Munich's most important church is the Frauenkirche, a 15th-century edifice topped with two onion domes. Investigate the Dark Footprint inside, allegedly made by the Devil himself. Among the museums, the Alte Pinakothek, re-opened in 1998 after refurbishment, is reckoned to be among the top half-dozen art galleries in the world. As well the German masters are featured, there is a stunning array of works by Rubens and several notable Italian masterpieces. Of a different kind are the BMW and Deutsches Museums. The former catalogues the history of the city's famous car-maker, while the latter is the world's largest museum of science and technology, featuring such items as original Wright Brothers planes.

A few miles west of the centre is the Schloss Nymphenburg, once a summer palace for the Wittelsbach family, who ruled Bavaria for nearly 1,000 years, and now worth visiting for its frescos, portrait gallery and parklands. Further north is the suburb built for the 1972 Summer Olympics. The 950-foot tower here affords some excellent views, and, for a small fee, you can visit the Olympic Stadium, home of Bayern Munich F.C.

For the liveliest nightlife, forget the world-famous Hofbrauhaus, where Hitler made his first public speech. This, like the Oktoberfest, has a pronounced tourist accent. Head instead to the trendy northern district of Schwabing to enjoy the street performers, bars, jazz clubs and beer gardens. But, after a day on the hoof, a good beer, an excellent dinner and a relaxing evening can be had in most parts of the city.

Al fresco relaxation is one of the pleasures of the Munich summer. You're never far from a restaurant or café with pavement tables, or one of the many, boisterous beer gardens for which the city is famous.

One of Munich's biggest draws is the Glockenspiel, one of the largest carillon clocks in Europe, with enamelled copper figures that dance to the chimes three times a day. It is part of the New Town Hall in Marienplatz.

MUNICH

Major Events
Fasching (January–mid February): annual spring homage to Bacchus, with balls, parades and festivities.
Ballet Festival Week (late March–early April): high-profile festival, featuring the Kirov Ballet in 1999.
Oktoberfest (mid September–early October): the world's most famous beer festival.

How to get there – and get around
By air: scheduled flights to Munich Airport (17 miles out) from Heathrow, Gatwick, Luton, Birmingham and Manchester (longest flight 2¼hrs).Taxis to Munich centre cost around DM90 (taking 20 mins); buses run every 20 mins, costing DM10 (40 mins).
Public Transport: excellent train (S-bahn)/metro (U-bahn) links support Munich's buses and trams. One-day tickets cost DM8; a strip of 10 tickets costs DM15. Tickets must be validated by a machine on the vehicle. Taxis are plentiful and reasonable.

Suggested Hotels
Hotel Rafael, Neuturmstrasse.
Tel: (089) 29 09 80 Fax: (089) 22 25 29
Top-grade hotel on the site of an old art gallery. Very expensive.
Hotel Palace, Trogerstrasse.
Tel: (089) 41 97 10
Fax: (089) 41 97 18 19
Elegant hotel in a smart residential area close to the city centre. Expensive.
Hotel Cristal, Schwanthalerstrasse.
Tel: (089) 55 11 10
Fax: (089) 55 11 19 92
Stylish, modern hotel near the main railway station. Expensive.
Hotel Fidelio, Schwanthalerstrasse.
Tel: (089) 53 02 31 Fax: (089) 53 56 57
Quiet, homely hotel very close to the centre and station. Moderate.

Suggested Restaurants
Tantris, Johann Fichterstrasse.
Tel: (089) 36 20 61
Michelin-rated international cuisine and a classical music ambience. Expensive.
Preysing Keller, Innere Wienerstrasse.
Tel: (089) 45 84 52 60
Excellent food in a basement atmosphere. Expensive.
Ratskeller, Marienplatz.
Tel: (089) 22 03 13
Weinstube atmosphere on a grand scale, with seating for over 1000 diners. Inexpensive.

The Romantic Rhine, Germany's most majestic waterway has long been a short break favourite, with its dramatic gorge, picturesque towns, crumbling castles and mythical tales of princes, sirens and mighty warriors. You can, of course, drive, sail or take the train through the main parts of the Rhine Valley, but a few days provides a much better perspective. As a base, Mainz is a decent choice, not just because it anchors a part of the river than Cologne, which has already been mentioned in this book, but because, it is a city well worth attention in its own right. Book accommodation in advance (the Tourist Office can help), as hotels are not in abundance.

History and Culture

The Rhine, 820 miles long and stretching across four countries, has long been a major trade route through Europe. Boats have been navigating its course since Roman times. Settlements developed along the river at key points.

The city of Koblenz takes its name from the confluence of the Rhine and the beautiful Mosel, while Mainz, further south, stands where the River Main joins its larger neighbour. Today, Mainz is a thriving city, capital of the local region.

Sightseeing

The 11th-century Mainz cathedral is a beauty, an enormous Romanesque hulk in red sandstone, dominating the market place. You also have to see the Gutenberg Museum, dedicated to the city's most famous son, printer Johannes Gutenberg, which puts various early books on display and houses one of his early presses in the basement. A film tells the story of the famous Gutenberg Bible, dating from around 1452, one of the few surviving copies of which is kept under top security on the site.

To thoroughly appreciate the scenery of the Rhine, you must take to the water. You can hop aboard a boat at Mainz, take a short cruise between

The figure of the Madonna and Child adorns a house wall on Augustinerstrasse, one of the many well-preserved streets in the fine, old centre of Mainz that avoided serious war damage.

RHINELAND

LORELEY

Boppard and Bingen (2–3 hours) along the Rhine Gorge. Here you can spot both natural and man-made features that have taken on personalities of their own: the Marksburg fortress, the twin castles of Liebenstein and Sterrenberg, known as the Hostile Brothers after two squabbling siblings; the Mouse Tower and Katz castle; and the mystical Lorelei Rock. This craggy headland was reputedly the home of the *Lorelei,* an enchanting siren who lured Rhine rivermen to their deaths on the rocks below. The other great Rhine legend is, the *Nibelungen*, inspiration for Wagner's *Ring* sequence of operas.

Off the water, explore small villages that dot the river banks. Take a glass of Rhineland wine with a hearty meal in one of the local restaurants and bars.

Koblenz, further north, is an appealing, if not dramatically stunning, city. It has an old centre, which makes for a pleasant amble, and the waterfront gardens are equally enjoyable. Although three quarters of the city was bombed out in 1944, it has preserved some fine churches. Its Weindorf (wine village) is popular with tourists and the summer festival (second Saturday in August), when the river is set alight, should not be missed. For a bird's-eye view of the city and the river at this point, cross over to the east side and take the cable car up to the fortress at Ehrenbreitstein.

Providing you time your visit to beat the crowds (try spring and autumn; a lot of attractions are closed in winter), and avoid the midday crushes of tour groups, the Rhine will very likely take a hold on you. If the natural beauty, charismatic old buildings or the allure of the vine don't get you, maybe the spells of the *Lorelei* and her legendary chums will.

PREVIOUS PAGE: The famous Lorelei Rock on the east bank of the River Rhine. Here sailors were supposedly drawn to their doom by the enchanting songs of the Lorelei siren. It is just one of the many landmarks along this stretch of the river with importance in local folklore.

Rhineland

Major Events (all Mainz)

Mainz Carnival (mid February): three days of pageant and parade, including the famous 'Rose Monday' carnival to herald the onset of Lent.

Johannisnacht (mid–late June): joint celebration of mid-summer and the printing pioneer Gutenberg, with music, fairs and fireworks.

Mainzer Weinmarkt (late August–early September): festival of wine-tasting plus a traditional fairground.

Weihnachtsmarkt (December): open-air Christmas market in front of 1000-year-old St Martin's Cathedral.

How to get there – and get around

By air: scheduled flights to Frankfurt International Airport (20 miles east) from Heathrow, Gatwick, Stansted, London City, Birmingham, Edinburgh, Glasgow and Manchester (longest journey 2 hrs). Frequent taxis (costing around DM40 and taking 25 mins) and trains (DM8; 30 mins) run to Mainz.

By rail: Eurostar to Brussels, then change for Cologne. There change for Mainz (total journey about 8 hrs).

Public Transport: Mainz has good bus services (a Mainz Card gives free local transport along with entrance to museums, swimming pools, etc., at around DM10 for 24 hrs weekdays, or for the whole weekend). Reliable, reasonably-priced taxis.

Suggested Hotels (all Mainz)

Hilton International, Rheinstrasse.
Tel: (061) 31 24 50
Fax: (061) 31 24 55 89
Large and luxurious hotel, close to the river, Gutenberg Museum and cathedral. Expensive.

Hyatt Regency, Malakoff-Terrasse.
Tel: (061) 31 73 12 34
Fax: (061) 31 73 11 73 6
New addition to Mainz's top-of-the-range accommodation. Expensive.

Mainzer Hof, Kaiserstrasse.
Tel: (061) 31 28 89 90
Fax: (061) 31 22 85 55
Well-appointed hotel to the north of the city centre, close to the Rhine. Moderate.

Suggested Restaurants (all Mainz)

All the major hotels have good restaurants serving both international and Rheinland-Pfalz food. Try also:

Zum Goldstein, Kartäuserstrasse.
Tel: (061) 31 23 65 76
Good quality local fare and a pretty beer garden. Moderate.

Altstadtcafé, Schönbornstrasse.
Just turn up at this popular café which is frequented by students – but none the worse for that. Inexpensive.

The 16th-century streets of Rothenberg ob der Tauber, on Germany's beautiful Romantic Road, have been so stunningly preserved that they have been described as a museum piece in themselves.

THE ROMANTIC ROAD

The concept of the 'Romantic Road' was dreamed up by the German authorities in 1950 as a means of attracting visitors to the remarkably well-preserved medieval towns of northern Bavaria. Today you'll have to resign yourself to share the attractions with busloads of other visitors. Don't be deterred, however. These great little towns are well worth the hassle.

History and Culture

The designated Romantic Road area stretches from Würzburg in the north down to Füssen, nestling in the Bavarian Alps. However, the most interesting part is the northern end, from Würzburg to Rothenberg ob der Tauber, which makes an excellent base. Würzburg was founded on the banks of the River Main. Its present appearance stems from the 16th century, but the city was badly damaged during World War II and much has now been restored. It is a worthy gateway to the Romantic Road. Rothenberg is an even greater marvel. Thankfully spared during the war, it presents the only existing 16th-century townscape without the intrusion of a modern building. It owes its survival to the mercy of the general Johann Tilly during the Thirty Years' War in the early 1600s. Tilly was all set to raze the city to the ground, but agreed to spare it if someone could drink three litres of the local wine in one draught. One brave soul, the former burgomaster Nusch, did just that. His achievement is celebrated every Whitsun in the Meistertrunk festival.

Sightseeing

A good way to begin to take in the magic of Rothenberg is to stroll around its old walls, which are dotted with

fortified and turreted towers. Within the old city, with no concrete intrusions to spoil the effect, you are transported back 400 years as you gaze at the old town hall, the prosperous mansions in Herrngasse, and lovely St James's church and other Gothic places of worship. Look for the clock on the Ratsherrntrinkstube. Its figurines re-enact the famous wine-drinking feat that saved the city.

Würzburg is 40 miles to the north. Its architectural highlight is the splendid Residenz, home of the ruling prince-bishops in the 18th century. Parts are truly sumptuous, a feast of crystal, marble and gold, with paintings of the town by Tiepolo. The Italian master's work can also be found in the palace's Hofkirche. Above the city, on the other side of the river, looms the prince-bishops' previous residence, the Marienberg fortress, which protects the ancient Marienkirche, a round chapel.

You should also explore the rolling countryside and its settlements further south. The two most worthwhile places near Rothenberg are Dinkelsbühl and Nördlingen.

The old half-timbered houses of Dinkelsbühl, variously adorned with balconies, floral window boxes and painted façades, sit beautifully within a complex of ramparts and watch towers. Nördlingen also has strong walls and elegant towers, and, like it's sister towns up and down the road, offers a museum to make sense of the history that survives all around. The town actually sits in the Ries Basin, a deep circular well 12 miles across, which was created either by volcanic activity or by a meteor.

The local wine is very good, but, unlike the redoubtable burgomaster Nusch, you'll probably find three litres just a bit too much.

The Romantic Road

Major Events (all Rothenberg)

Shepherd's Dance (Sundays throughout the year): music and dancing in colourful costumes in the Market Square, staged once every month.

Der Meistertrunk (late May): the 'Master Draught' re-enactment of the legendary drinking feat.

Kinderzeche (mid July): costumed children's festival at Dinkelsbühl to commemorate the sparing of the town during the Thirty Years' War.

The Imperial City Festival (September): Rothenburg's biggest celebration – a pageant devoted to its medieval past

Christmas Market (late November–late December): one of Germany's most popular Christmas Markets.

How to get there – and get around

By air: scheduled flights to Nuremburg (Nürnburg) Airport (45 miles away) from Heathrow and Luton (2 hrs), then 2 hrs by bus or train (change at Würzburg and Steinach) to Rothenberg. Alternatively, there are flights to Frankfurt Main Airport (70 miles away) from eight UK airports (longest journey 2 hrs), then trains (3 hrs, change at Steinach) to Rothenberg. Car hire is a better option.

Public Transport: Rothenberg is easy to explore on foot, and buses link other towns up and down the Romantic Road.

Suggested Hotels (all Rothenberg)

Eisenhut, Herrngasse. Tel: (09861) 70 50 Fax: (09861) 7 05 45
The Romantic Road's most famous hotel (inn). Very expensive.

Goldener Hirsch, Untere Schmiedgasse. Tel: (09861) 70 80 Fax: (09861) 7 81 00
Not as attractive on the outside as some of Rothenburg's inns, this is nevertheless extremely comfortable. Expensive.

Reichs-Küchenmeister, Kirchplatz. Tel: (09861) 97 00 Fax: (09861) 8 69 65
Very old inn with ultra-modern amenities. Moderate.

Suggested Restaurants (all Rothenberg)

Bärenwirt, Hotel Bären, Hofbronnengasse. Tel: (09861) 9 44 10
Hotel restaurant with a fine national and international reputation. Expensive.

Ratstube, Marktplatz. Tel: (09861) 55 11
Rothenburg's most popular tavern bar, serving straightforward Franconian food and a wide variety of local wines. Moderate.

Reichs-Küchenmeister, Kirchplatz. Tel: (09861) 97 00
This hotel's *weinstube* offers local fare in an unpretentious manner. Inexpensive.

The pretty city of Trier is one of Germany's forgotten gems. However, its excellent Roman remains, including the ancient Porta Nigra gateway, and its position on the lovely Mosel river, in wine country, should not be overlooked.

Considering that Trier was once one of the most important cities in the world, it's surprising that it is so poorly known these days. At one time, it was capital of the Western Roman Empire, but these days it seems to get lost in a no man's land on the border of Germany, Luxembourg and France.

History and Culture

According to legend, Trier was established in 2000 BC, but it is more likely that the Emperor Augustus founded the city after defeating the local Treveri tribe in the 1st century BC. It grew prosperous over the next three centuries but then was overrun by Germanic warriors, before being revitalised under Diocletian and Constantine, who, between them, endowed the city with new defensive walls and placed it well and truly on the map as the capital of Gaul. With the decline of the Roman Empire, Trier was once again subject to invasions and it has never recovered its former prestige.

Sightseeing

Trier's focal point is its colourful market place – the Hauptmarkt – with a splendid fountain in the middle. Stretching out from here are streets leading to the finest churches and the city's most distinctive attraction, the truly ancient Porta Nigra. This blackened gateway (as its name implies) marked the very edge of Roman domination in the 2nd century. An enormous structure, it is remarkably well-preserved and visitors can wander

Trier

around inside at various levels to see how it was once converted to a church in memory of St Simeon, who took refuge in the gateway in the 11th century. Of the churches, the Romanesque cathedral and the 13th-century Church of Our Lady are the most important, and they stand side by side. The airy cathedral is claimed to be the oldest Christian place of worship north of the Alps – its foundations are as old as the Porta Nigra although it has been repeatedly rebuilt and restyled over the centuries. Behind the altar you may be able to peer at the Robe of Christ, allegedly the garment worn by Christ when being tried by Pontius Pilate.

Just off Karl-Marx-Strasse stands the Karl-Marx-Haus, where the political philosopher was born. It now houses a museum of his life and works.

Trier also maintains an excellent example of a Roman bathhouse, as well as a fine Roman basilica, built for Emperor Constantine, who took up residence here. Visit the Landesmuseum for yet another dose of fabulous Roman finds, then head off across the modern ring road to see the great amphitheatre.

A great excursion from Trier, takes you down the Mosel Valley, its steep banks teeming with vines that cling on around every bend of the river's course. Attractive little villages dot the banks, most offering free tastings in their many wineries. Take the boat down to the twin town of Bernkastel-Kues, for a thoroughly relaxing and peaceful day's sightseeing. Admire the ruins of 11th-century Landshut castle, then head back to Trier for evening, where you can sample the very latest local vintage over a good, hearty German meal.

TRIER

Major Events
Opera and Theatre in Antiquity (July): season of open-air performances among the Roman ruins.
Trierer Moselfest (early July): celebration of the Mosel Valley and the towns that thrive on the river.
Trier Wine Festival (late July–early August): festivities surrounding the grape and its produce.
Trier Wine Market (mid–late September): grape harvest festival
Weihnachtsmarkt (late-November–December): picturesque, traditional Christmas fair and market.

How to get there – and get around
By air: Scheduled flights to Luxembourg-Findel Airport from Heathrow, Gatwick, Stansted and Manchester (80–90 mins; see Luxembourg), then airport coach direct to Trier (30 mins).
By car: several ferries from Channel ports to Calais, Boulogne, Dunkirk and Ostend (1½–4 hrs), or via the Channel Tunnel on Le Shuttle (35 mins), and then by (mostly untolled) motorway through France and Belgium to Trier (5 hrs).
By rail: Eurostar to Brussels (2 hrs 40 mins); change for Luxembourg then Trier (about another 4 hrs)
Public Transport: Trier is easily explored on foot, but efficient buses and taxis are readily available.

Suggested Hotels
Dorint, Porta Nigra Platz.
Tel: (06) 51 27 01 0
Fax: (06) 51 27 01 170
New luxury hotel right opposite the Porta Nigra. Very expensive.
Ramada, Kaiserstrasse. Tel: (06) 51 94 95 0 Fax: (06) 51 94 95 666
Centrally situated modern hotel with good facilities. Expensive.
Deutscher Hof. Tel: (06) 51 97 78 0
Fax: (06) 51 97 78 400
Modern, comfortable hotel. Moderate.
Blesius Garten, Olewigerstrasse.
Tel: (06) 51 36 06 0 Fax: (06) 51 36 06 33
Pleasant hotel, just away from the centre, close to the amphitheatre. Moderate.

Suggested Restaurants
'Pfeffermühle', Zurlaubener Ufer.
Tel: (06) 51 2 61 33
Haute cuisine in atmospheric surroundings. Expensive.
Schloss Monaise, Trier-Zewen.
Tel: (06) 51 82 86 70
Imposing château out of the centre, with a range of well-priced menus. Moderate.
Gutsweinstube & Weingut von Nell, Trier-Olewig. Tel: (06) 51 3 23 07
Traditional, suburban wine cellar serving hearty local fare. Inexpensive.

Athens, the cradle of civilisation, yet seemingly a city in chaos. There is so much here which travellers want to see, yet many visitors, quite wrongly, are deterred by the traffic in the throbbing streets and the notorious pollution in the air. Gazing down on this manic mix of ancient and modern is the historic Acropolis with its roots in pagan myths and legend. The winding lanes of the Pláka, Síndagma Square with its café tables, stylish boutiques in the Kolonaki area, the flea market of Monastiráki, 19th-century neo-classical mansions, and, of course, the finest reminders of a great ancient age all make Athens well worth the effort.

History and Culture

The first settlement in these parts dates from a staggering 5000 years BC. By around 700 BC, Athens was already a major force, capital of the region known as Attica. Later overshadowed and overpowered by Rome, the city fell into a gradual decline. In the Middle Ages, it was occupied by the Turks, who held on to it until the Greeks forced them out in 1833, making Athens the capital of their new country a year later. Today, Athens is a confused but entertaining mix of classical world power and modern capital city.

Sightseeing

The Acropolis is the place to start. This rocky plateau has been dominating Athens physically and spiritually for around 7000 years. It was always a religious focal point, even if the religion tended to change with the people. Today, it is home to a fine collection of classical buildings, most notably the famous Parthenon. It was from here that the famous marbles (a frieze and other sculptures) were looted and taken to the British Museum by Lord Elgin. Also on the Acropolis is the Erechtheion, built on the site of a legendary battle between the gods Athena and Poseidon, and home to a collection of shrines. The other great Acropolis temple is that of Athena Nike, the marvellous carvings of which are now housed in the Acropolis Museum, along with other treasures.

In the shadow of the Acropolis is the Theatre of Dionysius, dating from the 6th century BC. Let your mind wander and imagine Aeschylus, Euripides, Sophocles and Aristophanes premiering their work here. On the other side of the hill stands the Agora, the great market place and political centrepiece of old Athens. Next door is the Roman Forum, from the 1st century AD.

If you haven't had your fill of ancient treasures, make for the National Archaeological Museum; otherwise head away from the classical centre. The most characterful part of Athens is undoubtedly Pláka. When the sun goes down, Pláka bursts into life. The tavernas switch on their fairy lights, piped bouzoúki music billows out, and the entertainment continues into the small hours. Even though tourists are the target here, it is still a good place to dine.

North-east of Pláka is the political centre of Athens, Síndagma Square. Here, crowds gather to watch the semi-comic spectacle of the changing of the tall guards, the Evzones. Dressed in tassled hats, short skirts and pom-pomed shoes, they perform a march seemingly devised by Basil Fawlty.

Athens has a pollution problem, partly caused by its lack of green space. Only the lovely National Gardens provide leafy respite from the traffic, so, perhaps, take the metro to the port of Athens at Piraeus for a seafood lunch, or the funicular up to Likavitós Hill. If the smog clears, the views from here are terrific.

The Corinthian colonnade, the last surviving section of the once magnificent Temple of Olympian Zeus, near the Acropolis. The temple was planned as early as the 6th century BC, but it was the Romans who completed the work in 132 AD.

Tucked in the shadow of the mighty Acropolis is the fascinating Pláka area of Athens, a warren of often steep streets and little squares that takes on a new, lively atmosphere when darkness falls.

ATHENS

Major Events
Epiphany (January 6): swimmers retrieve a cross at the blessing of the sea at Piraeus.
Carnival (February–March): pre-Lent spectacle of masked fun.
Dora Stratou (late May–October): performances of traditional Greek songs and dances by the Dora Stratou company.
Athens Festival (June–October): theatre, opera, ballet and dance – the biggest of many summer celebrations of music in and around Athens.
Classical Concerts and Opera (September–June): seasons at the Mégaron (Athens Concert Hall) and the Greek National Opera.

How to get there – and get around
By air: scheduled flights to Athens-Athinai Airport (6 miles out) from Heathrow and Gatwick (2 hrs 50 mins), then by bus (20–30 mins; GDR160) or taxi (20–25 mins; GRD1500) to Athens centre.
Public transport: Athens has a bus and trolley-bus network (single tickets GDR150), but only a one-line metro at present (centre–Piraeus; single tickets GDR75). The taxis are cheap, but beware of unlicensed operators.

Suggested Hotels
Grande Bretagne, Síndagma Square.
Tel: (01) 321 5555 Fax: (01) 322 0211
Still one of the best addresses in Athens, despite some loss of ambience in recent years. Very expensive.
Athenaeum Inter-Continental, Syngrou Avenue.
Tel: (01) 920 6000 Fax: (01) 924 3000
Luxurious hotel in the business district with a great view of the Acropolis. Expensive.
Athenian Inn, Háritos.
Tel: (01) 723 8097 Fax: (01) 724 2268
Comfortable hotel in a quiet, yet central, location. Moderate.
Parthenon, Makri.
Tel: (01) 923 4594 Fax: (01) 644 1084
Popular and cheerful hotel near the Acropolis. Moderate

Suggested Restaurants
L'Abeuvoir, Xenokratous.
Tel: (01) 722 9106. French-orientated menu in a classy setting. Expensive.
Tavérna Xinos, Agelou Geronta.
Tel: (01) 322 1065
Classic Greek menu in a setting of live bozoúki music and serenading troubadours. Moderate.
Neon, Dorou. Tel: (01) 522 9939
One of a chain of cafeteria-style restaurants, but with highly-rated cuisine and surroundings. Inexpensive.

PELOPONNESE

The name Peloponnese means 'island of Pelops' (a prominent figure in local mythology) and today this part of Greece is indeed an island, thanks to the cutting of the Corinth Canal in 1893. The Peloponnese is a theme park for anyone interest in Greek history. Outside of Athens, this was the one of the hotbeds of ancient civilisation, meaning that there are archaeological sites galore. The most comfortable town in which to make your base is Nafplio, a pleasant little resort on the Gulf of Argolis.

History and Culture

The Peloponnese has cities dating back to the dawn of European civilisation. Corinth, for instance, has evidence of buildings constructed in the 6th century BC, although the settlement is undoubtedly older still, while the treasures of Mikínes date from 1600 BC and recall the might of the Mycenaean civilisation. The peninsula was the subject of a 27-year war in the 5th century BC, as the struggle for power between the regions of Greece reached a climax. The town of Nafplio is said to have been founded by the grandson of Poseidon. It has seen many changes of ownership in its long lifetime: the Byzantines, the Franks, the Venetians and the Turks all occupied this port, until it was liberated by the Greeks in 1822. Nafplio then became the new country's capital, until power was transferred to Athens in 1834.

Sightseeing

Lace up your sensible shoes, don your sun hat and pick up your guidebook, for this is a short break dominated by the rocky remnants of the past. From Nafplio it is but a short ride to Epídhavros and Mikínes. At Epídhavros, one of Ancient Greece's great spa centres was established, in homage to Asclepius, the god of healing. People came from miles around to make sacrifices and spend some time in the hospital, the remains of which have been uncovered amidst groves of pines and oleanders. Overshadowing the sanctuary, however, is the remarkable amphitheatre, constructed in the 4th century BC and unearthed at the end of the 19th century. The arena could seat 14,000 spectators and the acoustics are astounding. Even from the back row, 55 tiers up, you can hear a coin being dropped in the centre of the theatre.

Mikínes is the new town close to the old Mycenae of Greek legend, a city allegedly founded by Perseus. Today, you can still enter the old city by the famous Lion Gate and wander through the vestiges of the royal palaces and past the tombs of ancient kings.

Heading further north from Nafplio brings you to historic Corinth. The old city is a fine collection of crumbled temples, baths, fountains and market places, a few miles outside the modern town. You can wander around freely and examine these last traces of a once-proud civilisation. High above the town is the old fortress of Acrocorinth. This is even better preserved than the old city below, and is worth a visit to take in the strategic position it occupies. The road twists, turns and bumps its way to the top, and the lanes inside the ruins are equally steep, but the views are marvellous. From Corinth it is but a short drive to the spectacular Corinth Canal, which was forced through the narrow isthmus that once joined the Peloponnese to the rest of Greece. The short-cut saves hours at sea for merchant and other vessels, and to peer down the sheer walls onto passing cruise ships is an enjoyable pastime in itself.

Nafplio is a very pleasant little town, hugging the waterside. The broad expanse of seafront is overshadowed by the bulk of the Palamedes Fort, a bastion built by the Venetians. The heart of the town is Síndagma Square, with some fine historic buildings dotted around. The town is an excellent base, despite its somewhat faded grandeur, and, apart from ruin rambling you can also use it as a springboard for island hopping. A hydrofoil service runs to Spétses and other offshore settlements. If you don't think you can handle the hustle and bustle of Athens, Nafplio provides a much gentler introduction to wonders of historic Greece.

PREVIOUS PAGE: The Lion Gate was the entrance to the old city of Mycenae and once formed part of a series of ramparts. The heads of the lionesses have been lost over the centuries, taking away some of the majesty, but the power of the gateway would not have been lost on visiting strangers.

The harbour at Nafplio is dominated by the offshore Boúrtzi fortress. It was designed in the 15th century to defend the entrance to the port and was the residence of the city's public executioner during the 19th century.

Peloponnese

Major Events
Piano Festival (June): annual festival of music in Nafplio.
Argos Festival (June): cultural events including theatre, dance, opera and the visual arts at Argos.
Epídhavros Festival (July–August): entertainment of a wide nature, but including ancient Greek drama.
August in Nafplio (August): classical music, theatre, dance, shadow theatre and traditional music.

How to get there – and get around
By air: scheduled flights to Athens-Athinai Airport (see Athens, p.114) from Heathrow and Gatwick, then by bus via Corinth and Argos, or hydrofoil from Piraeus port (end of the Athens metro line), to Nafplio (both take about 4 hrs).
Public Transport: everything within Nafplio is within strolling distance, but buses run out to other centres and there is a hydrofoil link to some islands. Car hire is recommended for greater flexibility.

Suggested Hotels
Xenia Palace, Acronafplia.
Tel: (0752) 28 981 Fax: (0752) 28 987
Easily Nafplio's best hotel, even though it is some way out of town, with wonderful views of the bay. Expensive.
Agamemnon, Akti Miaouli.
Tel: (0752) 28 021
The harbourside location makes all the difference to this comfortable hotel. Moderate.
Byron, Plateia Agiou Spiridona.
Tel: (0752) 22 351 Fax: (0752) 26 338
Pleasant, small hotel in a quiet location. Inexpensive.

Suggested Restaurants
Savouras Psarotaverna, Leoforos Bouboulínas. Tel: (0752) 27 704
Hugely popular fish restaurant whose menus (and tariffs) fluctuate wildly with the day's catch. Moderate–expensive.
Hellas, Síndagma Square.
Tel: (0752) 27 278
One of the best and most popular restaurants, set in the busy square. Moderate.
Noufara, Síndagma Square.
Tel: (0752) 23 648
Restaurant that catches the eye of the strolling public. Inexpensive.

Budapest

Even before the Iron Curtain was lifted, Budapest's secret was out. Now, with the Cold War thankfully a distant memory, Hungary is open to all-comers and its capital city is one of Europe's greatest finds.

History and Culture

Budapest is not one city, but two: Buda, the historic heart, on the hilly west bank of the Danube, and Pest, the more modern, commercial half, on the other side of the river. They came together in 1872. The first settlement here was Roman, then the Magyars of the 9th century set the foundation for the city we see today. The Mongols razed it to the ground but Budapest resurfaced with a new Renaissance face, only to suffer more strife at the hands of the Turks and the Habsburgs in the 16th and 17th centuries. Budapest was the second city in the Austro-Hungarian Empire, until the aftermath of World War I saw Hungary siphoned off as a separate country. An attempt to liberalise the Soviet regime after World War II led to the cruel Red Army invasion in 1956, but Hungary was never at ease within the Eastern Bloc. An element of capitalism had crept in long before it seized the chance to take back its independence in 1989.

Sightseeing

Budapest is such a stunning city that you'd be tempted to just wander and soak up the atmosphere. However pleasing that might be, there is a lot to pack in. Buda is the obvious place to begin, not least because its elevated position allows you to gain a perspective of the whole city. Take the world's second oldest funicular up to Castle Hill, the historic heart, a maze of cobbled streets and fine old buildings. Here you'll find the old Buda Palace, reconstructed after the war and now containing Budapest History Museum, which brings the city's checkered past to life, and the National Gallery, home to works by the country's finest artists. Also on the Buda plateau is the Matthias Church. The highly ornate interior of this 13th-century structure is dazzling. Just behind the church is the so-called Fisherman's Bastion, a turreted confection affording brilliant views over Pest and, directly below, the narrow old streets of Watertown, once home to the local fishermen.

The most striking image of Pest is the prickly neo-Gothic parliament building along the banks of the Danube. Beyond it lie some of the best shopping streets (particularly the pedestrianised Váci utca) and plenty of other interesting sites. St Stephen's basilica is a massive edifice dedicated to the king who converted Hungary to Christianity. In the National Museum, to the south, is the crown the Pope gave to Stephen 1,000 years ago. Along with other priceless treasures on show here today, this was smuggled out of the East after the war and held safely in America, until its return the in 1978.

The most relaxing place to stroll is on an island between the two halves of the city. Margaret's Island was once the home of Roman nobility. These days it is a largely traffic-free haven with swimming pools and the odd beer garden. Budapest is built on a series of thermal springs and spa activity is prolific. Join the locals in the resting of tired feet in one of the many bathhouses. There are complexes on Margaret Island as well as one in the City Park over in Pest, where you'll also find even more museums, a fairytale castle and a funfair.

Throughout the day, you are likely to be tempted into one of the ubiquitous coffee houses and seduced by some of the cakes and pastries. Evening entertainment is as cosmopolitan as you wish. The Magyar Opera House hosts high-standard classical performances. At the other end of the scale, Budapest also offers dozens of smoky little bars and buzzing jazz clubs.

Hungarian dining centres around the national dish, goulash, but is much more varied than at first glance, although the essential spice, paprika, does tend to crop up a lot on the menus. Pork, goose, local coarse fish, savoury pancakes and cabbage are among the staples of the local diet. The wines are perfectly good and very cheap.

The enormous dome of Budapest's St Basilica, the largest place of worship in the city. There are great views from the tower. In the Basilica's museum is the holy relic of St Stephen's right hand, plus priceless treasures returned from safe-keeping in the USA by President Carter.

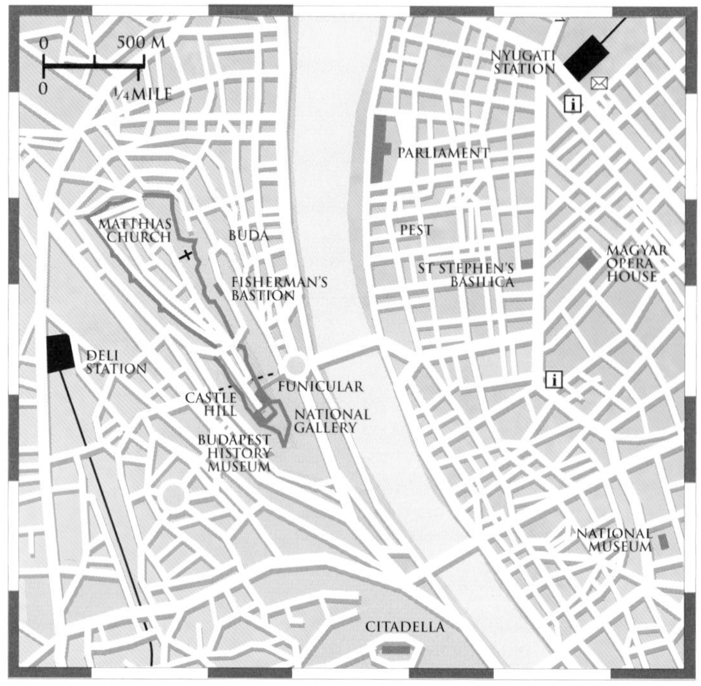

BUDAPEST

Major Events

Budapest Spring Festival (mid late March): celebration of the onset of spring.

Danube Carnival (early June): week-long folk festival in the city.

Budapest Summer Opera and Ballet Festival (early August): a feast of music and dance.

Living Crafts (late August): craft show and fair at Buda Castle.

Budapest Wine Festival (September): tribute to Hungary's long association with the grape.

Budapest Autumn Festival (October–early November): music, theatre and dance.

How to get there – and get around

By air: scheduled flights to Budapest Ferihegy Airport (10 miles out) from Heathrow and Gatwick (2 hrs 50 mins). Buses and taxis (taking 15 mins and costing HUF600–3,000) run to the city centre. Mini-buses are most frequent and cost HUF1200.

Public Transport: buses, trams, trolley buses and metro make up a comprehensive and cheap network but taxis are not so reliable.

Suggested Hotels

K&K Opera, VI Révay u.
Tel: (1) 269 0222 Fax: (1) 269 0230
Modern, exclusive hotel near the Opera House in Pest. Expensive.

Gellért, Gellért tér.
Tel: (1) 185 2200 Fax: (1) 166 6631
Famous for its Danube location, art nouveau style and its spa bath: a very popular grand hotel. Expensive.

King's Hotel, VII Nagydiófa.
Tel/Fax: (1) 352 7675
Comfortable, modern hotel in the centre. Moderate.

Radio Inn, VI Benczúr u.
Tel: (1) 342 8347 Fax: (1) 322 8284
Just out of the centre, this little-known hostelry, owned by the national radio station, offers excellent value. Inexpensive.

Suggested Restaurants

Gundel, XIV Allatkerti u.
Tel: (1) 322 1002
Re-opened after the Communist era and striving to match the elegance of its greatest days. Expensive.

Bagolyvár, XIV Allatkerti u.
Tel: (1) 321 3550
Next door to the Gundel, and under the same ownership: a taste of the same *haute cuisine* without the cost. Moderate.

Fészek, Kertész u. Tel: (1) 322 6043
Fine examples of Hungarian cooking in a busy city-centre atmosphere. Inexpensive.

Reykjavík

It is not surprising to learn that Reykjavík is one of the fastest-growing short break destinations. One hesitates to use the word 'unique', but its attractions are highly individual. Where else can you bathe by the side of a spouting geyser, catch sight of the Northern Lights and walk over a creaking glacier, all in one weekend?

History and Culture

Iceland was first settled by Norsemen in the 9th century and became officially part of Norway in the 13th century. Along with Norway, it was then subsumed into the Kingdom of Denmark, only receiving independence within the Danish state in 1918. Since 1944, it has been its own sovereign country, a republic with the oldest parliament in the world (*circa* 930) that concerns itself strongly with fishing and whaling matters in its surrounding waters. Over the centuries, Iceland has become accustomed to natural disasters, as the Earth's thin crust regularly erupts to create new mountains and islands, or, more frighteningly, to occasionally consume part of the landscape.

Sightseeing

The first thing experienced travellers will tell you about Reykjavík is that it is not particularly exciting in itself. After the immediate appeal of its colourful Lego-block houses, there is not a great deal to do here. There is a good museum, with an excellent collection of Viking artefacts, and a National Art Gallery where local artists are put under the spotlight, but beyond these the capital city is largely featureless. However, as a base for exploring Iceland, it is first class. Once you've found your bearings, hire a car (not cheap, so book a fly-drive) or sign up for one of the many excursions around the island.

Head for the Gulfoss Waterfall, probably the island's star attraction. Here the River Hvitá crashes down over 100 feet, its fine spray creating brilliant rainbows against the stark, rocky landscape. Daredevils can white-water raft in the waters below. Next, don't miss Geysir, the water spout after which all geysers are named. In actual fact, the original gusher stopped billowing many years ago, but there is another one nearby that shoots a plume of water into the air at three-minute intervals. Completing the main tourist trilogy in southern Iceland is the Pingvellir National Park, original site of the Althing parliament and a place of great historical and geographic interest. Here, you can hike around canyons, visit caves and enjoy even more waterfalls and springs.

If you've ever fancied swimming in the effluent pool of a power station, Iceland gives you that rare chance. It's actually a much more enjoyable experience than it sounds. Icelandic power plants pump natural hot water into the towns and the so-called Blue Lagoon has been formed from the run-off of one such utility. The water is blissfully warm and steamy, and a dip here on a cold day is truly invigorating. Filled with salts, the water is acknowledged to help cure psoriasis and other ailments.

Iceland is also a great place for spotting wildlife. You can catch seals and walruses flopped on the rocky shoreline, and there are enough species of bird here to thrill an ornithologist for life.

If you time your visit for March or October, there is a chance that you will witness the famed Northern Lights. These vibrant streams of coloured lights are caused by the combination of solar winds and the Earth's magnetic field. They are very beautiful, but can be a little unnerving. The other great natural phenomenon, the Midnight Sun, is a feature of the summer months. Iceland sits on the fringe of the Arctic Circle and experiences woefully long nights in winter, but plenty of light in summer, when the evenings never come to an end. The weather in Iceland, is not its best feature, with rain a common visitor, but the Gulf Stream ensures that it is surprisingly comfortable in winter. However, be prepared for climatic extremes, which can more than put a damper on your visit.

PREVIOUS PAGE: Iceland's largest lake is Pingvallavatn, 25 miles east of the city of Reykjavík. Covering around 50 square miles, it is fed by River Oxará and several underground streams.

Just a short ride from Reykjavik city centre is the open-air Arbaer Folk Museum. Established in 1957, it incorporates numerous old buildings – such as this priest's house – from all over Iceland.

Reykjavík

Major Events

First day of Summer (mid–late April): celebration with a cast of thousands in parades all over Iceland.

Seaman's Day (early June): day in honour of those whose efforts are integral to Icelandic life, with flotillas of vessels all heading for port.

National Independence Day (June 17): the country celebrates the anniversary of its peaceful break from Denmark

Harbour Festival (July): fun and frolics in the port of Reykjavík as the bond with the sea is acknowledged again.

Viking Festival (July): annual celebration of Nordic folklore at nearby Hafnarfjörour.

RúRek Jazzfestival (mid September): jazz fans converge on Reykjavík.

How to get there – and get around

By air: scheduled flights to Reykjavík-Keflavík International Airport (25 miles out) from Heathrow and Glasgow (longest flight 3 hrs 5mins), then airport buses (45 mins; about IKR750) or taxis (about IKR6000) to Reykjavík.

Public Transport: Reykjavík is easily explored on foot but there are buses and taxis in the town and (rather expensive) coach services to other towns, as well as (comparatively cheap) internal flights from Keflavík.

Suggested Hotels

Hotel Island, Armúli.
Tel: 568 8999 Fax: 568 9957
Upmarket hotel in the business centre, next to a popular nightclub. Expensive.

Grand, Sigtún. Tel: 568 9000
Fax: 568 0675
Modern, well-appointed hotel. Expensive.

Fosshótel Lind, Rauðarástigur.
Tel: 562 3350 Fax: 562 3351
Comfortable, modern hotel, near the main shopping street. Moderate.

Suggested Restaurants

Restaurant Perlan, Öskjuhlíð.
Tel: 562 0200
Reykjavík's best eaterie, with its reputation extending beyond Iceland.
Very expensive.

Hotel Holt, Bergstaðastræti.
Tel: 552 5700
Excellent restaurant providing the best of Iceland and elsewhere. Expensive.

Restaurant Argentina, Baronstíg.
Tel: (no code) 551 9555
Popular restaurant with locals and tourists alike. Moderate.

CORK AND KERRY

The southwest of Ireland is the most visited part of the country. At times, in summer, the tourist crush can be oppressive in cities like Cork and on scenic stretches like the Ring of Kerry. But, time your visit well, aiming for spring – when the Gulf Stream warms the southwest – early summer or autumn, to find the rural Ireland you've been looking for.

History and Culture

Focal point of the region is Cork, Ireland's second largest city. But, with only 175,000 inhabitants, compared with Dublin's 3 million, it's a very poor second in the size stakes. This easy-going city was founded as a monastic settlement in the 6th century and developed as a fortified trading post under the Vikings and Normans. Today, it has stretched out from its original base around the two channels of the River Lee and climbed up slopes to the north and south, but the centre remains the old island site known as 'the flat'. Here, evidence of Cork's mercantile past remains in the form of old warehouses and stone quays.

Cork is known for its pub scene, where the cares of the world are talked away over a drop of the black stuff. The city is home to two breweries – Murphy's and Beamish – and the stouts from both are widely available. Other parts of Southwest Ireland tend to focus more on edible nourishment, with some of the finest restaurants in Europe tucked away around the bays of Cork and Kerry. The harbour village of Kinsale has become a gourmet capital in its own right.

Sightseeing

Cork is easy to explore on foot, and its handful of attractions are within easy reach of each other. The Old City Gaol, the Opera House and St Finn Barre's Cathedral, with its gingerbread house facade, top the list, along with numerous markets, Bishop Lucey Park and the fine Crawford Art Gallery, displaying modern Irish and other works. St Anne's Chapel sits on top of a steep hill, north of town, in the Shandon area, and, if you climb to the top of the tower, for a small fee you can buy the privilege of playing the bells, using music cards provided. However, the real pleasure of Cork is in wandering its jumbled streets, crossing its old bridges, relaxing over a leisurely pint, meeting its talkative people and just enjoying the spirited atmosphere of the city. In contrast, whistlestop tourists flock to famous Blarney Castle, just five miles away, and literally bend over backwards to kiss the Blarney Stone.

Voyaging further west, the other tourist honey pots in the region are Killarney and the Ring of Kerry, an undeniably beautiful 110-mile stretch of waterside roadway, skirting the Iveragh peninsula. It is sadly often diminished by traffic at the height of the season, but, even when it's busy, if you make a few detours, you can still take in some of the wonderful landscapes of the west coast. There are fishing villages, untarnished offshore islands and more folklore and tradition than a sackful of leprechauns. It's not too difficult to lose yourself in the wild flowers, tufty grasses, cliff-faced headlands or sandy beaches, beneath the cries of the abundant birdlife, with a stiff Atlantic breeze freshening the air. It's a great area for cycling, and walking the Gap of Dunloe, between the Purple Mountains and Ireland's highest range, Macgillicuddy's Reeks, is one of the greatest pleasures of a summer afternoon.

The Ring of Kerry is as stunning as the Irish Tourist Board claims it to be. The little fishing villages along its course tend to be overloaded in summer months, but, even at these busy times, there are always quiet corners of the countryside to be enjoyed.

Blarney House viewed from Blarney Castle. Up here is the famous Blarney Stone, which, if kissed, is said to bestow the gift of eloquence. However, it is not easy to reach and those seeking its blessing need to lean backwards, grasp an iron rail for support and poke their heads through a small opening in the parapets.

Cork and Kerry

Major Events

Celtic Flame Festival, Cork (late February): national festival of traditional music.

Cork International Choral Festival (March): annual celebration of choral singing.

International Gourmet Festival, Kinsale (late September/early October): famous get together for food-lovers from around the world.

Guinness Cork Jazz Festival (late October): major international festival with some 100 bands performing .

How to get there – and get around

By air: scheduled flights from nine UK airports to Cork; flights from Stansted, Luton and Manchester to Kerry (Farranfore). Taxis from Cork Airport to the city (taking 12 mins), and from Kerry Airport to Killarney (15 mins), are reasonable and a better bet than the infrequent buses (especially from Kerry).

By car: ferries to Cork from Swansea and to Rosslare (130 miles north-east of Cork) from Liverpool, Holyhead, Pembroke and Fishguard.

Public Transport: Cork city buses are cheap and regular, if at all needed. Taxis have a minimum fare of IR£1.80. Bus services between centres, although regular, are not always frequent. Cork and Killarney are linked by train, but again, not too often. Car-hire, at reasonable rates, is recommended.

Suggested Hotels

Park Hotel, Kenmare.
Tel: (064) 41200 Fax: (064) 41402
Luxurious hotel, world-renowned for its seafood restaurant, overlooking the Kenmare estuary. Very expensive.

Jurys Hotel, Western Road, Cork.
Tel: (021) 276622 Fax: (021) 274477
Cork's premier hotel, on the banks of the River Lee, just five mins from the centre. Expensive.

Aghadoe Heights, Aghadoe, Killarney.
Tel: (064) 31766 Fax: (064) 31345
Acknowledged as one of Ireland's outstanding hotels, with a fine gourmet restaurant, lake and mountain views, and golf and fishing laid on. Expensive.

Trident Hotel, World's End, Kinsale.
Tel: (021) 772301 Fax: (021) 774173
Comfortable hotel overlooking pretty Kinsale harbour, with all rooms offering a sea view. Moderate.

Arbutus Lodge, Montenotte, Cork. Tel: (021) 501237 Fax: (021) 502893
Stylish townhouse in its own gardens 15 mins from the centre. Award-winning restaurant. Moderate.

Suggested Restaurants

Blue Haven Hotel, Pearse Street, Kinsale. Tel: (021) 772209
Hotel/restaurant with a plethora of awards to its name. Seafood tops the menu. Expensive.

Foley's Seafood and Steak Restaurant, High Street, Killarney. Tel: (064) 31217
Long-standing, family-run restaurant. Moderate.

Bully's, Looney's Cross, Bishopstown Road, Cork. Tel: (021) 546838
Multi-award-winning Italian-influenced restaurant and wine bar. Inexpensive.

Val O'Shea's Bar and Bistro, Bridge Street, Tralee. Tel: (066) 21559
Award-winning, first class pub grub in ambient surroundings. Inexpensive.

DUBLIN

The images and icons of Dublin are very familiar. Elegant Georgian buildings, a literary heritage that takes in the likes of Joyce, Swift and Shaw, and noisy pubs serving pints of stout as black as the night outside. It's a good-living, inspirational city and all the better for being on our very doorstep.

History and Culture

The city on the River Liffey was established by Celtic traders in the 2nd century, though its name is derived from the Vikings, who came here in the ensuing centuries. They called it *Dubh Lihn*, meaning Black Pool. However, the greatest outside influence on the city has come, inevitably, from across the Irish Sea. Blame the English for the Georgian architecture and for founding Trinity College. And now the face of 'Dublin's fair city' is changing yet again, as an economic upturn and Ireland's membership of the European Union have introduced a cosmopolitan buzz.

No less than four Irish authors have won the Nobel Prize for Literature, but it's hard to know whether Dublin's famous literati were writers who liked to drink, or drinkers who liked to write, for many of them were regulars in the local pubs. A nightly literary tour pays tribute to the famous scribes and encourages plenty of consumption of Dublin's gift to the quaffing world, the mighty Guinness. The Guinness Hop Store museum is the city's most frequented attraction.

The pubs of Dublin are a tourist attraction in themselves and are a world away from the fake Irish pubs now seen in the UK. Plenty offer authentic Irish music, but others concentrate on another great Irish gift to the world – conversation.

Sightseeing

Studying the river from one of its bridges is a good way to begin a city tour, as the Liffey splits the city into north and south. The south is the more appealing, centring around Grafton Street, with its quality shopping, the fashionable night-life of Temple Bar, and College Green, backing onto Trinity College. Here, on illuminated display in the Library, is the 1000-year-old *Book of Kells*.

Close to the college are Dublin's two cathedrals, both of them – somewhat improbably in this Catholic city – Protestant. St Patrick's dates from 1191, and lists Jonathan Swift as one of its deans in the 18th century; Christ Church is even older, dating from 1038, and was founded by the Norsemen who settled in Dublin.

If Ireland takes inordinate pride in its men of literature, its artistic benevolence is more altruistic. The National Gallery is home to works by the great Italian, Spanish and French, as well as Irish, painters, and the Hugh Lane Municipal Gallery also doffs its cap to overseas talent, whilst not forgetting the nation's own. The latter sits in the northern part of the city, where O'Connell Street is the main thoroughfare and the famous Abbey Theater and The Writers' Museum uphold yet again Dublin's literary and dramatic traditions.

To paint an unashamedly glowing picture of Dublin would be to deliberately mislead, because, for all the outstanding Georgian architecture and the latest fashionable quarters, there are also crass new buildings and some very bleak suburbs. But the city, on the whole, is a joy, full of character and one not to miss.

DUBLIN

Major Events
St Patrick's Festival (mid March): Ireland's biggest annual celebration – music, street theatre, dance, sports, pageants, carnival parades.
Dublin Film Festival (mid/late April): best of Irish and international cinema.
James Joyce Summer School (mid/late July): lectures and seminars at University College, Dublin.
Dublin Theatre Festival (early/mid October): celebration of Dublin's rich theatrical heritage .

How to get there – and get around
By air: scheduled flights from airports to Dublin Airport (longest flight 70 mins). Buses leave for Dublin city centre (30 mins drive) every 15 mins during the day and charge about IR£2.50; taxis (from the terminal building) cost around IR£12.
By car: ferries to Dublin, Dun Laoghaire (10 miles south-east of Dublin) and Rosslare (95 miles south) from Liverpool, Holyhead, Pembroke and Fishguard.
Public Transport: Dublin has good bus and rail services. Rambler and Day Bus Tickets – with unlimited travel – are also available. Taxis are plentiful and reasonable, from a minimum IR£1.80 fare.

Suggested Hotels
Shelbourne, 27 St Stephen's Street.
Tel: (01) 676 6471 Fax: (01) 661 6006
Arguably Dublin's most distinguished hotel, with an address to match. Very expensive.
Berkeley Court, Lansdowne Road, Ballsbridge.
Tel: (01) 660 1711 Fax: (01) 661 7238
Luxurious hotel, set in Dublin's business district. Very expensive.
Gresham, 23 Upper O'Connell Street
Tel: (01) 874 6881 Fax: (01) 878 7175
Busy, yet refined, long-established hotel in the heart of Dublin. Expensive.
Royal Dublin, O'Connell Street.
Tel: (01) 873 3666 Fax: (01) 873 3120
Comfortable hotel, close to the shops, restaurants and theatres. Moderate.

Suggested Restaurants
Eamonn O'Reilly's One Pico,
1 Upper Camden Street. Tel: (01) 478 0307
Highly acclaimed Le Routier Gold Medallist cuisine. Expensive.
The Grey Door Irish Restaurant,
22/23 Upper Pembroke Street.
Tel: (01) 676 3286
Traditional and contemporary Irish fare in a popular restaurant of long-standing. Private dining rooms available. Moderate.
Kilkenny Shop Restaurant, Nassau Street. Tel: (01) 677 7066
Award-winning self-service restaurant near Trinity College, specializing in home-made fare. Inexpensive.

BOLOGNA

Standing just off Bologna's Piazza Maggiore is one of the city's best-known landmarks, the Neptune Fountain. The giant figure of the sea god is surrounded by four sirens. These splendid bronze sculptures were produced in 1566 by the artist Giambologna.

Bologna is a city with character. Not for nothing is it known for its rich cuisine, or its left-wing politics. The capital of the region of Emilia-Romagna is an academic centre, home of the oldest university in Europe, where the likes of Dante, Petrarch and Tasso once studied. It's also one of Italy's best pre served cities. Here is a city that has attractions to rival the best in the country, but with an attitude and atmosphere all of its own.

History and Culture

Bologna's history predates even Roman times. The Etruscan capital of Felsina stood on the site the city occupies today. The Romans developed the region, with one of their major 'trunk' roads, the Via Aemilia, running through the middle of the area. In the Middle Ages, the powerful Bentivoglio family called the shots. In their era, and under later Papal control, the city we see today took shape. The countryside around the city is famously lush and plentiful, ideal for cereal crops and animal farming. As a result, the towns of the region have gained a reputation for excellent dining. Bologna is acclaimed as Italy's gourmet capital.

Sightseeing

Bologna's old centre is very distinctive, with ochre-coloured stonework, rows of porticoed buildings and two giant towers, which no longer stand straight. The Asinelli and Garisenda towers are the last survivors of the tall city structures built for defence and social status by the wealthy families of the 12th century. Climb to the top of the Asinelli for the best view for miles.

The city's main square is Piazza Maggiore, fronting the monumental

church of San Petronio, dedicated to Bologna's patron saint. Begun in the 14th century, its size and beauty threatened to undermine St Peter's in Rome and so the Church diverted funds to the city's university to save face. If you look closely, you can see where the plans were changed and how the church had to be modified. Outside is the famous Neptune Fountain, featuring bronze sculptures by the artist Giambologna.

The other major churches to see are San Giacomo Maggiore, San Domenico and the abbey of Santo Stefano. San Giacomo houses the tombs of the Bentivoglio family, while San Domenico is the resting place of St Dominic, who died here in 1221. It contains some wonderful marble works by Pisano and by a young Michelangelo. Santo Stefano is actually four medieval churches in one.

Bologna's National Gallery is one of the best in Northern Italy and primarily features local artists. For a more modern view of art, pay a visit to the Morandi Museum, dedicated to the works of one of Italy's best-known 20th-century artists.

These paradoxical themes of ancient and modern are combined in the university. You can visit intriguing sites like the historic Anatomical Theatre, where dissections were carried out, and the Astronomy Museum in the Observatory, where you can see early star maps and primitive instruments. The area around the University is littered with good value bars and restaurants frequented by today's students. Even these modest eateries tend to live up to the Bolognese standard. Look for such local specialities as pork dishes and rich pasta like tortellini, said to have been invented by a local cook in the image of the beautiful navel of Venus.

Bologna's culinary heritage is not just propagated in the many fine restaurants. The markets, too, heave with plump offerings. Visit the stalls on Via Clavature for a visual banquet. At the other end of the shopping scale, just off Piazza Maggiore, you'll find the best designer boutiques.

Bologna

Major Events
Carnevale dei Bambini (February–March): carnival dedicated to children.
Teatro Comunale Season: (January–June): opera and concerts at the city's famous theatre.
Bologna Est: (July–September): annual summer festival of music and dance, theatre and street entertainment.
Children's Song Festival (October): annual celebration of the music of youth.
La Mostra Bella (end-October–early-November): important antiques fair.

How to get there – and get around
By air: scheduled flights to Bologna Airport (4 miles out) from Heathrow, Gatwick and Stansted (flight time 2 hrs 10 mins). Buses (taking 30 mins and costing around LIT7000) and more expensive taxis (taking 20 mins) run to Bologna centre.
Public Transport: Bologna is easy to explore on foot, but a reasonable and reliable bus service links the outer suburbs to the centre.

Suggested Hotels
Al Cappello Rosso, Via Fusari.
Tel: (051) 26 18 91 Fax: (051) 22 71 79
One of the finest hotels, near Piazza Maggiore. Expensive.
Grand Hotel Baglioni, Via dell'Indipendenza.
Tel: (051) 22 54 45 Fax: (051) 23 48 40
Traditional and stylish hotel, close to the heart of medieval Bologna. Expensive.
Donatello, Via dell'Indipendenza.
Tel: (051) 24 81 74 Fax: (051) 24 81 74
Close to all the sights. Moderate.

Suggested Restaurants
Donatello, Via Augusto Righi.
Tel: (051) 23 54 38
Restaurant serving high-class regional cooking for almost a century. Expensive.
Trattoria da Baroni, Via Morgagni.
Tel: (051) 23 88 98
Award-winning, restaurant. Expensive.
Lamma, Via dei Giudei.
Tel: (051) 26 83 62
Central restaurant with a vaulted ceiling and good, basic local fare. Inexpensive.

The seafront at Vernazza, generally considered to be the most attractive of the Cinque Terre. It is typical of the five villages with its pastel-shaded houses squeezed in at the water's edge.

The Cinque Terre

The Cinque Terre – literally 'Five Lands' – is one of Italy's latest tourist discoveries. These five little *villages* – no more – cling to the rugged cliffsides of the Ligurian coast, to the south and east of Genoa. Their attraction is their very simplicity, allied to their highly improbable setting. For years the villages were only accessible by boat, and still no road joins all five together. The train, however, does, making the region very easy to reach from Genoa and an excellent place to for a short break that's just that little bit different.

History and Culture

The Cinque Terre are the villages of Monterosso al Mare, Vernazza, Corniglia, Manarola and Riomaggiore. Just a little further south is the much better known, but still small, town of Portovénere, before the headland gives way to the Italian naval city of La Spezia and more lively resorts on the other side of the gulf. The Cinque Terre began life as mere fishing ports. They have also prospered from agriculture, with the almost vertical cliffs to their rear somehow being cultivated with vines, citrus trees and olive groves. The terracing is so steep in places that grape harvesters have been known – it is said – to abseil down the cliff. Today, the villages remain largely unspoilt and the people still follow age-old traditions and customs. However, times change. The young people have begun to leave in search of a more

exciting life, and the mark of tourism is gradually being applied.

Sightseeing

For most people, the greatest pleasure is taken along the footpath that spectacularly links the five settlements, unfurling around rocky headland after rocky headland. It takes about five hours to ramble from one end to the other, with the occasional beach allowing you to stop and cool off. With trains running past every half an hour or so, you can stretch the walk to a couple of days, by stopping to wander the streets of each village in turn, pausing for a leisurely lunch in one of the tiny squares, and then ambling on to the next stop, taking the train back to the start when you're through.

Your base here might be Portovénere, which, although small, does have more facilities to offer the traveller than the Cinque Terre themselves. It's not the prettiest of towns, but there is plenty of atmosphere. Make your way over to the promontory, where the black-and-white-striped, 13th-century church of San Pietro looks back along the coast to the Cinque Terre.

Skipping La Spezia, with its shipbuilding and military connections, to the south lies the little resort of San Terenzo, only a fishing village at the time the Romantic poet Shelley stayed there. He drowned off the coast when returning from seeing his friend, and fellow poet, Leigh Hunt at Livorno. The next resort along is even more popular. Lérici is dominated by a castle, seemingly etched out of the cliff by the Pisans in the 12th century, and is much more commercial than its modest neighbours to the north.

It will come as no surprise to hear that most restaurants around here focus on seafood. Indeed, many of the restaurants are very simple establishments, the sort of eating places that would be described as a *trattoria* in other parts of Italy, although the prices have become elevated as the visitor presence has increased. Nevertheless, the food is known to be good and, washed down with excellent wine from the vines you passed on your coastal trek (once praised by the great Italian writer Boccaccio no less), it rounds off a very fulfilling and healthy few days in the open air.

The Cinque Terre

Major Events

Palio del Golfo (August): La Spezia's historic rowing competition.

How to get there – and get around

By air: scheduled flights to Genoa-Cristoforo Colombo Airport from Gatwick only (2 hrs 50 mins), but there are many flights to Rome-Fiumicino Airport (see Rome) with transfers to Genoa (1hr). Trains to La Spezia (1hr 40 mins), from where buses or taxis take you to Portovénere (20 mins).

Public Transport: Portovénere and the Cinque Terre should be explored on foot. The local train runs from La Spezia to Lévanto stops at each of the Cinque Terre and there is a ferry from Portovénere across the bay to Lérici.

Suggested Hotels (all Portovénere)

Grand, Via Garibaldi. Tel: (0187) 792610 Fax: (0187) 790661
Probably the finest hotel in Portovénere. Expensive.

Royal Sporting, Via Olivo.
Tel: (0187) 790326 Fax: (0187) 529060
Some would put this on a par with the Grand; a fine hotel with great views. Expensive.

Paradiso, Via Garibaldi.
Tel: (0187) 790612 Fax: (0187) 792582
Smaller hotel overlooking the bay. Moderate.

Suggested Restaurants (all Portovénere)

Grand, Via Garibaldi. Tel: (0187) 792610
Excellent hotel restaurant serving international cuisine. Expensive.

Trattoria La Marina-da Antonio, Piazza Marina. Tel: (0187) 790686
Restaurant well-respected locally for its Ligurian cooking. Moderate.

Taverna del Corsaro, Calata Doria.
Tel: (0187) 790622
Seafood is a speciality at this restaurant at the end of the peninsula. Moderate.

DOLOMITES

If you thought that the Dolomites were just another mountain chain, a more-of-the-same subdivision of the Alps, think again. The Dolomites have an identity all of their own. For a start, they look different. Instead of the usual cleanly-cut peaks, these mountains appear fragile and crumbly, as if they might all turn to dust before your eyes. Furthermore, the land around them is populated by people who speak a different language and enjoy a different heritage from the rest of their country. As you weave your way through the valleys, you'll think you are in Austria, not Italy, and this cultural paradox adds spice to a few days in this breathtakingly beautiful area.

History and Culture

The Dolomites are a limestone formation with a distinctively delicate, powdery look. The effect of the weather has added unusual features to the highest peaks, the wind, ice, snow and rain carving sharp furrows into the rock faces, and glaciers cutting deep, clean valleys below. The territory around the mountains has long been a source of pique between Austria and Italy. Originally, it was colonised by the Counts of Tirol, but was ceded to Italy after World War I. The people have refused to give up their Germanic identity, however, even when brow-beaten by Mussolini and his Fascists. Today, you will still see the Austrian flag hoisted on the balcony of many, typically alpine, chalet homes. German is spoken, and lots of the towns have dual German-Italian names.

Sightseeing

The best base for a trip (on account of its excellent facilities) is Cortina d'Ampezzo, at the southern end of the Dolomite region and well and truly in the Italian sector. But head north to Brunico (otherwise known as Bruneck) and Bressanone (Brixen), or west to Bolzano (Bozen), and you'll enter a different world.

The year splits in two around here: the times when you can ski, and the times when you can't, and Cortina switches identity accordingly. In the winter, the snowy slopes become a blaze of colour, as strident-suited skiers make the mountains their own. The amenities are excellent, thanks to the fact that Cortina staged the Winter Olympics in 1956. You can still see the ski jump and the bobsleigh run. When the weather warms up, the mountains become a magnet for hikers, out to savour the rarefied air and the stunning panoramas.

Of the other Dolomite centres, the market town of Brunico is one of the most appealing. Standing guard above its narrow streets is the dominant shape of the 14th-century castle, while the church of St Ursula features some lovely old sculptures. Bressanone also has a cluster of cramped medieval streets that surround its cathedral, where the cloister dates from the 12th century and is adorned with fabulous frescos from some 300 years later.

Along the majestic Great Dolomite Road from Cortina, which passes the mighty Marmolada – the highest peak in the range (11,000 feet) – is Bolzano. Characteristically Tirolean, it is centred around a fine Gothic cathedral, which stands in the main square, Piazza Walther, where pavement cafés serve *apfel strudel*.

Away from the urban centres, the Dolomites are peaceful and truly beautiful. All kinds of unusual flora and fauna live here, from edelweiss and red mountain lillies to roe deer and royal eagles. There are some stunning lakes with crystal clear waters (such as at the little resort of Alleghe), chairlifts to take you to the higher reaches and views to make your heart sing.

Appetites whetted by energetic walks and gulps of sharp, fresh air can be happily assuaged in the region's excellent restaurants, very many, of course, specialising in the hearty alpine fare of the Tirol, but plenty featuring pasta dishes. The wines from the region are very good, too, the best ones white, crisp, dry and very refreshing after a day in the mountains.

PREVIOUS PAGE: The somewhat fragile-looking Dolomite mountains were named after the French geologist Déodat Dolomieu. Their natural beauty attracts thousands of visitors each year for hiking, rambling and, of course, winter sports.

Skiers relax near the Falzarego Pass. The Dolomite region has some of Italy's best skiing areas, with major international events taking place at locations such as Cortina d'Ampezzo and Val Gardena.

Dolomites

Major Events
Winter Polo Cup (February): Cortina's polo-in-the-snow contest.
Carnevale (February): processions and entertainment in Cortina to preface Lent.
Gara di Fondo (February): the Dobbiaco–Cortina cross-country ski marathon.
Bobsleigh and Ski-jumping (winter): world-class events held anually in Cortina.
Festa dell'Uva (October): celebration of the grape harvest in Bolzano.

How to get there – and get around
By air: scheduled flights to Venice-Marco Polo Airport from Heathrow, Gatwick and Stansted (2 hrs 40 mins), then bus to Cortina (1hr 50 mins). A free hotel courtesy bus operates on Saturdays during the winter season.
Public Transport: Cortina is easy to explore on foot. Buses and taxis are available for outlying areas, and coaches link to most other Dolomite centres. However, car hire is recommended for access to out-of-the-way areas.

Suggested Hotels (all Cortina)
Miramonti Majestic, Via Peziè.
Tel: (0436) 4201 Fax: (0436) 867019
Despite being a mile out of town, this is Cortina's most sought-after address. Very expensive.
De la Poste, Piazza Roma.
Tel: (0436) 4271 Fax: (0436) 868435
Arguably the most popular first-class hotel in the centre of Cortina. Expensive.
Aquila, Corso Italia.
Tel: (0436) 2618 Fax: (0436) 867315
Cosy hotel, with a heated indoor pool, in central Cortina. Moderate.

Suggested Restaurants (all Cortina)
The hotel restaurants of the Miramonti Majestic and De la Poste (above) have excellent reputations for their food and ambience. Expensive.
Da Beppe Sello , Via Ronco.
Tel: (0436) 3236
Popular restaurant with an intimate atmosphere. Moderate.
Croda Café, Corso Italia.
Tel:(0463) 866589
Good value pasta and pizza – a handy lunchtime choice. Inexpensive.

Florence

Florence is a glorious place. But a couple of days won't really be enough to do justice to its beauty and artistic merit. A long weekend is better, given a little forward planning and the purchase of a useful guidebook. Only with these can you hope to understand why this wonderful Italian city has captured the imagination of poets and novelists for centuries.

History and Culture

Florence was founded as a Roman military town. The River Arno gave easy access to the sea and provided irrigation for agriculture and industry. Wool and other textiles became the city's crop and, by the year 1000, Florence was an important merchant and banking centre. The city gave rise to strong and wealthy families, one of which, the Medici, assumed control of state affairs and set the course for the greatest outpouring of creative activity since the classical age. They were lovers of the arts and sponsored talents like Brunelleschi, Botticelli and the great Michelangelo.

Sightseeing

Florence has changed little since the 15th century. A climb to an elevated square like Piazzale Michelangelo affords a vista of shimmering ancient architecture: brown battlements, imposing red domes and proud stretches of creamy marble. The Arno drifts beneath elegant bridges and highlights the most famous crossing of all, the heavily-laden Ponte Vecchio. Cathedral Square is a good starting point. Here you can view the squat little baptistery where the city's most famous son, Dante, was christened. Its East Door attracts the most attention. Sculpted in gilded bronze by Ghiberti, its ten panels depict Biblical scenes so skilfully that Michelangelo declared it worthy of being the 'Gate of Paradise'. The panels are now copies, the originals being safely tucked away in the Cathedral Works Museum. A few strides across the piazza is the famous belltower designed by the influential Giotto, its facade iced with coloured marble. The cathedral itself is a vast barn of a church whose finest feature is the massive dome, ingeniously constructed without the use of exterior scaffolding by Brunelleschi.

When you've had your fill of the religious zone, head to the old civic centre, based around the Piazza della Signoria. Here generations of Florentines assembled for proclamations, insurrections and the occasional burning at the stake. The old square is littered with statues. The best known is Michelangelo's strong but delicate *David*, but, like Ghiberti's door panels, this is a copy. The original has been taken into the Academy of Fine Arts for protection. Behind the piazza stands the Uffizi art gallery, a crash course in art history in one building. The best strategy is to read up a little beforehand and head for the really important features, such as Botticelli's *Venus* and *Spring*, or the portrait of Venus by Titian.

On a short trip to Florence, it's best to ration your art intake. A few hours of overkill in the Uffizi may dampen your appetite for the city's other artworks, so mix up your cultural itinerary with a spot of shopping or a leisurely bite to eat. But, refortified, pop into the Bargello museum and admire works by Donatello, and don't miss the religious frescos by Fra Angelico in San Marco, or Michelangelo's Medici tombs in San Lorenzo.

As for most cities, there are times to avoid in Florence. High summer is a hot tourist crush, and spring and autumn provide better access to the main attractions. No one with a hope of a bargain should seriously consider Florence for a shopping trip, but the city earns respect for its silks and leather goods and has colourful markets galore. After dinner, join the locals on their evening *passeggiata*, the leisurely stroll through the squares and along the river. It's when you allow yourself the chance to take stock like this that the treasures of Florence become most precious, and you realise you've barely scratched the surface.

The battlemented tower of the Palazzo Vecchio soars above the old centre of Florence at night. The building was constructed in the early 14th century as the city's Town Hall and fulfils that function to this day

Michelangelo's acclaimed statue of David, which once stood in Piazza della Signoria and is now housed in the Academy of Fine Art It was completed in 1504 as a symbol of how the 'Davids' of Florentines had overcome their 'Goliath',the city's tyrannical republican rulers, after the fall of the Medici

Florence

Major Events
Explosion of the Carriage (Easter Sunday): colourful religious spectacle, involving a mechanical dove and fireworks at the cathedral.
Maggio Musicale (May–June): major arts and music festival throughout the city.
Estate Fiesolana (mid June–August) music, drama and arts festival based in Fiesole.
Football in Costume (19, 24 and 28 June): medieval, rough-and-tumble team game for districts of the city

How to get there – and get around
By air: scheduled flights to Pisa-Galileo Galilei Airport and Florence Peretola Airport (3 miles out) from Gatwick and Stansted. Trains run from Pisa Airport to Florence (costing around LIT6500 and taking 1 hr); cheap buses run from Florence Peretola Airport to the city centre (15 mins).

Suggested Hotels
Helvetia e Bristol, Via dei Pescioni. Tel: (055) 28 78 14 Fax: (055) 28 83 53 Luxurious hotel near the cathedral. Very expensive.
Monna Lisa, Borgo Pinto. Tel: (055) 247 97 51 Fax: (055) 247 97 55 Renaissance palace with a modern extension. Expensive.
Beacci Tornabuoni, Via de' Tornabuoni. Tel: (055) 21 26 45 Fax: (055) 28 35 94 Centrally situated, very comfortable former palace. Moderate.
Hermitage, Vicolo Marzio. Tel: (055) 28 72 16 Fax: (055) 21 22 08 Hotel housed at the top of a medieval building, with cheaper rooms on the lower floors. Near the Ponte Vecchio. Moderate.

Suggested Restaurants:
Enoteca Pinchiorri, Via Ghibellina. Tel: (055) 24 27 77 Long-famous, formal restaurant with a stunning wine list. Very expensive.
Cibrèo, Via del Verrocchio. Tel: (055) 234 11 00 Traditional Tuscan cooking, but no pasta, in a relaxed atmosphere. Moderate.
La Taverna del Bronzino, Via delle Ruote. Tel: (055) 49 52 20 Excellent food in an orderly but not too formal setting (a Renaissance palazzo once connected with the artist Bronzino). Moderate.
I Quattro Amici, Via degli Orti Oricellari. Tel: (055) 21 54 13 Specialised fish restaurant, founded by four friends, as its name suggests. Moderate.

Proof of Lucca's ancient past can be found in Piazza San Michele (pictured), which sits on the site of the old Roman forum, and just north of here, the Piazza Anfiteatro, an odd-shaped square constructed around the base of the city's former amphitheatre.

LUCCA AND PISA

The strange thing about Lucca is that it never seems crowded with tourists, despite its obvious attractions. Perhaps the lure of Florence, Pisa and Siena is simply too great. Yet Lucca is one of the great Italian cities, beautifully preserved, untarnished by modern developments, architecturally rich and, as just stated, thankfully fairly quiet.

History and Culture

Lucca was a Roman colony as long ago as 177 BC. After time under Florence in the Middle Ages, the town bought its own freedom and prospered as a small city state until Napoleon strolled in and handed it over as a gift to his sister. Later part of Tuscany, it joined the new Italy in 1861, three years after the composer Giacomo Puccini was born here. Over the centuries, Lucca's great rival was Pisa, just 15 miles to the south. Mighty Pisa was once one of the great Italian maritime republics, its menfolk taking a lead during the Crusades. To commemorate victories in battle, the city erected the magnificent 'Pisan-Romanesque' buildings that make the city such a draw today.

Sightseeing

Lucca's main monuments can easily be found on its grid-like streets (a legacy of its Roman days), but, before venturing into the heart of the city, it is a good idea to take a stroll around the fine 17th-century ramparts. Tree-lined and shady, they convey an excellent first impression of this lovely city. Chief among the attractions is San Martino, the city's 11th-century cathedral. Like the major edifices in Pisa, this is an excellent example of the ornate Pisan-Romanesque style, its asymetrical facade adorned with tiers of tiny arches and squeezed in beside the battlemented belltower, which has been standing here for over 1000 years. Inside the cathedral is the celebrated Volto Santo, a wooden crucifix said to bear the visage of Christ. Lucca also has several other fine churches,

including the eccentric-looking San Michele in Foro, on the site of the old Roman forum, and San Frediano, beautifully adorned with bright 13th-century mosaics. Near here is Palazzo Pfanner, an imposing 17th-century mansion housing a costume museum and some of the silk textiles that once made Lucca wealthy. Its formal gardens are some of the finest in Italy. Don't miss a wander down Via Fillungo, the main shopping street, filled with tempting boutiques, or the pretty Via del Fosso, with its central canal.

A short train ride away is Pisa, home of the Leaning Tower. The city's attractions are nearly all housed in one square. As you turn into the Piazza del Duomo, four remarkable, brilliant white wedding cake structures stand out against the lush green lawns that surround them. The biggest is the cathedral, begun in the mid-11th century and one of Italy's most stunning buildings. Inside, the highlights include the intricately carved pulpit by Giovanni Pisano and an early 14th-century mosaic of Christ by Cimabue. Adjacent is the slightly younger baptistery, with traces of Gothic to add to its Romanesque beginnings. The marvellous pulpit by Nicola Pisano catches the eye.

The Leaning Tower is actually the cathedral's belltower. It was begun in 1173 and was already starting to lean before the third storey was added 100 years later, thanks to its shallow foundations. If you look closely, you can see how the architects tried to compensate by 'straightening' the building from here up. Despite efforts to rectify the situation in recent years, the Tower now inclines at around 17 feet from the vertical and has been closed to the public since 1990. Whilst it is a shame that you can no longer climb to the top, you can make yourself just as giddy by lying on the grass below and watching the clouds float above the Tower. It's a weird sensation.

Lucca and Pisa

Major Events

Sagra Musicale Lucchese (April–July): annual celebration of sacred music.

Luminaria di San Ranieri (June 16–17): the Arno river is lit up for the feast of St Ranieri in Pisa.

Gioco del Ponte (late June): medieval tug-of-war contest across the main bridge in Pisa.

Estate Musical Lucchese (July–September): classical concerts form the core of Lucca's musical summer.

Luminaria di Santa Croce (August 14): torchlit religious procession through the streets of Lucca.

Volto Santo (mid September): religious procession from Lucca'sSan Frediano to the cathedral.

How to get there – and get around

By air: scheduled flights to Pisa-Galileo Galilei Airport from Gatwick and Stansted (about 2 hrs 25 mins), then bus to Pisa (20 mins) and bus or train to Lucca (30 mins).

Public Transport: central Lucca is transport-free, but excellent bus and train networks radiate out to Pisa (30 mins) and the other main Tuscan centres.

Suggested Hotels (all Lucca)

Locanda L'Elisa, SS del Brennero.
Tel: (0583) 37 97 37 Fax: (0583) 37 90 19
Classy hotel, the best in central Lucca.
Very expensive.

Grand Guinigi, Via Romana.
Tel: (0583) 4991 Fax: 49 98 00
Classic hotel with good facilities.
Expensive.

Napoleon, Viale Europa.
Tel: (0583) 31 65 16 Fax: (0583) 41 83 98
Quality hotel close to the railway station.
Moderate.

Suggested Restaurants (all Lucca)

Puccini, Corte San Lorenzo.
Tel: (0583) 31 61 16
Popular up market restaurant, with seafood specialities. Expensive.

Buca di Sant'Antonio, Via della Cervia.
Tel: (0583) 558 81
Well-regarded city-centre restaurant.
Moderate.

Giglio, Piazza del Giglio.
Tel: (0583) 49 40 58
Known for its value-for-money food.
Moderate.

MILAN

Milan is Italy's most stylish city. This is the design capital, the economic powerhouse of the country, a city with more in common with other parts of Western Europe than its compatriots in the South of Italy. With its nose for business, it's not the warmest or friendliest of Italian destinations, but it has plenty going for it – from the best shopping to the world's greatest opera house, from a stunning cathedral to some of this art-rich country's finest masterpieces.

History and Culture

Milan's origins lie with the Celts, who settled here around 400 BC. On the same site, the Romans established Mediolanum, where, in the 4th century, the famous Edict of Milan was issued by Constantine, allowing Christians the right to practise freely for the first time. In the Middle Ages, two ruthless families, first the Visconti and then the Sforzas, took control and the city became a major force and began to develop its cultural base. In later centuries, however, it fell to the Spanish and then the Austrians, who were only finally expelled in 1859, just before Milan helped found the new Kingdom of Italy. Milan was hit by bombs during World War II, but was quickly back on its feet in the post-war years, becoming the driving force for Italy's economic 'miracle' of the 1950s, a position it is keen not to relinquish.

Sightseeing

Milan's cathedral is a huge pincushion, a fantastic and distinctive Gothic giant founded in the 14th century but not finished for 500 years. Once seen, it is never forgotten, a mass of pinnacles and spires that cover one of the largest churches in the world. Even older is the church of the city's patron saint, St Ambrose. He began building it himself way back in 379 AD, although the structure you see today is much more modern – from the 10th century. More beautiful still is the little Renaissance church of San Satiro, with lovely frescos and an octagonal baptistery.

Milan's magnificently Gothic cathedral. When you've explored the interior head for the roof, from where there are excellent views not just over the city but as far north as the Alps, on a clear day.

The other great historic building in Milan is the Castello Sforzesco, built by the ruling Sforza family in the 15th century on the site of the palace of the Viscontis. It houses the Civic Art Gallery whose prize exhibit is Michelangelo's unfinished *Rondanini Pietà* sculpture. The best collection of artworks in the city can be found at the Brera Gallery, almost a rival to Florence's Uffizi. Here you can see true masterpieces by Raphael, Piero della Francesca, Caravaggio, Tintoretto, Canova and others. Yet Milan's best-known painting is not here either. Leonardo's magnificent *Last Supper* adorns a wall of the convent of Santa Maria delle Grazie and should not be missed. More of Leonardo's works can be admired in the Science and Technology Museum, where models of his inventions – such as his famous flying machine – can be viewed.

Milan is, of course, the home of La Scala, the world's most famous opera house. Some of the best-known works have premiered here since its opening in 1778 but, if you want to see a performance, you will need to book months in advance. As a poor, but interesting enough, alternative, you can always visit the Theatre Museum, where props and other operatic items can be studied.

While you're in Milan, shopping must feature highly on the agenda. Make for the fabulous Galleria Vittorio Emanuele II. Note its complex mosaic floors and stroll around some of the swishest shops in Italy. Having said this, the main designer outlets are found elsewhere. Versace, Gucci, Armani, Ferragamo and others occupy a complex of streets known collectively as the 'Quadrilatero'.

In the unlikely event that you have any more time on your hands – especially if you take in the other great museums and churches not mentioned here – it's easy to day-trip out to the Italian lakes. Maggiore and Como are both easily accessible and provide a welcome break from the pace of this dynamic, chic city.

Milan's Galleria Vittorio Emanuele II, dedicated to the first king of Italy, is one of the world's great shopping centres. Its novel metal and glass architecture has inspired copies all around the world.

Milan

Major Events

San Siro Stadium (August–May): watch AC Milan and Inter alternate at the great stadium each weekend in this football-mad city.
Season at La Scala (September–July): the great operas, ballets and recitals.
Formula One Motor Racing (September): the Italian Grand Prix takes place at the famous Monza track, north of Milan, at a critical stage of the season.
Festa di Sant'Ambrogio (December): colourful market to celebrate the patron saint's day.

How to get there – and get around

By air: scheduled flights to Milan-Linate Airport (4 miles out) from Heathrow, Gatwick,Stansted, Birmingham and Manchester. Buses (taking 20 mins and costing around LIT4500) and taxis (15 mins; LIT20000) run into Milan centre. However, many flights may go into the new terminal at Milan-Malpensa Airport (30 miles out; bus 55 mins; LIT13000).
Public Transport: Milan has an efficient network of metro, buses and trams (single tickets LIT1500; 10 tickets LIT 14,000; 24-hr ticket LIT6000), but taxis can be expensive.

Suggested Hotels

Duca di Milano, Piazza della Repubblica. Tel: (02) 62 841 Fax: (02) 65 55 966
Super-luxury hotel in the heart of Milan. Very expensive.
Fenice, Corso Buenos Aires. Tel: (02) 29 52 55 41 Fax: (02) 29 52 39 42
Modern hotel, 15 mins' walk from the sightseeing centre. Moderate.
Cavour, Via Fatabenefratelli. Tel: (02) 657 20 51 Fax: (02) 659 22 63
Modern hotel just around the corner from La Scala. Moderate.
Gran Duca di York, Via Moneta. Tel: (02) 87 48 63 Fax: (02) 86 90 344
Comfortable, central hotel. Moderate.

Suggested Restaurants

Peck, Via Victor Hugo. Tel: (02) 87 67 74
High-quality Italian cuisine. Expensive.
Alfio, Via Senato. Tel: (02) 76 00 06 33
Well-patronised seafood restaurant. Moderate.
La Cucuma, Via Pacini. Tel: (02) 29 52 60 98
Good value pizza parlour. Inexpensive.

NAPLES

For travellers not content with flopping on a beach, the Bay of Naples must rank among the best seaside destinations. Unfortunately, its attributes are only too well recognised and the crowds tend to take over in the summer months. However, with the spring and autumn so comfortable, there's no excuse for giving the romantic Bay of Naples a miss. Naples, itself, is a truly fascinating city with much to commend it, but it is also a hassle. For a more relaxing break stay somewhere else around the bay. Sorrento, although a honey pot for the package tour crowds, is nonetheless a pleasant resort, with everything that you need.

History and Culture

The Bay of Naples was first colonised by Greek settlers, as early as the 8th century BC. The Romans later took a shine to the area and set up holiday homes around the gulf. However, the history of this very lovely bay is indelibly marked by the events of the year 79 AD, in which the volcano Vesuvius, which dominates the skyline, blew its top and devoured the towns of Pompei, Herculaneum and Stabiae. In the Middle Ages, Naples was made the capital of a Spanish-controlled kingdom that included Sicily. It then became part of the new Italy in 1860.

Sightseeing

There's not a great deal to see in Sorrento itself, but it's an excellent base for hitting the major attractions. Just across the water is the famously ritzy island of Capri, where personalities as diverse as the Emperor Tiberius and singer Gracie Fields have set up home. Peering over the sheer cliffs to the deep azure waters way below, clambering up the little lanes fragranced by orange and lemon trees, and taking a chairlift to the top of the highest point, Monte Solaro, are just three of the pleasures of this undeniably beautiful, rocky little island. But, if crowds don't appeal, try the neighbouring islands of Ischia and Procida, which are much less touristy.

From Sorrento, you can also take a bus over the 'Milky Mountains' to the celebrated Amalfi Drive. This cliff-hugging road twists and turns its way along the jagged peninsula, skirting above picturesque fishing towns like Positano, which tumble down to the crystal clear sea, all the way to Amalfi. This lovely, little town was once a major rival to Venice, Genoa and Pisa. Here the remains of St Andrew are stored in the multicoloured, 13th-century cathedral.

A short hydrofoil ride, or an hour on the excellent Circumvesuviana train, will whizz you into the heart of Naples. After a day in this rather chaotic city, you'll be pleased you are staying elsewhere, but you'll also understand why its inhabitants love it so much. The 14th-century cathedral is a beauty and contains the remains of the patron saint, San Gennaro. Phials of his dried blood are said to miraculously liquefy twice a year.

Anyone with an interest in ancient history should not miss the Archaeology Museum, an internationally important collection of Greek and Roman finds, while above the city is the Capodimonte Museum, with an excellent display of canvases by Botticelli, Raphael, Titian and other Italian greats. Yet all these major sights, plus the royal palace and the San Carlo Opera House, and countless other churches and museums, pale into significance against the bay's greatest treasure, the amazingly well-preserved Roman city of Pompei.

Engulfed by the debris from Vesuvius in 79 AD, Pompei is a city stranded in time. You can admire almost intact buildings, with their vivid wall paintings and mosaic works, see the old amphitheatre, the cobbled streets and the ancient baths, and transport yourself back nearly 2000 years to civilisation Roman-style. Don't stint on time. Give yourself a day to take it all in and consider paying a local guide to tell you all about it.

The magnificent Bay of Naples is a treasure chest of tourist attractions, blessed with a wonderful climate. If you have time, climb the slopes of mighty Vesuvius to take home a view you'll never forget.

Marina Grande is the main port of the isle of Capri. Here passengers disembark from Naples, Sorrento and other parts of the bay. The colourful houses and bobbing boats make a colourful introduction to this lovely island and , from here, you can take a boat Capri's famous Blue Grotto, a cave lit by the azure glow from sunlight filtered through seawater

Naples

Major Events
Festa di Sant'Antonio (January 17): parade in honour of St Anthony in Naples
Grieving Madonna Procession (Good Friday): religious ritual on the island of Procida.
Festa di San Gennaro (early May and September 19): the amazing spectacle of the liquefaction of the patron saint's dried blood in Naples cathedral.
Festa della Santa Maria del Carmine (July 16): lively event during which the Naples belltower is illuminated.
Neapolitan Song Contest (early September): colourful folksong competition for couples held in Naples.
International Cinema Convention (October): homage to the silver screen at Sorrento.

How to get there – and get around
By air: scheduled flights to Naples-Capodichino Airport (7 miles out) from Gatwick only (3 hrs 20 mins), but there are many flights to Rome-Fiumicino Airport (see Rome) with transfers to Naples (45 mins). Buses (25 mins) and taxis (15 mins) run to Naples centre. From there take the Circumvesuviana train around the bay (1 hr; LIT4200), or hydrofoil across it (30 mins; LIT12000), to Sorrento.
Public Transport: Naples has a metro, bus, tram and funicular network (LIT1500 for any 3 journeys in a 90-min period). The Circumvesuviana links towns around the bay, while hydrofoils and ferries sail to Capri, Ischia and Procida.

Suggested Hotels (all Sorrento)
Excelsior Vittoria, Piazza Tasso.
Tel: (081) 807 10 44
Fax: (081) 877 12 06
Super-deluxe hotel in on the main square, with a lift to the sea. Very expensive.
Michelangelo, Corso Italia.
Tel: (081) 878 48 44
Fax: (081) 878 18 16
Very comfortable, first-class hotel on the main street. Expensive.
Conca Park, Via Capo.
Tel: (081) 807 16 21
Fax: (081) 807 13 65
Large, popular hotel with a pool. Moderate.

Suggested Restaurants (all Sorrento)
La Solara, Via Capo.
Tel: (081) 533 80 00
Panoramic views and tempting pasta dishes. Expensive.
Central, Corso Italia. Tel: (081) 807 33 31 Handily placed, with plenty of house specials. Moderate.

Palermo

Sicily may be part of Europe but it has more than a touch of Africa about it. The climate is hot, the people are dark and many of the buildings have an Arab appearance. This is hardly surprising, since the Saracens were just one of the races who conquered this prominent island, along with the Greeks, Romans and Normans. They left a rich cultural inheritance and a very cosmopolitan culinary heritage, which can be enjoyed in or around the much-maligned capital city of Palermo.

History and Culture

Palermo was founded by the Phoenicians, eight centuries before the birth of Christ. Today, it is a wonderful mish-mash of architectural styles inherited from the various invaders that have darkened its doorstep. In recent times, Palermo has struggled under the mantle of being the Mafia capital. The Mafia has been cleaned up by the authorities in the last decade, and, although its influence remains strong, don't expect to be confronted with violence. Instead, you'll find the people welcoming and friendly.

Sightseeing

Although its initial appearance from the sea, cradled in a cup of mountains on the fringe of the water, is an attractive sight, once you've disembarked (be it from boat, train or aeroplane), Palermo is not an immediately appealing location. It is noisy and confusing. But step back from the crowd, find your bearings, and it becomes a grossly underestimated city with a great deal to offer. Many streets are medieval, and rich in Norman and Arab influence. The beautiful palaces and churches are not as well preserved on the outside as in other parts of Italy, but, inside, they are truly beautiful.

Make a start at the cathedral, founded in the 12th century. Here lie the remains of the kings of Sicily. Just across a palm-filled park sits the Palazzo dei Normanni, today home of the Sicilian regional government, but previously the royal palace. As its name suggests, it was mostly constructed by the Normans, but its roots are actually Arabic. Much of the palace is now closed to the public, but the Palatine Chapel is accessible. Its interior is a feast of mosaics, marble, gold and glass. Palermo's other superb buildings include the churches of San Giovanni degli Eremiti, topped by five domes, and La Martorana, with its 12th-century Byzantine mosaics. The city's powerful baroque churches should not be overlooked either.

Palermo has a very good regional art gallery, and a more unusual, but entertaining, Marionette Museum. You can visit the Archaeological Museum, or take a bus and head out of the city to the well-preserved Greek temple and amphitheatre at Segesta, 40 miles to the west. Nearer to Palermo is Monreale, a Benedictine cathedral founded in 1172. Inside, the mosaic work and gilded ceilings make it one of the highlights of the island.

Back in the city, you must see the Vucciria market. It's more an Arab souk, selling anything from fruit to household junk. When night falls, the pace slows and Palermo takes on yet another air. Seafood features prominently in the restaurants alongside flavoursome fresh vegetables. Eastern spices such as saffron find their way into many recipes. For dessert, try the local speciality, cassata. The local wines don't have a great international reputation, but they are seriously underrated.

PREVIOUS PAGE: The Moorish influence on Sicilian architecture is evident in the bulbous red domes of the church of San Giovanni degli Eremiti in Palermo. The church was built in 1132 on the site of a former mosque.

The Benedictine cathedral at Monreale is one of the treasures of Sicily. Don't miss its magnificent mosaics, the work of master craftsmen, and the 900-year-old cloisters, which are remarkably well preserved.

PALERMO

Major Events
Palermo di Scena (June–September): packed summer festival of music and theatre.
Festino di Santa (early–mid July): celebration of the patron saint, culminating in processions and fireworks.
International Sport Film Festival (October): annual movie showcase.
Winter Music (November–March): Sicily Symphony Orchestra season with guest conductors and soloists, and operas, ballet and dance.

How to get there – and get around
By air: many scheduled flights into Rome-Fiumicino Airport (see Rome); connections to Palermo Airport (19 miles out) take 1hr. Buses to the centre are frequent and cost around LIT6,500. Taxis and hire car services are also available.
Public Transport: Palermo has a reliable bus service (single LIT1,500, or LIT 4,500 per day); taxis have a minimum fare of LIT6,000.

Suggested Hotels
Grand Hotel Villa Igiea, Salita Belmonte.
Tel: (091) 54 37 44 Fax: (091) 54 76 54
Palermo's grandest hotel with terrific sea views, although slightly out of the centre. Very expensive.
Centrale Palace, Corso Vittorio Emanuele.
Tel: (091) 33 66 66 Fax: (091) 33 48 81
Central hotel with good amenities. Expensive.
Cristal Palace, Via Roma.
Tel: (091) 61 12 580 Fax: (091) 61 12 589
Popular, centrally situated hotel. Moderate.
Orientale, Via Maqueda.
Tel: (091) 61 65 727
Small, but central hotel for the budget conscious. Inexpensive.

Suggested Restaurants
Capricci di Sicilia, Piazza Sturzo.
Tel: (091) 32 77 77
Well known for its Sicilian and international cuisine. Expensive.
Casa del Brodo, Corso Vittorio Emanuele. Tel: (091) 31 16 55
Well-thought of, mid-range restaurant in the heart of Palermo. Moderate
Italia, Via Oroglio.
Tel: (091) 58 98 85.
Typical of a crop of well-priced eating places. Inexpensive.

Inside Parma's Palazzo Pilotta is the Teatro Farnese, a 17th-century copy of the Teatro Olimpico, which the famous architect Palladio constructed in Vicenza. Entirely made of wood, the baroque theatre demands a visit, even when there is no show being performed.

Parma

Parma is not that far from Bologna or Milan, both already featured in this book, and could feasibly be tagged onto the end of a visit to either. However, this splendid little city has everything you could want for a few days' break and is worth the extra effort of getting here – especially if you have a love of opera.

History and Culture

Parma was founded by the Romans in 183 BC, and was an independent city state in the Middle Ages. It later belonged to the Papacy, and even passed into Spanish hands for a while before joining the new Kingdom of Italy in 1861. Two culinary items of world renown stem from this sophisticated little city: ham and cheese. Parma ham is acknowledged as one the mainstays of classic Italian cuisine. The meat is cured in the warm air of the hills around the city and is traditionally served with melon or figs for a perfect first course. Parmesan cheese is even more famous, hard and tangy, grating into power over pasta dishes and into soups. Expect to find these and much more on the menus of a city that almost rivals mighty Bologna in the restaurant department.

Sightseeing

Being small, Parma is also compact and easy to take in. With all the sights concentrated in the historic centre, you won't need to waste time taking buses out to the suburbs. The most attractive square is the Piazza del Duomo and features one of the most magnificent cathedrals (11th century) in all of Italy,

adorned with artwork by Correggio and his pupils. The master's *Assumption of the Virgin*, painted in the 1520s, is worth the visit alone. The thrusting, steepled bell-tower stands guard at the cathedral's side, towering over the octagonal Romanesque-Gothic baptistery, built in pink Verona marble and adorned with important reliefs depicting the months of the year. To the east of the square is San Giovanni Evangelista, a domed, 16th-century monastery church with some important frescos, including Correggio's *Dormition of St John*.

Parma did not escape the ravages of World War II. One casualty was the Palazzo Pilotta, close to the river and home of the powerful Farnese family in the 16th century. Thankfully, it has been cleverly renovated and rebuilt and houses the Teatro Farnese. Palazzo Pilotta is also home to the National Gallery, exhibiting excellent pieces by the likes of Leonardo, Fra Angelico, Bronzino, Tiepolo, Van Dyck and El Greco. For even older treasures, pop into the Archaeology Museum, which offers prehistoric bits and pieces and items from Etruscan tombs.

This is not the end of the city's attractions. The church of Santa Maria della Steccata has an elegant dome designed by Sangallo the Younger and contains frescos by Parmigianino. There are other churches, too, almost as well endowed with masterpieces, but, for a breath of fresh air – which you need after a fresco overdose – Parma also has some fine formal gardens in the Parco Ducale.

Parma is a city that exudes well being. The people are prosperous and in tune with the artistic jewels they have on their doorstep. They also have a reputation for being very selective, a trait highlighted in their enthusiasm for good music. The city has a magnificent opera house, the Teatro Regio, where its audience tends to show its true emotions if not pleased with the performances. Perhaps they have the right to do so. After all, this was the birthplace of Verdi and Toscanini and is the final resting place of Paganini. The city is certainly not cheap, a break here gives you the chance to wallow in comfortable, extremely civilised surroundings, with much to observe and relatively few other tourists with which to share the sights.

Parma

Major Events

Opera at the Teatro Regio (October–May): classics by Verdi and international composers.

Concerts at the Teatro Regio (summer): Parma has being playing host to the homeless Orchestra and Chorus of La Fenice, Venice.

Parma Theatre Festival (September–October): international drama event.

How to get there – and get around

By air: scheduled flights from various UK airports to Rome-Fiumicino Airport (see Rome, p.154). Flight transfers to Parma (Giuseppe Verdi) Airport take an extra hour. Alternatively, there are flights to Milan (see p.143), then trains to Parma (1 hr 40 mins), or to Bologna (see p.130), then trains to Parma (1½ hrs).

Public transport: Parma has a reasonable, reliable bus service.

Suggested Hotels

Grand Hotel Baglioni, Viale Piacenza. Tel: (0521) 29 29 29 Fax: (0521) 29 28 28 Exclusive hotel overlooking the Parco Ducale. Very expensive.

Palace Hotel Maria Luigia, Viale Mentana. Tel: (0521) 53 10 08 Fax: (0521) 23 11 26 Upmarket hotel with good facilities near the city centre. Expensive.

Park Hotel Stendhal, Via Bodoni. Tel: (0521) 20 80 57 Fax: (0521) 28 56 55 Comfortable, well-appointed city-centre hotel. Moderate.

Suggested Restaurants

Il Canova, Viale Piacenza. Tel: (0521) 29 29 29 The Grand Hotel's excellent restaurant. Expensive.

Santa Barnaba, Via Trento. Tel: (0521) 27 03 65 Popular restaurant specialising in regional fare. Moderate.

Trattoria del Tribunale, Borgo Politi. Tel: (0521) 28 55 27 Good value food in the centre of town. Inexpensive.

BENEDICTVS XIV
PERFEC

Has there ever been a more compelling city than Rome? Its wonderful mix of ancient remains, medieval churches, bold baroque fountains and the greatest artworks the world has ever seen means that there is something to fascinate at every turn. It's a hot, bustling, sometimes choking city but it's a place that everyone who loves travelling just has to visit at least once.

History and Culture

Rome was founded in 753 BC, but was destroyed by the Gauls in the 4th century BC. The city then re-established itself and, soaring in power, built an empire that stretched from the Straits of Gibraltar to the Black Sea, and from Scotland to the Sahara. From the 4th century AD, Rome fell into decline and the Dark Ages saw the city repeatedly raped and plundered. It reawakened in the Renaissance, as interest in classical art placed it on the 15th-century tourist map. Great artists came to the city and added their own touches of brilliance, before the onset of the 17th-century baroque period in which Gianlorenzo Bernini and his rivals refashioned Rome with highly ornate churches and monuments. After this peak, Rome endured yet another economic trough but was saved by the unification of Italy, which saw it installed as the capital in 1870.

Sightseeing

Rome's Trevi Fountain, where visitors toss in a coin in to guarantee a return to the Eternal City. Frank Sinatra sang about 'Three Coins' here, and Anita Ekberg splashed around in its water for Fellini's film masterpiece *La Dolce Vita*.

To enjoy Rome, you need time – a bare minimum of four clear days to cover just the highlights. The big names are obvious: the Colosseum amphitheatre, the international symbol of Rome; the Forums, a rubbly reminder of daily life 2,000 years ago; St Peter's basilica, graced by Michelangelo's beautiful dome and fronted by Bernini's colonnaded square; the baroque Trevi Fountain, the flower-filled Spanish Steps, dotted with scribbling artists; and so on. These, of course, should not be missed. But there are other priceless exhibits in this urban museum which just cannot be overlooked. The Vatican Museums could easily eat up your whole holiday, particularly through its Raphael Rooms and, of course, Michelangelo's unsurpassed ceiling and *Last Judgement* fresco in the Sistine Chapel. The astonishing ancient Pantheon is still as solid as a rock today. Fantastic churches like Santa Maria Maggiore, San Lorenzo, St Paul's and St John in Lateran are all dripping in history and artworks, and the treasures of the Capitoline museum take you back to the glory of Ancient Rome.

Culture shock can take the pleasure out of a vacation, so spare some time for more hedonistic pleasures, like the classy shopping on the Via Condotti, or the atmospheric restaurants and tavernas in the winding old streets of the Trastevere district. For a novel experience, visit the enormous flea market at Porta Portese on Sunday mornings (but watch your pockets!).

The great squares like Piazza Navona, and Campo dei Fiori, are always worth a wander, and provide welcome respite from the hurly-burly of Piazza Venezia. Possibly the greatest pleasure of them all, however, is to stroll around the old backstreets, discovering an almost forgotten piece of ancient architecture.There's simply no city like it. When your time is up, you'll understand why they call Rome 'the Eternal City' – you will need an eternity to see it all properly.

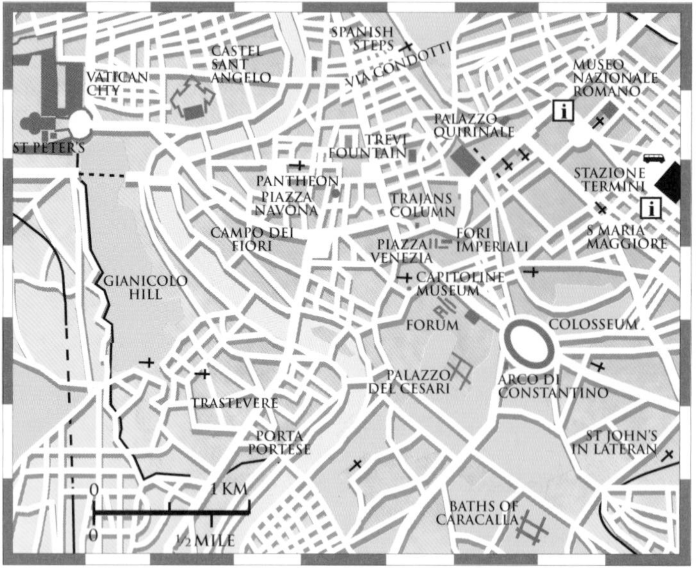

Rome

Major Events

Teatro dell'Opera di Roma (January–May; and November–December): great operas under the baton of Siropoli.

Papal Address (Easter Sunday): the Pope speaks to the world.

Tevere Expo (end June): local crafts, music, fireworks and food on the banks of the Tiber.

Open Air Opera (July–August): performances at Rome's Olympic Stadium.

Estate Romana (July–August) open-air performances every night for two months – classical music, theatre, dance and rock.

La Befana (December–January): famous Christmas fair in Piazza Navona.

How to get there – and get around

By air: scheduled flights to Rome-Fiumicino Airport (16 miles out) from Heathrow, Gatwick, Stansted, Luton, Edinburgh and Manchester (longest journey 3 hrs), then by bus (45 mins; LIT7,000), train (35 mins; LIT13,000) or taxi (45 mins; LIT14,000–16,000) to the city centre.

Public transport: Rome has plenty of good bus services, but they can be a hassle. Buy tickets from kiosks beforehand and stamp them in the machine on the bus. The efficient metro is the easiest way to get about, but it runs in only two directions. Single interchangeable tickets for bus and metro cost LIT1,500; 24-hr LIT6,000; one week LIT24,000. Taxis are expensive and not so reliable.

Suggested Hotels

De la Ville Inter-Continental, Via Sistina.
Tel: (06) 67331 Fax: (06) 6784213
Super-luxury hotel at the top of the Spanish Steps and near the Via Condotti. Very expensive.

Scalinata di Spagna, Piazza Trinità dei Monti.
Tel: (06) 6793006 Fax: (06) 69940598
Popular, tiny hotel on top of the Spanish Steps. Expensive.

Columbus, Via della Conciliazione.
Tel: (06) 6865435 Fax: (06) 6864874
Right on the Vatican's doorstep and once a cardinal's residence. Moderate.

Suggested Restaurants

Les Etoiles, Hotel Atlante Star, Via Vitellischi. Tel: (06) 6893434
Starry restaurant overlooking the dome of St Peter's. Expensive.

Sans Souci, Via Sicilia.
Tel: (06) 4821814
Star-spotting restaurant, with a worthy reputation. Expensive.

Dal Bolognese, Piazza del Popolo.
Tel: (06) 3611426
If the Sans Souci gets the stars, Dal Bolognese attracts the starlets with its pasta dishes. Moderate.

Da Lucia, Vicolo del Mattonato.
Tel: (06) 5803601
Traditional Trastevere trattoria offering basic Roman dishes. Inexpensive.

SIENA AND SAN GIMIGNANO

Numerous bars and cafés ring the Piazza del Campo in Siena, providing excellent vantage points for admiring the architecture of the Palazzo Pubblico, the Torre del Mangia and the wonderful square itself.

Although Florence is undeniably the star in the Tuscan firmament, Siena can run the great city close. From the outset, its appearance and atmosphere are much more modest, but Siena is no less beautiful than its larger neighbour, some would say even more attractive. It also makes a good base from which to explore the relatively undiscovered delights of central Tuscany. You can head north-west to the dramatic little town of San Gimignano, or make a trip east to the often of Arezzo. And in between there's some glorious Tuscan countryside to be explored.

History and Culture

Siena was founded by the Etruscans, but it really came into its own during the Middle Ages as an important centre for the wool and banking trades. As a political rival to Florence, it was in constant conflict with the city on the Arno, once famously defeating the Florentines in 1260 but thereafter always in their shadow. Plague and tyranny were the hallmarks of the centuries that followed. A declined Siena was eventually forced into the Medici's Grand Duchy of Tuscany, finally joining the new kingdom of Italy in the 1860s.

Sightseeing

The appearance of Siena is distinctive, so distinctive that the orange-brown-coloured brickwork has given its name to the pigment known today as 'burnt Sienna'. Its lovely old buildings are arranged in an arc around the central square, the Piazza del Campo. This shell-shaped arena slopes down to the historic town hall, the Palazzo Pubblico,

which houses some excellent medieval artworks, including a primitive map of the world from the 14th century. Soaring above the palazzo is the lofty belltower, the Torre del Mangia. The views from the top are superb, but the climb up and down is not for the claustrophobic.

It is here in the square that Siena's world-famous Palio horse race is run twice every summer. This historic pageant features representatives from each of Siena's 17 districts and the race is a matter of great honour and prestige. It only lasts a minute or two, but the excitement generated by the preceding parades is electric. While the Palio may be the reason travellers want to visit Siena, it is also the best excuse for staying away. Close to race days, the crowds are unbearable and obtaining a hotel room or restaurant table is a nightmare.

Around the corner from the Piazza del Campo is the city's magnificent cathedral, looking like a giant humbug in its black and white-striped marble shell. It is one of Italy's finest. Elegant works by Pisano, Pinturicchio, Donatello and the great Michelangelo contribute to its interior beauty.

Other delights await in this corner of Tuscany. San Gimignano is a medieval delight. Thirteen towers dominate the horizon, the survivors of dozens that once fashioned the face of the town. San Gimignano is a city to wander around, popping into lovely old churches like the Collegiata and Sant'Agostino to see the fabulous frescos, and visiting the Civic Museum for yet more ancient masterpieces.

In the opposite direction from Siena is Arezzo. Despite severe wartime damage, the city still has plenty of interest, with, once again, more classic paintings than you can shake a guidebook at. To art lovers, the *Legend of the True Cross* cycle of frescos by Piero della Francesca, in the church of San Francesco, is worth the plane fare to Italy on its own.

Finally, you can't ignore the fact that this is wine growing territory. The Chianti district sits just to the north of Siena and its estates beckon you with offers of free tastings and tours.

Siena and San Gimignano

Major Events
Palio di Siena (July 2 and August 16): the world famous horse race.
Siena Jazz (July and August): summer jazz in the town.
Settimana Musicale Senese (late August): highly-acclaimed classical music festival held annually in Siena.
Giostra del Saracino (1st Sunday in September): Arezzo's medieval pageant featuring jousting contests.

How to get there – and get around
By air: scheduled flights from Gatwick and Stansted to Florence-Peretola Airport (2 hrs 20 mins), then bus to Siena (50 mins), or to Pisa-Galileo Galilei Airport (2½ hrs), then bus to Siena (1 hr).
Public transport: Siena's medieval city centre is virtually traffic-free, but reasonable bus services link outlying areas and other Tuscan towns.

Suggested Hotels (all Siena)
Certosa di Maggiano, Via Certosa.
Tel: (0577) 288180 Fax: (0577) 288189
Easily Siena's most sought-after hotel: small, exclusive and set in a former Carthusian monastery dating from 1314. Very expensive.
Park, Via Marciano.
Tel: (0577) 44803 Fax: (0577) 49020
Luxury, villa-style hotel with all amenities. Expensive.
Duomo, Via Stalloreggi.
Tel: (0577) 289088 Fax: (0577) 43043
Comfortable hotel, close, as its name suggests, to Siena's cathedral. Moderate.

Suggested Restaurants (all Siena)
Al Marsili, Via del Castoro.
Tel: (0577) 47154
Siena's best restaurant, full of Tuscan delights. Expensive.
La Torre, Via Salicotto.
Tel: (0577) 287548
Typical Sienese eaterie in the heart of the old town. Moderate.
Nello, Via del Porrine.
Tel: (0577) 289043
Well-priced, central restaurant with good pasta dishes. Moderate.

The streets of Taormina are, understandably, at their busiest at the height of summer. The place is flooded with visitors clamouring to enjoy the spectacular views. But visit at other times and you can linger as long as you like over the marvellous panoramas of volcano and sea.

TAORMINA

To hear that Taormina is the most popular resort on Sicily is not surprising. Draped splendidly over the cliffs on the edge of the Ionian Sea, it has charmed tourists for centuries. Consequently, you do best to avoid the high season and time your visit for spring or autumn, or even winter, when the weather is still pleasantly hospitable. What makes it so popular? A combination of things: a stunning setting; flower-filled streets of centuries-old mansions; a crumbling old castle on a craggy rock; unsurpassed Roman remains; fine sandy beaches; and mighty Mount Etna, the highest volcano in Europe.

History and Culture

It was the Greeks who first put Taormina on the map. They came here in the 8th century BC and constructed the town's famous amphitheatre 500 years later. The Romans replaced them, and replaced the amphitheatre, too, with one of their own. There followed a host of other foreign influences, as Sicily was fought over by the Arabs, Normans, French and Spanish, before the city and its neighbourhood were 'liberated' by Garibaldi and Sicily joined the new Italy in 1861.

Sightseeing

However appealing the rest of the town may be, there is one major sight in Taormina, and that is the Teatro Greco. The site of this amphitheatre is very well preserved but nothing remains of the Greek original whose name it still bears. Instead, you can see its Roman replacement, from the 1st century AD. The stage, the arena and the pens where the gladiators and wild beasts were kept before fights are still visible, as are the gutters for sweeping away the gory remains after the blood bath. The various concerts and the

international film festival which are staged here today belong, thankfully, to a different world. Even more fantastic than its historic architecture is the setting of the amphitheatre. Framed behind the arena is the magnificence of snowy-peaked Mount Etna.

There are other Roman items of interest in the town, too. Near the tourist office is the *odeon*, a small-scale theatre used originally for musical performances and now partly absorbed into the church of Santa Caterina. Then there's the *naumachia*, which was an artificial pond constructed to stage mock sea battles. Taormina's main street features monuments from a later age, in the form a fine collection of old mansions.

Below Taormina runs a string of good beaches, but more accessible and better bathing can be discovered just out of town – at Mazzarò, where a cable car lowers you to the sea, or at Naxos, where Garibaldi's men landed in 1860. To reach Mount Etna, you can take a bus or hire a car. You can no longer climb right up to the crater itself, thanks to the recent history of violent eruptions that threatened to engulf the surrounding towns and villages. You can, however, don some sensible footwear, wrap yourself up in something warm and spend a good few hours hiking up the slopes. Minibuses provide an easier way to the top and, once you're there, you can flirt with danger and examine the lava and other volcanic debris. Providing all caution notices are heeded and everyone acts sensibly, there is no threat to life or limb. However, more visitors will be content with the good second-best option of touring the base of the volcano on the Circumetnea train, which runs from Catania to Riposto.

Back in Taormina, there are plenty of decent restaurants and bars – not the cheapest in Italy, but easily affordable for the budget-conscious, if you shop around in the tucked-away streets and piazzas. Yet the best value in town remains the fabulous panorama.

Taormina

Major Events
Carnevale in città (February): masked processions celebrating the coming of Lent.
Settimana Santa (late March–early April): pageantry surrounding the festival of Easter.
Festa della primavera (May): celebration of spring in a specifically Sicilian way.
Estate a Taormina (June–September): music, dance and street theatre all summer long.
TaorminArte (July–August): international festival of cinema, music, theatre and dance in the Teatro Greco.
Natale a Taormina (December): Christmas festivities with gospel singing and street theatre.

How to get there – and get around
By air: scheduled flights to Rome-Fiumicino Airport (see p.154), then transfer to Catania-Fontanarossa Airport (1 hr 10 mins); by bus and/or bus and train for the 40 miles (via Catania) to Taormina (50 mins–1 hr 20 mins). Some charter flights leave Gatwick and Manchester direct for Catania.
Public Transport: Taormina is easy to explore on foot, but bus and train services link the town to Messina, Catania and other centres.

Suggested Hotels
Timeo, Via Teatro Greco.
Tel: (0942) 23801 Fax: (0942) 24838
Among Taormina's most exclusive hotels, adjacent to the amphitheatre. Expensive.
San Domenico Palace, Piazza San Domenico.
Tel: (0942) 23701 Fax: (0942) 625506
Well-appointed luxury hotel, a former monastery, with views over smouldering Etna. Expensive.
Bristol Park, Via Bagnoli Croce.
Tel: (0942) 23006 Fax: (0942) 24519
Popular, comfortable hotel, also with great views. Moderate.

Suggested Restaurants
All the above hotels have well-respected kitchens. Expensive.
Other suggestions:
La Piazzetta, Via Paladini.
Tel: (0942) 626317
Good, robust Sicilian fare. Moderate.
San Pancrazio, Via San Pancrazio.
Tel: (0942) 23184
Good value pizzas. Inexpensive.

TRIESTE

The traditional images of Italy don't apply in Trieste. This is a city with a split personality. A stone's throw to the east lies the border with Slovenia, yet many of its traditions and lifestyles derive from Austria and Central Europe. All this makes for a fascinating mix in a city that, at first glance, has clearly seen better times, but a city that has an atmosphere quite unlike any other in Italy.

History and Culture

The Romans, in typical fashion, set up base in Trieste in 178 BC. They called it Tergeste but eventually lost it to the various marauding hordes that worked their way through Italy during the Dark Ages. Undoubtedly the greatest influence on the city has come from Austria, which took over the region in the 14th-century and did not relinquish its grip until after World War I. The Austrians developed Trieste as the major southern port of their empire and turned it into the chief city on the Adriatic. There has always been friction here, however. Having acquired the area in 1918, Italy was aggrieved to cede part of the territory to Yugoslavia after World War II, an annoyance that was only put to rest in 1975 when the frontier question was properly settled.

Sightseeing

Something that will immediately strike you as you wander through the streets of this once great city is the rich, beckoning aroma of coffee. One field which Trieste has made its own is coffee importation. They take bean roasting very seriously here, and the city has an elegant café society not far removed from that in Vienna.

Once refreshed with a strong cup or two, head for the city's San Giusto fortress. On a terrace up above the

Although Trieste's grandeur has been on the wane for some years, the city is still stately and has its own distinctive charm. This façade, from the Cassa Marittima Adriatica, shows the prosperity the city once enjoyed. For even more monumental buildings, look around the city's main square, the Piazza dell'Unità.

harbour, this castle was built by the Venetians during their brief rule over the city in the 14th century. Although the museum it now contains is only worth a cursory glance, the views from the ramparts are wonderful. Next to the castle are the remains of a Roman law court from the 1st century (there is also a Roman theatre at the foot of the hill). Up here, too, is the city's cathedral, actually two churches knocked into one during the 14th century. The Gothic rose window, the fine frescos and the Venetian-style mosaics are all well worth a look. Just down from the cathedral is the city's Museum of History and Art, a mixed bag of good archaeological finds from around the world, including Greek vases, sculpture from the Himalayas and some Egyptian manuscripts. This is not Trieste's best museum, however. That honour falls to the Revoltella, which specialises in local furnishings and works of art. Meanwhile, down at the harbourfront is the more popular aquarium, focusing very effectively and entertainingly on Adriatic marine life.

Five miles out of Trieste stands the splendid white Castello di Miramare. The castle was once the summer residence of the Austrian Archduke Maximilian and was built in the mid-19th century, just before he went off to be Emperor of Mexico and was assassinated.

After a couple of days exhausting Trieste, it's time to pack your passport and some warm clothing and head east. Just a couple of hours away by train are the not-to-be-missed caves at Postojna in Slovenia. These are no ordinary little stalagmite and stalactite showrooms: they are enormous caverns with rock formations that amaze you with their drama and beauty. A mini-train takes you over a mile deep into the mountain where a tour begins.

In one respect, Trieste is as much Italian as any other city, and that is in the love of good food. Yet, once again, many of the restaurants and wine bars here tend to offer a splash of Austrian colour, in the form of goulash-type stews and dumplings on their menus. The local wines are excellent and often underestimated.

TRIESTE

Major Events

International Operetta Festival (June–August): operetta and stage musicals in the opera house.

Barcolana Autumn Cup Regatta (October): massive sailing event featuring over 1000 vessels of all shapes and sizes.

How to get there – and get around

By air: scheduled flights to Trieste-Ronchi dei Legionari Airport (20 miles out) from Gatwick only (2 hrs 40mins), but there are many flights from the UK to Rome-Fiumicino Airport (see 154) with transfers to Trieste (1 hr 10 mins). Buses run to Trieste centre (35 mins).

Public Transport: Trieste has an adequate bus service, although the Lower Town can be easily negotiated by foot.

Suggested Hotels

Savoia Excelsior Palace, Riva del Mandracchio.
Tel: (040) 77 941 Fax: (040) 63 82 60
Trieste's most elegant hotel, still serving in the grand manner. Very expensive.

Jolly, Corso Cavour.
Tel: (040) 760 00 55 Fax: (040) 36 26 99
Part of the modern hotel chain. Expensive.

Centro, Via Roma.
Tel: (040) 63 44 08 Fax: (040) 76 00 237
Pleasant, but modest, 18-room hotel in the centre. Inexpensive.

Suggested Restaurants

Antica Trattoria Suban, Via Comici.
Tel: (040) 543 68
Just east of the city centre, but well regarded. Expensive.

Hostaria 'Alla Voliga', Via della Fornace. Tel: (040) 309 606
Near San Giusto castle and specialising in fish and polenta. Moderate.

Galleria Fabris, Piazza Dalmatia.
Tel: (040) 364 564
Popular restaurant-pizzeria. Inexpensive.

The city of Fiat cars and the Juventus football club comes as a pleasant surprise. True, Turin is indeed an industrial city, one of the powerhouses of the Italian economy, but the centre is remarkably stately, harking back to the age of baroque. The city also has some of the finest museums in Italy, and it sits on the doorstep of the lovely alpine Aosta region. For a short break, Turin it is as good as anywhere in Italy.

History and Culture

Although Turin was once a Roman colony, it did not begin to prosper until the 15th century, when it became part of the principality of Savoy. A hundred years later, it became the Savoy capital and, after shrugging off an occupation by Napoleon, went on to lead Italy's fight for independence in the 19th century. Its reward was the status of Italy's first national capital, from 1861 to 1865. Today, Turin is the capital of the region of Piedmont and important for its motorcar construction, other heavy industries and fashion. Tourism does not yet feature large in its portfolio, but that deserves to change.

Sightseeing

The Mole Antone-lliana, with its pinnacled dome, dominates the city's skyline. It was planned as a synagogue, but now houses exhibitions. Its viewing platform should be an early port of call, to familiarise yourself with the city.

Undoubtedly the city's best museum is the Egyptian Museum. This is one of the world's greatest treasure troves of Egyptian finds, with the highlights a reconstruction of the Rock Temple of Ellessya, the tomb of Kha from 14 centuries before Christ, and a marginally younger black granite statue of Ramses

Turin has some of the finest streets and baroque squares in Italy, all laid out in a grid pattern. Its elegant arcades come in very handy when the weather turns inclement, as it is apt to do in the rainy north.

II. The museum fights for attention with the Galleria Sabauda, in the same building. Here, there are masterpieces by the likes of Tiepolo, Tintoretto, Mantegna, Veronese, Bellini, Van Eyck, Van Dyck and Rembrandt. For even more antiquity, make for the Palazzo Madama. This medieval fortress was converted into an elegant. Inside is the Museum of Ancient Art, with paintings, sculptures, furnishings, jewellery and other artistic items from the dawn of civilisation to the 19th century. You can also tour the Palazzo Reale, the home of the House of Savoy royalty before Italian unification.

Motor enthusiasts will not want to miss the Automobile Museum, two miles from the centre. Here, in the city that put the 'T' in FIAT (Fabbrica Italiana Automobili Torino), you can view fabulous early Maseratis, Bugattis, Lancias and, of course, Fiats. Turin's cathedral is home to a treasure of a different sort: the famous Turin Shroud, the ancient piece of fabric that bears the imprint of a crucified man, with a crown of thorns on his head and a spear wound in his side. For centuries it has been alleged that this is the imprint of Christ and that the garment is the cloth in which His body was wrapped after crucifixion. Carbon dating tests have proved that the shroud is no more than 700–800 years old, but its sacredness has been undiminished by this.

Back in the city, the grand avenues and elegant squares at the heart of Turin were just made for walking. Stroll by the fine arcades; admire the baroque architecture in the Piazza San Carlo; gaze at the fashions in the stylish shops; pause for a coffee at one of the many fine cafés. There is a surfeit of excellent restaurants to choose from, and the local specialities include risotto, and beef cooked in Barolo, the excellent local red wine.

TURIN

Major Events

Festa di San Giovanni (mid June–mid July): festival for the patron saint, celebrated since medieval times.
Giorni d'Estate (June–September): summer open-air festival of music, theatre, dance and cinema throughout Turin.
Newport Jazz Festival Torino (early–mid-July): Rhode Island Italian-style, in one of Europe's greatest jazz jamborees.
Settembre Musica (September): conclusion of the Turin summer with classical, jazz, ethnic rock and avant-garde music.
Teatro Regio (November–September): classic concert, ballet and opera season.
Artists' Light in Turin (mid November –mid January): annual foray of contemporary artists into the streets of Turin.

How to get there – and get around

By air: scheduled flights to Turin (Torino)-Caselle Airport (10 miles out) from Gatwick only (2½ hrs), then bus (30 mins) to Turin centre. Alternatively, there are flights to Milan (see page 143), from where buses take 75–90 mins.
Public Transport: Turin is easy to explore on foot but buses and trams are efficient (single LIT1400; 24-hrs LIT4800) and taxis reasonable.

Suggested Hotels

Diplomatic, Via Cernaia.
Tel: (011) 561 24 44 Fax: (011) 54 04 72
Top-of-the-range hotel. Very expensive.
Grand Sitea, Via Carlo Alberto. Tel: (011) 517 01 71 Fax: (011) 54 80 90
Luxurious hotel, a favourite with businessmen as well as tourists. Expensive
Turin Palace, Via Sacchi.
Tel: (011) 562 55 11 Fax: (011) 561 21 87
Famous historic hotel, close to the railway station. Moderate–expensive.
Victoria, Via Nino Costa.
Tel: (011) 561 19 09 Fax: (011) 561 18 06
Comfortable city-centre hotel. Moderate.

Suggested Restaurants

Del Cambio, Piazza Carignano.
Tel: (011) 54 66 90
Turin's most famous . Expensive.
L'Osto del Borg Vej, Via Tasso.
Tel: (011) 436 48 43
Small restaurant with all the flavours of the Piedmont. Moderate.
Porto di Savona, Piazza Vittorio Veneto.
Tel: (011) 817 35 00
Friendly atmosphere and excellent views from the terrace. Inexpensive.

The Gothic medieval cathedral in the lovely city of Orvieto has to be seen to be believed. The dazzling façade features exquisite carvings of scenes from the Bible and incredibly rich mosaics.

UMBRIA

As the streets and hills of Tuscany have become increasingly crowded with British holidaymakers, experienced Italophiles have begun to turn elsewhere for their annual break. Umbria has been the answer for many, and understandably so. This rich, green region north-east of Rome and south-east of Florence is truly beautiful. It's an area in which to absorb the very best of Italy: a scorching summer sun, the cool of hallowed old churches and cathedrals, breathtaking ancient artworks, and simple, rustic food that bursts with flavour.

History and Culture

This beautiful landscape was originally inhabited by an ancient tribe known as the Umbrians. Their forgotten language is depicted on a series of stone tablets discovered near the town of Gubbio. The Etruscans also lived in Umbria, then the Romans. In the Middle Ages, the region gave birth to a collection of individual city states, before the Papacy assumed control of the territory. It became part of Italy in 1869.

Sightseeing

Perugia is the most logical place in which to set up base. The settlement is typical of the region, perched high on a hill with a history of conquest and confusion. The elevation affords dramatic views that tempt you out, but the city, known as an intellectual centre, will keep you busy for a few days in itself.

As in nearly every Italian city, the cathedral is the place to start a tour. Perugia's 15th-century spiritual heart stares across at the secular centre, in the form of the massive, 13th-century town hall, the Palazzo dei Priori. The latter houses an art gallery with works by Fra Angelico, Pinturricchio, Piero della Francesca and other Renaissance masters. The church of San Domenico

and the Archaeology Museum, with its Etruscan and Roman finds, should not be ignored either.

From Perugia it is an easy drive to the region's best-known town, Assisi. Those who have already visited St Francis's home will have been heart-broken to hear of the damage caused by 1997's earthquake, which reduced some of the priceless frescos in the famous basilica to dust. Restoration work is still underway meaning some of the high-lights are today out of bounds. However, Assisi just has to be visited because, despite the heavy tourist presence and tacky souvenir stalls, the town always maintains an air of tranquillity. Francis's tomb sits in the lower section of the massive basilica, which dominates the western fringe of Assisi. Across the town is the atmospheric church of St Clare, Francis's spiritual companion, and the area around Assisi is dotted with other sites of St Francis pilgrimage. The little chapel he founded is now encased in the baroque hulk of the church of Santa Maria degli Angeli at the foot of the Assisi hill, while over to the east is the Eremo delle Carceri refuge, where Francis lived and meditated.

To the south of Perugia is the lovely little town of Spoleto, home of an international performing arts festival every summer, while heading towards Rome brings you to the delightful city of Orvieto.

These are only the bare highlights. Every village you pass has its places of interest: wonderful medieval churches, enchanting cobbled lanes, battlemented walls, incredible views, even the occasional Roman ruin. Each place also has more than its share of good restaurants, turning out rustic specialities washed down with fine wine.Umbria is becoming more popular each year. Enjoy before it becomes too busy.

UMBRIA

Major Events
Festa dei Ceri (May): historic race for teams carrying large candles, held in Perugia and Gubbio.
Festa dei Due Mondi (end June–early July): Spoleto's festival of music, dance and drama.
Umbria Jazz (mid July): one of Europe's most important of jazz festivals, spread over 10 days and 100 concerts, in Perugia.
Umbrian Festival of Sacred Music (mid September): Perugia festival famed for its traditional sacred music, and its championing of composers like Britten, Hindemith and Stockhausen.
Antique Trade Fair (late October): well-established high-class market in Perugia.

How to get there – and get around
By air: scheduled flights to Rome-Fiumicino Airport from numerous UK airports (see Rome), but connections to Perugia-Sant'Egidio Airport (10 miles out) are infrequent. From Rome, car hire apart, the best way to get to Perugia is by a direct express bus (3 hrs). Trains from Rome are not as direct or fast.
Public Transport: Perugia is easy to explore on foot. Buses (costing around LIT1000) link the railway stations to the centre; taxis are fairly expensive. Cheap trains run from Perugia to Assisi (30 mins) every hour, but car hire is advisable for seeing other sites.

Suggested Hotels (all Perugia)
Brufani, Piazza Italia.
Tel: (075) 573 2541 Fax: (075) 572 0210
Perugia's finest, set in the centre of the ancient town. Very expensive.
Locanda della Posta, Corso Vannucci.
Tel: (075) 572 8925 Fax: (075) 573 25 62
Exquisite smaller hotel, beautifully appointed. Moderate.
Palace Hotel Bellavista, Piazza Italia.
Tel: (075) 572 0741 Fax: (075) 573 9092
Well-positioned and very comfortable. Moderate.

Suggested Restaurants (all Perugia)
Osteria del Bartolo, Via Bartolo.
Tel: (075) 573 1561
Elegant restaurant, long a local favourite. Expensive.
Canto delle Serene, Via Campo di Marte. Tel:(075) 505 5185
Well-regarded seafood restaurant. Moderate.
Altromondo, Via Caporali.
Tel: (075) 572 6157
Good-value Umbrian cooking. Moderate.

The medieval village of Todi, dramatically positioned on top of a steep hill, with unrivalled views over the Umbrian countryside. Like its neighbouring towns, Todi has its share of excellent old architecture, including a fine 13th-century cathedral.

VENICE

What can be said about magical Venice that has not been said before? It's been a wonderful holiday destination for centuries now, with the Victorian Grand Tourists only precursors to the masses that swarm all over St Mark's Square today. The major attractions are obvious – the Grand Canal, the Bridge of Sighs, spectacular St Mark's basilica – and should not be missed, even if you have to share them with the daytripping hordes. However, allow yourself time to discover hidden Venice. To do this, you must stay in the heart of the city, where you can enjoy the best times: the early morning and the late evening, when the bus crowds have gone.

History and Culture

As impressive as it is, Venice is only an Italian regional capital today, a far cry from its peak as one of the world's great seafaring nations. From a marshy haven for refugees fleeing Attila the Hun, Venice grew into one of the most prosperous settlements in Europe, using its position on the Adriatic Sea as a springboard to trade with the Middle East. From here Marco Polo set off to explore China; to here came exotic textiles, fragrant spices and a definite smack of the Orient, as seen in the fabulous mosaics of St Marks's. With the discovery of the New World and the opening up of new sea routes to India, the wealth of Venice began to dry up. Eventually, the once-proud nation fell victim to Napoleon and then the Austrians. Only in 1866 did Venice break free, when it joined the new Kingdom of Italy.

The Grand Canal is one of the world's most famous highways and is the main through-route in the city, running a length of 2½ miles, with an average width of around 230 feet. It's banks are lined with magnificent Gothic and Renaissance palaces.

Sightseeing

What was once a marshy haven is now, even 500 years past its heyday, a simply spectacular city. Everyone knows that Venice is built on a series of islands (over 100), and that its streets are canals, criss-crossed with bridges, but somehow the individual beauty of each of the Renaissance palaces at the water's edge tends to be lost in the general overview. You're more likely to hear about the gondola, but forget it, unless you want to pay through the nose for a half-hour of bobbing up and down to the strains of hackneyed local folksongs.

To get around Venice use the *vaporetto*, or water bus. The vaporetti are reasonably efficient and take you from A to B, either scenically or more directly. Then use your feet. Of course, spend time in St Mark's Square and in the basilica. The famous bronze horses (now copies outside) and the breathtaking Pala d'Oro altarscreen were both looted from Constantinople. Take a tour of the Doge's Palace and see the Titians, Tintoretto and Tiepolos, before crossing over the Bridge of Sighs, where condemned prisoners allegedly took their last glimpse of the world outside. Stroll down to the famous Rialto bridge, now stacked with tacky souvenirs, but then head off into the backstreets. Almost any direction will do, but the area just east of San Marco, around the Arsenal, where the boats that made Venice famous were built, is particularly interesting. You'll inevitably get lost – even with a map – but you'll also enjoy an insight into Venice life – the places people live, the little squares, the forgotten places of worship. Even well-known churches are usually abandoned by daytrippers, so the glory of the Frari, the Redentore or Santa Maria della Salute is not so obscured by crowds. You can't say you've 'done' Venice until you've set eyes on the priceless collection at the Accademia or the modern art in the Guggenheim art gallery. The Venetian islands are just just a short ride across the lagoon: the ancient cathedral on the island of Torcello; the lace island of Burano; the glass blowing island of Murano.

Venice is a notably expensive city, especially if you sit at a café in St Mark's Square, dine at a world famous restaurant, or follow royalty and film-stars by staying at one of the poshest hotels. But Venice is still affordable. You have to shop around, and, in the quieter backstreets, prices are no more inflated than elsewhere in Northern Italy. Imagine strolling back to your hotel along the waterfront after a candlelit supper and then, the next morning, throwing back the shutters of your room to beckon in the canal sounds of a new day. These are the moments that make Venice special.

Venice is beginning to show its age – it is, after all, 500 years beyond its heyday – but the grandeur of its remarkable buildings still shines through. Note the Eastern influence in the windows of this old palace.

VENICE

Major Events
Carnevale (mid February): major celebration of the onset of Lent – colourful costumes and masks abound.
Feastday of the Redeemer (mid July): traditional festival on the water to thank Christ the Redeemer for delivering Venice from the plague in 1576.
Historical Regatta (early September): 16th-century pageantry on the canals.
Venice Film Festival (September): highly prestigious film event.

How to get there – and get around
By air: direct flights to Marco Polo International Airport (6 miles out) from Heathrow, Gatwick and Stansted (2 hrs 40 mins). Buses take 15–30 mins to **Venice centre** (costing around LIT5,000), and are quicker and cheaper than taxis.
Public Transport: vaporetti (water buses) cost about LIT4500 per trip, or LIT15000 for 24 hrs and LIT30,000 for 72 hrs; *motoscafi* (water taxis) are expensive, and not necessarily exclusive.

Suggested Hotels
Cipriani, Isola della Giudecca.
Tel: (041) 520 77 44
Fax: (041) 520 77 45
Venice's most exclusive hotel. Very expensive.
Giorgione, Santi Apostoli. Tel: (041) 522 58 10 Fax: (041) 523 90 92
Highly rated hotel, with good facilities, close to the Rialto Bridge. Expensive.
Flora, Calle Larga XXII Marzo. Tel: (041) 520 58 44 Fax: (041) 522 82 17
Busy and popular hotel just off St Mark's Square. Moderate.
Do Pozzi, Corte do Pozzi.
Tel: (041) 520 78 55
Fax: (041) 522 94 13
Cosy hotel near the Grand Canal. Moderate.

Suggested Restaurants
Harry's Bar, Calle Vallaresso.
Tel: (041) 528 57 77
World-famous venue with a jet-set image. Home of the Bellini cocktail. Expensive.
La Caravella, Calle Larga XXII Marzo.
Tel: (041) 520 89 01
Decked out nautically to complement the seafood menu. Expensive.
Taverna la Fenice, Campiello de la Fenice.
Tel: (041) 522 38 56
Charming eating house within the shadow of the stricken Fenice Opera House. Moderate.
San Trovaso, Fondamenta Priuli.
Tel: (041) 520 37 03
Restaurant-pizzeria, popular with locals and visitors, near the Accademia. Inexpensive.

The entrance to the Castelvecchio, the imposing, yet beautifully proportioned, castle built by Verona's 14th-century, the Scaligeri, or della Scala, family. *Scala* is Italian for ladder, and little ladder symbols are entwined into the metalwork surrounding the Scaligeri tombs, near Piazza dei Signori.

Verona and Lake Garda

As romantic cities go, Verona has no competition, for this is the beautiful city of Romeo and Juliet. Shakespearean connections abound – he also knew *Two Gentlemen* from here – but the city has an even greater heritage than that provided by the Bard of Avon, one that belongs to the Romans. Right in the middle of the city stands one of the finest Roman amphitheatres still in existence. The magnificent pink marble Arena is in such good order that it is still used every summer for the *Stagione Lirica*, Verona's world-famous open-air opera festival. Should you somehow tire of this and the city's many other historic attractions – who on Earth would? – remember that the relaxing waters and shoreline of Lake Garda are only an hour or so away.

History and Culture

The Romans may have left some wonderful treasures to Verona, but the Middle Ages bequeathed even more. In the hands of the powerful Scaligieri family, the city was a force to be reckoned with in the 13th to 15th centuries. The family's castles and fortifications can be found all over the city. After their relatively peaceful rule fell into decline, Verona was traded between various occupying forces, ending up in the hands of the Austrians until it became part of the new Italian kingdom in 1866.

Sightseeing

Verona is one of the most stunning cities in a country of stunning cities. Often overlooked in favour of Tuscan treasures like Florence and Siena, or its near neighbour, mighty Venice, Verona's time has now come. Not only opera-lovers are discovering its secret. Its tight streets of ancient pink-hued buildings are welcoming a new generation of travellers. It is a city for wandering, with much of the old centre now pedestrianised, leading you from the main square, Piazza Brà, right into the old Roman centre.

The first port of call must be at the

Arena. Be sure to pay the modest fee and have a good look around. It's even more interesting in early summer when preparations are underway for the opera season. From the Arena, head towards the Piazza delle Erbe, now a market square. This was the site of the Roman forum, but the tall column topped by a Venetian lion reveals the identity of one of the city's later masters. Just off the piazza, you can step into a small, sadly graffiti-ridden courtyard watched over by what is alleged to have been Juliet's balcony. The balcony scene was undoubtedly a figment of Shakespeare's imagination, but Juliet's family, the Capuletti, did exist, as did the Montecchi, said to have been Romeo's clan.

Verona's old civic buildings hold pride of place around the Piazza dei Signori, with an elegant Renaissance arcade along one side and a statue of Dante the centre. The ornate tombs of the Scaligieri rulers are a little further along on the right. Take the lift to the top of the Torre dei Lamberti, for a dizzying panorama of this fabulous city. You can see the River Adige and its historic bridges, the old Scaligieri castle of Castelvecchio (now housing an excellent art gallery), the cathedral (home to a Titian masterpiece), the splendid dual church of San Fermo, near the Arena, and the 12th-century bell-tower of the church of San Zeno. If you can, visit this ancient sanctuary, which has a memorable altarpiece by Mantegna and acclaimed carved bronze doors.

With only a couple of days in the city, you'll hardly want to stray far from the centre, but a train trip out to Lake Garda provides a pleasant contrast. Lake-side towns like Peschiera, Sirmione, Desenzano, Salò and Malcesine have some enjoyable promenades, fine churches and/or castles and offer a chance to see the sometimes quite dramatic beauty of Italy's biggest lake. A hydrofoil service means you can quickly cross the water and absorb another perspective.

Verona and Lake Garda

Major Events
Teatro Filarmonico Winter Season (January–March): concerts, opera and ballet.
Primavera Festival (April–May): season of classical concerts and operas at the Teatro Filarmonico.
Shakespeare at the Teatro Romano (July–August): the bard traditionally played in Italian at Verona's smaller Roman amphitheatre.
Stagione Lirica (July–September): the world-famous open-air operas at the Arena.

How to get there – and get around
By air: scheduled flights to Verona-Villafranca Airport (6 miles out) from Gatwick only (flight 2 hrs); charter flights from other UK airports in summer. Buses costing around LIT8000, and taxis (LIT 40,000) run to the city centre. There are also flights to Milan and Venice, but with slow and awkward road/rail transfers.
Public Transport: Verona is easy to explore on foot but there is a reliable bus service. Inexpensive trains run regularly to Lake Garda.

Suggested Hotels
Montresor Giberti, Via Giberti.
Tel: (045) 80 06 900 Fax: (045) 80 03 302
Premier hotel close to the centre, but out of the tourist areas. Expensive.
San Marco, Via Longhena.
Tel: (045) 56 90 11 Fax: (045) 57 22 99
Well-appointed first-class hotel in a quiet district. Expensive.
Giulietta e Romeo, Vicolo Tre Marchetti.
Tel: (045) 80 03 554 Fax: (045) 80 10 862
Don't be put off by the touristy title – this is a friendly hotel close to the Arena. Moderate.

Suggested Restaurants
El Mocoleto, Via Stella.
Tel: (045) 80 30 066
Exclusive, high-class restaurant, close to the Arena. Expensive.
Lido di Verona, Via Galliano.
Tel: (045) 81 02 736
Good quality local and international dishes. Moderate.
Il Ritrivo, Vicolo Cieco San Pietro Incanario. Tel: (045) 80 09 494
Good seafood and pizzas in the city centre. Inexpensive.

It's been described as 'the crossroads of Europe' by some, but Luxembourg doesn't really live up to that image. Crossroads infers that traffic and people meet here, whereas, by and large, the converse is true. Luxembourg is by-passed by most continental travellers, who head west to france, north to Belgium or east to Germany. Frankly, it's their loss, because Luxembourg is a super destination for a relaxing short break.

History and Culture

This tiny Grand Duchy takes its name from 'Lucilinburhuc', the name given to a small fortress established here in 963. As war ravaged across Europe, and the area fell into the hands of French, Spanish, Austrian and Prussian conquerors, the little fortress was extended and restructured, creating in Luxembourg a 'Gibraltar of the North'. Luxembourg today is ruled by a Grand Duke and his cabinet, and is predominantly a country of thick forests, deep valleys and fortified hilltops.

Taking in the history and the panoramas forms the core of a visit to Luxembourg City, but National and Pescatore Museums do have some fine Flemish paintings. The shopping is good, too, with souvenir specialities including chocolates and local porcelain.

Sightseeing

Luxembourg City is a challenge for the walker. It is set on two deep canyons,

Luxembourg City church with the royal residence, the Grand-Palais-Ducal, which was previously the Town Hall. Tours can be taken of the palace when the Grand Duke is away in the summer.

LUXEMBOURG

which follow the Rivers Pétrusse and Alzette. The old heart of the city, with most of the sights, lies north of the Pétrusse. Here, the new, six-storey Historical Museum fills you in on the development of the city through interactive displays and multimedia exhibits, while visits to the 17th-century Notre-Dame Cathedral and the tiny, 11th-century St Michel church provide a taste of the city's religious past. But probably the most absorbing attraction are the Bock Casemates. This complex of tunnels was carved in a rock promontory some 300 years ago, and were used as air-raid shelters in World War II. The dark, steep passageways and staircases are not for the claustrophobic, but they do afford some stunning views.

Luxembourg's more modern suburb is across the bridges to the south of Pétrusse. In the gorge below is the Grund area, with its narrow streets of slate-roofed houses. If you don't feel up to the walk – and not many visitors do – there is a lift to take you down.

Luxembourg, the city, is a treat for a couple of days. There are several, well thought-out circular walks which take in all there is to see. To extend your visit, reach out into Luxembourg, the country, which is even more neglected by the holidaymaker than its capital. Drive or take a bus out to the well-restored town of Echternach, an hour away, with its reconstructed basilica and Roman villa. From here, a 30-minute ride takes you to the hilltop castle and chairlift at Vianden, majestically presiding over a winding river, thick Ardennes forestry and cobbled streets.

LUXEMBOURG

Major Events

Printemps Musical – Festival de Luxembourg (March–May): an eclectic range of musical concerts in Luxembourg City, from chanson to jazz and classical.
Emaischen (Easter Monday): a celebration of local traditions in Luxembourg City and Nospelt; young lovers swap gifts of whistling birds made of clay.
International Festival of Classical Music (May–June): an annual event in Echternach, preceding the dancing procession on Whit Tuesday in honour of St Willibrord.
Jazzrallye (July): various jazz-orientated evenings in cafés and around the public squares of Luxembourg City.
Streeta(rt)nimation (August): part of the 'Summer in the City', with street performances of pantomime, stilt-walking and other such arts.

How to get there – and get around

By air: scheduled flights Luxembourg-Findel Airport (4 miles out) from Heathrow, Gatwick and Stansted (80–90 mins), and Manchester (1 hr 55 mins). Transit into the centre by bus and taxi is easy and cheap.
By car: ferries from Channel ports to Calais, Boulogne, Dunkirk and Ostend, or via the Channel Tunnel on Le Shuttle; then by motorway to Luxembourg.
By rail: Eurostar to Brussels (2hrs 40mins); change for Luxembourg (a further 2hrs 55 mins)
Public Transport: A comprehensive bus/train/tram service with interchangeable tickets for unlimited travel is available at around LUF160 per day.

Suggested Hotels

Le Royal, boulevard Royal.
Tel: 2416161 Fax: 225948
Sumptuous hotel on a dominating city-centre site – the only hotel in the city with a pool. Expensive.
President, place de la Gare.
Tel: 486161 Fax: 486180
Superior, well-appointed hotel near the railway station. Moderate.
Français, place d'Armes.
Tel: 474534 Fax: 473464
Cosy, small hotel, handily-placed in the centre. Inexpensive

Suggested Restaurants

Restaurant Speltz, rue Chimay.
Tel: 474950
Atmospheric, city-centre gourmet restaurant, with private dining rooms. Expensive.
Restaurant Bonaparte, Bisserwee.
Tel: 227166
Good range of traditional fare and international dishes in elegant surroundings. Moderate.
Maison de Brasseurs, Grand-rue.
Tel: 471371
The Luxembourger's restaurant, offering many appetising local recipes. Inexpensive.

AMSTERDAM

Amsterdam is a city of contrasts and contradictions. On the one hand heavy culture takes hold in the form of some of the best art collections in the whole world; on the other more transitory pleasures beckon through the sleaze of the Red Light District and the pot-smokers' cafés.

History and Culture

Amsterdam takes its name from the dam on the River Amstel, the basis for the founding of the city in the 13th century. Its golden age was in the 17th century. Dutch merchants ruled the commercial waves and Amsterdam was at the centre of their empire. It may not have reached such giddy heights since, but the city is still evidently rich.

Sightseeing

A good focal point when planning a tour is the Centraal railway station. From here the city radiates outwards like a giant fan. To the west are the attractive sidestreets of the Jordaan quarter; to the east, the fleshpots of the Red Light District; straight ahead is the avenue known as the Damrak, leading to Dam Square. This wide expanse is the city's main plaza, the site of the original dam. It is flanked by the royal palace and the Nieuwe (new) Kerk, an airy 15th century church, used these days mainly for exhibitions. For the record, the city's Oude (old) Kerk can be found in the Red Light District. Dating from 1325, it is well worth a visit but, if you've led a sheltered life until now, close your eyes as you walk through the streets around it.

Four major canals fence in the Dam Square area: the Singel, the Herengracht, the Keizersgracht and the Prinzengracht. These can be toured in a glass-topped boat, which provides a useful introduction to the city. You glide past streets of tall, beautifully gabled old houses that are deliberately narrow, designed to save paying excess tax on property width. Beyond these canals are situated the main museums. Along the Museumplein you'll find the world-famous Rijksmuseum, the excellent Van Gogh Museum and the Stedelijk Museum, the last featuring a marvellous collection of works by artists such as Matisse, Picasso, Monet, Chagall and local painters. The Van Gogh Museum is split into two floors. The Rijksmuseum is a wonderful gathering of classic canvases, with the highlight being the famous *Night Watch* by Rembrandt. Rembrandt is also remembered in his former home, now a museum showing some of his possessions and a small collection of his lesser works. It stands on the fringe of the old Jewish quarter and near the excellent flea market at Waterlooplein. Amsterdam's other great museums pay tribute to the persecuted, none more so than the schoolgirl diarist Anne Frank. To visit the little attic refuge she and her desperate Jewish family lived in for two years before being betrayed and transported to Auschwitz is a very moving and humbling experience. Less vivid, but remarkable nonetheless, is the Amstelkring Museum – or 'Our Lord in the Attic' – which, although looking like any other canalside house from the outside, conceals a complete church on the top floor, with pews, pulpit and organ. Here the banned Roman Catholics of the 17th century held their clandestine services.

Apart from the arches of the canal bridges, Amsterdam is famously flat, so flat that cycling is not so much a local pastime but a way of life. Take advantage of this by hiring a bike (or taking the bus, if this appeals more) and heading off north, across the water to the lovely fishing village of Volendam, on the banks of the Ijsselmeer, the former Zuider Zee. Although it gets swamped by tour bus crowds, Volendam remains picturesque and bracing. You can also wheel your way through the village of Edam.

Back in the city, the nightlife is all-embracing and there areplenty of entertainments, at a variety of prices. You can dine on the extremely varied international cuisine (particularly good Indonesian food), or just slope off for a wonderfully complex Dutch beer in one of the atmospheric 'brown cafés'.

PREVIOUS PAGE: Amsterdam's canals provide a useful introduction to the city. Boat tours slowly take in all the major sights, with commentaries provided in various languages. You can board at quays around the city.

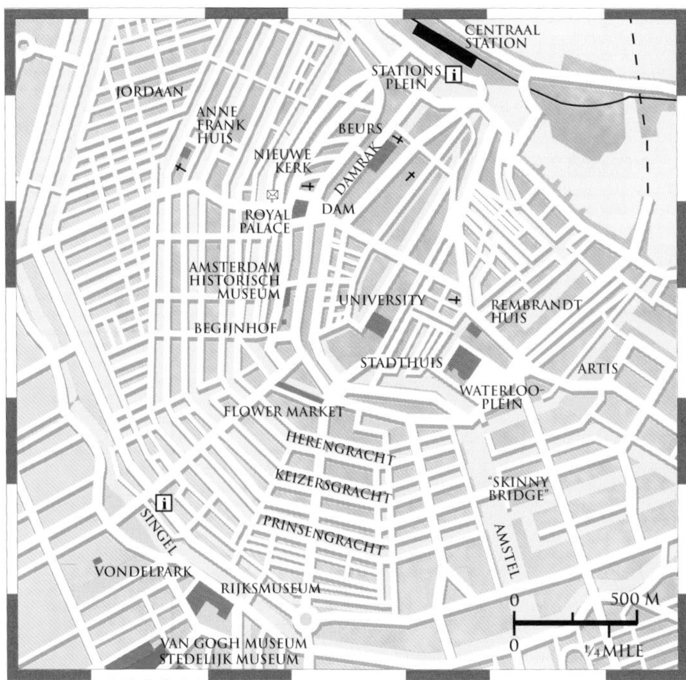

Amsterdam

Major Events
Stille Ommegang (mid March): religious procession to St Nicholas's church.
Koninginnedag (April 30): the Queen's Birthday – a fair on Dam Square.
Holland Festival (June):innovative theatre, opera, music, dance and film.
Amsterdam Arts Adventure (June–August): celebration of the performing arts in Amsterdam's theatres, parks and churches – and on the canals.
Prinsengracht Canal Concert (August): annual concert spectacular on the water.

How to get there – and get around
By air: scheduled flights to Amsterdam–Schiphol Airport (9 miles out) from 21 British airports (longest flight 1hr 20 mins), then by train (17 mins; around NLG7), bus (30–40 mins; NLG8.50) or taxi (30 mins; NLG50) to Amsterdam centre.
By car: ferry from Harwich to the Hook of Holland (3 hrs 40 mins), or from Hull to Rotterdam (13 hrs), then 1 hr by (untolled) motorway; or ferry from Newcastle direct to Amsterdam (16 hrs).
By rail: Eurostar to Brussels Midi (2 hrs 40 mins), then change for the hourly train to Amsterdam (3 hrs).
Public Transport: Amsterdam has an excellent bus and tram network, but only a small metro (single tickets from NGL3; 1-day NG12; 2- to 8-day options NGL 15–40). Taxis (from stands only) start at around NGL6.

Suggested Hotels
Amstel Inter-Continental, Professor Tulpplein.
Tel: (020) 622 60 60 Fax: (020) 622 58 08
Wonderful, 19th-century hotel, the haunt of the rich and famous. Very expensive.
Schiller, Rembrandtplein.
Tel: (020) 554 07 00 Fax: (020) 624 00 98
Well-positioned, quality hotel, recently refurbished. Expensive.
Amstel Botel, Oosterdokskade.
Tel: (020) 626 42 47 Fax: (020) 639 19 52
Floating 3-star boat near Centraal station. Moderate.

Suggested Restaurants
La Rive, Amstel Inter-Continental. Tel: (020) 520 32 73
Amsterdam's most-fêted eaterie. Expensive.
't Swarte Schaep, Korte Leidsedwarsstraat. Tel: (020) 622 30 21
Sophisticated Dutch restaurant, which belies its homely surroundings. Expensive.
De Oesterbar, Leidseplein.
Tel: (020) 623 29 88
Famous fish restaurant which pleases both the eye and the palate. Moderate.

The flat green land of lakes and pastures around Groningen is more interesting than it first appears. Among its attractions is the Fraeylemaborg 17th-century, moated mansion, near the small town of Slochteren, 12 miles to the east.

FRIESLAND

Now here's a short break you won't find in many travel brochures. The very north of the Netherlands is an often forgotten place. Yet Friesland and its neighbouring province of Groningen provide a wonderfully relaxing, low-stress destination that offers a taste of a quite different Netherlands to the high-jinx world of Amsterdam and the business-like sophistication of The Hague. There are two major centres to visit: Friesland's capital Leeuwarden, and the provincial capital, Groningen, the latter providing the best base for a very unusual, off-the-beaten-track few days' holiday.

History and Culture

There's a distinct air of difference up here. The remoteness of the area – even more remote until the dyke was built across the mouth of the Zuider Zee in 1932 – has preserved individuality, perhaps highlighted best by the fact that the people of Friesland still use their own language, described as a cross between German and early English. Groningen, a once independent merchant state, was badly damaged by World War II bombing, although many fine old buildings happily survived. Today, the city is a thriving university seat that has much to commend it.

Sightseeing

The remarkable Groningen Museum, built as a sequence of pavilions, a startling conglomeration of steel, glass, aluminium and red brick, was put together by a group of guest architects. Step inside to see the fine collection of ceramics, silverware, jewellery and paintings (including the *Adoration of the Magi* by Rubens). The city's hub is the

Grote Markt, home to a huge market on Saturdays. The ancient Martinikerk, with parts from the 12th century, stands in one corner and houses an internationally famous organ, dating from 1480, and some lovely old frescos. More interesting artefacts can be discovered in the Noordelijk Scheepvaart Museum, a splendid archive that recounts Dutch trading links with the East Indies and other seafaring matters. As you stroll around the streets, you'll appreciate the lack of traffic. Cars were banned here nearly 20 years ago and Groningen is much the better for it. Now the many bars and restaurants can spread their tables out into the streets, which means the nightlife in summer takes place at least partly in the open air and is enjoyably upbeat as a result.

Around Groningen, the land is flat and wet, with only the occasional raised farm to break the horizon. Neighbouring Friesland is equally flat and open, but, in fairness, does have some interesting coastal towns, which are well worth a day trip. Harlingen is a good choice, an old harbour town and naval base, now adorned with fresh fish stalls and centuries-old houses. Off the coast here are the lovely Friesian islands, tranquil havens of beach and dune

The Friesland capital, Leeuwarden, is a compact, comfortable provincial centre, split into various quarters by a series of canals. It was the home of the spy Mata Hari when she was young, and her undercover activities are showcased in the city's Friesland Literary Museum. The heritage and culture of this isolated region are explored in the very good Fries Museum, the Princessehof, houses a sparkling collection of ceramics, Ming porcelain and 15th–17th-century Dutch tiles.

Friesland

Major Events (all Groningen)
Dialect Song Festival (May): traditional North Netherlands competition.
Country Week (June): every year Groningen adopts a different country as its theme for a week.
South American Carnival (July): Rio comes to Groningen every July
Noorderzon (mid–late August): performing arts festival.
St Maarten's Celebration (November 11): a saint's day toasted by innkeepers everywhere.

How to get there – and get around
By air: scheduled flights to Amsterdam-Schiphol Airport (see p.174), then by train to Amsterdam and Groningen, possibly changing at Amersfoort (3 hrs).
By car: ferry (3 hrs 40 mins) from Harwich to the Hook of Holland, or from Hull to Rotterdam-Europoort (13 hrs), then about 3 hrs on (untolled) motorways, including the spectacular 20-mile stretch over the Afsluitdijk (Barrier Dam), to Groningen.
By rail: Eurostar to Brussels Midi (2 hrs 40 mins), then trains every hour to Groningen (change at Amsterdam; about 6 hrs).

Public Transport: Groningen is easy to explore on foot, but very reasonably-priced buses and trains link to Leeuwarden (50 mins) and other towns.

Suggested Hotels (all Groningen)
Martinihal Mercure, Expositielaan.
Tel: (050) 525 8400 Fax: (050) 527 1828
Well-appointed luxury hotel. Moderate
Hotel de Ville, Oude Boteringestraat.
Tel: (050) 318 1222 Fax: (050) 318 1777
Smart, new hotel in the heart of old Groningen, with good facilities. Moderate.
Bastion, Bornholmstraat.
Tel: (050) 541 4977 Fax: (050) 541 3012
Popular hotel near the town centre. Inexpensive.

Suggested Restaurants (all Groningen)
La Canard, Schuitendiep.
Tel: (050) 312 3730
Quality French restaurant. Moderate.
Het Goudkantoor, Waagplein.
Tel: (050) 589 1888
Local menus feature at this famous café-bar. Moderate.
Bali, Rademarkt. Tel: (050) 313 3355
Spicy Indonesian food in the town centre. Moderate.

Delft china is world famous. Its distinctive blue and white design originated in the 17th century and is still a major tourist attraction today. However in their porcelain preoccupation , the majority of visitors somehow manage to ignore the other delights of this pretty town, including its lovely churches.

The small Dutch towns of the Randstad ('Rim Town') – the area to the south of Amsterdam – are ripe for the discovering. The obvious centre is The Hague, home of the Netherlands government, but don't miss wonderful Leiden, or the chance to see how Delft pottery is made in the town that gave it its name.

History and Culture

Without the careful planning practised by the Dutch authorities, it would be easy for these small towns to merge into one. As it is, they all enjoy their own individual personalities. The major city, The Hague, has been the political centre of the country since the 16th century and is now a rather low-key, but cultured, place to visit. Leiden has grown up as an academic city, and Rembrandt was born here. Delft is world renowned for its porcelain, but also has a famous artistic son, Jan Vermeer.

Sightseeing

The Hague doesn't strike the visitor as being an exciting city. There are too many bureaucrats here to allow that. But it is very civilised and has a number of excellent museums. In the Mauritshuis, a magnificent Renaissance mansion on a lake, you'll find most of the royal collection of artworks, including canvases by Rembrandt, Vermeer, Hals, Cranach, Van Dyck and Rubens. The remainder of the collection is stored at the Schildergallerij Prins Willem V, which is virtually wall-papered with paintings. You can also visit the Gemeentmuseum for a much more esoteric range of artworks, and

THE HAGUE, DELFT AND LEIDEN

there are some good science museums in the city, too. Tours are provided daily at the International Court of Justice, if you want to see how global wrongs are put right. A few miles outside The Hague is the resort town of Scheveningen, once a modest fishing port, now the most popular beach area in the Netherlands.

Leiden is a delightful canal city with a fine medieval quarter and some user-friendly museums, covering local history, archaeology, and even notable Egyptian treasures. There's also a windmill museum, and a lush botanical garden. The religious centrepiece is the huge Pieterskerk, where the Pilgrim Fathers, en route to the New World, once said prayers. Near Leiden are the famous Dutch bulbfields that attract coachloads of flower fanciers every year. Spring is the obvious time to visit, when the bulbs, thriving on the sandy soil, come into flower. Special signposts indicate the best vantage points, although the undoubted centre is the Keukenhof Gardens.

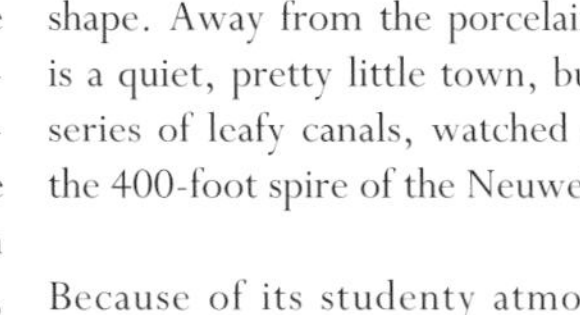

In the opposite direction from The Hague is Delft. Chinese porcelain reached the city in the 17th century and the inspiration it provided for local craftsmen led to the blue and white designs that went on to make the town famous. You can still tour the workshops and see how the process takes shape. Away from the porcelain, Delft is a quiet, pretty little town, built on a series of leafy canals, watched over by the 400-foot spire of the Neuwekerk.

Because of its studenty atmosphere, Leiden is probably the best bet for nightlife in the area. However, The Hague has plenty of excellent restaurants, and not all of them in the high-price bracket.

The Hague, Delft and Leiden

Major Events

North Sea Regatta (early–mid May): week of sailing races at Scheveningen, including the North Sea Race.

International Kite Festival (mid June): colourful spectacle at Scheveningen.

North Sea Jazz Festival (early July): one of the superior jazz festivals, attracting acts from around the world to The Hague.

Music Scheveningen (mid July): Dixieland and old-style jazz around the bars, cafés and streets of Scheveningen.

Prince's Day (late September): the Opening of the States General in The Hague with Queen Beatrix taken in the Gold Coach to make the Queen's Speech.

How to get there – and get around

By air: scheduled flights to Amsterdam-Schiphol Airport (see p.175), then by train (40 mins) direct to The Hague.

By car: Ferry (3 hrs 40 mins) from Harwich to the Hook of Holland, or from Hull to Rotterdam-Europoort (13 hrs), then 20 mins by road to The Hague.

By rail: Eurostar to Brussels Midi (2 hrs 40 mins), then change for hourly trains to The Hague (2 hrs).

Public Transport: The Hague and the other cities are easy to explore on foot. Buses and trams link The Hague to Scheveningen, and reasonably-priced trains run very regularly to Leiden (35 mins) and Delft (15 mins).

Suggested Hotels

Des Indes Inter-Continental, Lange Voorhout, The Hague. Tel: (070) 3632932 Fax: (070) 3451721
Centrally-situated, luxury hotel with many facilities. Very expensive.

Kurhaus, Gevers Deynootplein, Scheveningen. Tel: (070) 4162713
Famous seaside hotel in the suburb of Scheveningen. Expensive.

Corona, Buitenhof, The Hague. Tel: (070) 3637930
Well-regarded hotel in the centre. Moderate.

Duinzicht, Alkmaarsestraat, Scheveningen. Tel: (070) 3506999
Comfortable hotel convenient for the beach. Inexpensive.

Suggested Restaurants

Kurhaus Restaurant, Kurhaus Hotel, Gevers Deynootplein, Scheveningen. Tel: (070) 4162713
Hotel restaurant renowned for its sumptuous buffets. Expensive.

Duckdalf, Dr Lelykade, Scheveningen. Tel: (070) 3557692
Well-respected fish restaurant. Moderate.

Garoeda, Kneuterdijk, The Hague. Tel: (070) 3465318
Indonesian cooking with a distinctly old-colonial atmosphere. Moderate.

The old city walls provide a good introduction to Maastricht and its past. The earliest section dates from the 13th century; other parts were added during the war against Spain 300 years later.

It's likely that a very small minority of British people had heard of Maastricht before European heads of state agreed a treaty there in 1991. These days, more and more UK folk are discovering the Netherlands' most southerly city and it's being increasingly featured on touring itineraries.

History and Culture

This beautiful little city, in the south-eastern corner of the Netherlands dates from Roman times, its name derived from the Latin *Mosae Trajectum*, meaning crossing of the River Maas. The river still flows through the heart of town. When Charlemagne was Holy Roman Emperor in the 9th century, he had a base at nearby Aachen, and Maastricht, as a result, was endowed with some fine Romanesque churches. Today, Maastricht is increasingly cosmopolitan, specialising in the ceramics and textile trades, gearing itself up for the conference business and developing its image as the heart of Europe.

Sightseeing

The first sight to see is the topography of Maastricht. It is one of the few Dutch cities with elevated land. The main part of town is on the west bank of the river and the whole city is so compact it can be crossed on foot in half an hour. The city walls provide a good overall introduction, and a guide to their tree-lined walkways is available from the Tourist Office.

Two wonderful Romanesque churches form the highlights of the city's archi-

MAASTRICHT

tecture. St Servatius was expanded in the Middle Ages but still has a 10th-century crypt and contains the bones of the eponymous saint, who died in 384 and was the city's first bishop. The Onze Lieve Vrouw (Our Beloved Lady) church, close to the river, was founded in the 10th century. It is the most atmospheric and elaborate of the city's churches, with an allegedly miraculous statue of the Virgin Mary at its entrance. Maastricht also has a small Protestant church, the simple St Janskerk, but Protestantism, unlike in the rest of Holland, is not the city's religion. The flamboyant religious festivals celebrated here throughout the year reveal that Maastricht is devoutly Catholic.

In Waldeck Park are the Casemates, a maze of tunnels, created by mining, which have provided a refuge for citizens in times of distress for hundreds of years. Guided tours take you through the most interesting parts in summer. More tunnels can be found in the sandstone mines on the nearby St Pietersberg hill. Again, there are tours in summer and you can see what is supposedly Napoleon's autograph on the wall.

The city also offers a handful of decent museums. The Bonnefanten Museum is the main archive, with works by local artists and some intriguing local Roman finds. But don't keep on the go. Maastricht is a place in which to relax and have fun. The nightlife is as vibrant as you want it, and there are some excellent restaurants in which to unwind and appreciate a genuine taste of the Netherlands.

Maastricht

Major Events
Maastricht Carnival (mid February): Holland's biggest carnival celebrating the onset of Lent.
World Music Theatre Festival (March– April): music from Africa, Asia and Latin America.
Feast of St Servatius (early May): Maastricht's premier week-long religious festival, with services and processions.
Cultural Summer Programme (June–September): cornucopia of events from the Geusselt Pop Festival, through street theatre, brass band music and a movie festival to a festival of religious music.

How to get there – and get around
By air: scheduled flights to Maastricht-Aachen Airport (6 miles out) from Stansted only (1hr 20 mins), but there are flights from many UK airports to Amsterdam from where there are frequent connections to Maastricht. Buses into Maastricht are irregular, but there are taxis.
By car: Channel Tunnel or ferries from various UK ports to Hook of Holland, Rotterdam, Zeebrugge, Calais, Dunkerque or Ostend, then motorway through Belgium/Holland to Maastricht (short crossings take 1½-4; long crossings up to 13 hrs; the shortest road journey is from Rotterdam/Hook – about 3 hrs).
By rail: Eurostar to Brussels, then change for Liège and Maastricht (about 4½–5 hrs).
Public Transport: Maastricht has adequate and reasonable bus services; taxis are plentiful and fairly inexpensive.

Suggested Hotels
Château St Gerlach, Joseph Corneli Allée, Valkenburg.
Tel: (043) 608 8888 Fax: (043) 604 2883
Eight miles east of Maastricht, this is one of Holland's best hotels. Very expensive.
Golden Tulip Derlon, Onze Lieve Vroueplein.
Tel: (043) 321 6770 Fax: (043) 325 1993
Elegant and luxurious, city-centre hotel close to the basilica. Expensive.
De Poshoorn, Stationstraat.
Tel: (043) 321 7334
Pleasant hotel above a café near the station. Inexpensive.

Suggested Restaurants
Beluga, Havenstraat.
Tel: (043) 321 33 64
High-quality international cuisine with a strong French influence. Expensive.
Restaurant Alsacien Beaumont, Wycker Brugstraat. Tel: (043) 325 4433
Classic, elegant French restaurant. Expensive.
Café Restaurant Reube, Tongersestraat.
Tel: (043) 325 2843
Traditional Dutch restaurant in intimate surroundings. Moderate.

The lively fish market, in the main square on the seafront at Bergen, is one of the city's major attractions. You can buy some ready-to-eat fresh seafood here, for a quick, inexpensive snack.

Bergen

Norway's second largest city, and its one-time capital, is surprisingly small. Squeezed onto a couple of narrow peninsulas between the mountains and the cold North Sea, Bergen looks more like a little fishing town. An overnight ferry from the UK will land you in the thick of the action. Bergen has plenty to offer, there are some excellent museums and a genuine taste of old Norwegian life. It's not been named European City of Culture in the year 2000 for nothing.

History and Culture

Bergen was founded in the 11th century and later became part of the Hanseatic League of European trading cities. It was also a big religious centre, home to dozens of churches and monasteries, and today is a university town. International trade apart, its wealth was built on shipbuilding and fishing, and the quayside fish market is still a major draw.

Sightseeing

The most charismatic quarter of Bergen is Bryggen, the old wharf area. Here, brightly painted timber-fronted houses and historic warehouses recall medieval times, when Bergen was in its prime. Parts of the original settlement have been incorporated into the Bryggen Museum. Nearby, the Mariakirken is a lovely church that has been in continuous use since the 1100s, and also here is the 16th-century Rosenkrantz Tower, built using Scottish labour and incorporating part of a 13th-century fortress.

The Hanseatic Museum provides a colourful insight into the life of a wealthy merchant 200 years ago while from a different era is the tiny Theta Museum, once the centre of Resistance activity to the Nazis and now commemorating the heroic efforts of its activists.

The new town around the other side of the Vågen sea inlet is less pretty and more functional, but does contain yet more fine museums. Rasmus Meyer's Collection has excellent pieces of Norwegian art, while the Municipal Art Museum, close by, exhibits international works by such notables as Picasso and Klee. Spend some time in the Aquarium, too, but you will be forgiven if you can't stomach a visit to the Leprosy Museum. A 10-minute bus ride from the centre is Old Bergen, a picturesque gathering of 18th- and 19th-century wooden houses and shops, some of which can be toured.

Above the town sits Mount Fløyen, reached by a funicular and well worth the effort. At the top is a wooded nature park. To get to Edvard Grieg's summer home, Troldhaugen, involves a 15-minute bus ride to Hopsbroen, then a 20-minute walk. The composer is also buried here.

Should you have longer to spare, a train ride out of Bergen is thoroughly recommended. Pick up a 'Norway in a Nutshell' value ticket and take a day's rail trip out to Myrdal. From here, hop on the branch line down to the waterside town of Flåm. It has to be one of Europe's most spectacular train journeys. The alternative is to catch one of the many boats that cruise the stunningly beautiful fjords.

Norway is never likely to be the cheapest place to visit, but its combination of Nordic history, friendly people and almost unbelievable scenery is hard to beat. Bergen is a good introduction.

Bergen

Major Events
Bergen International Festival (May): annual celebration of folklore, music, drama, ballet and arts.
Fana Folklore (June–August): famous summer folk-dancing in an idyllic woodland setting.
International Jazz Festival (late May): more than 60 concerts in under two weeks.
Recitals at Troldhaugen (June–August): three per week at the home of Grieg.

How to get there – and get around
By air: to Bergen Airport (12 miles out) from Heathrow, Stansted, Aberdeen and Newcastle (longest journey 2 hrs). Frequent taxis and buses to the town centre.
By car: ferry from Newcastle to Bergen (22 hrs).
Public Transport: Reliable bus services (the Bergen card gives free bus and funicular access along with a package of entrance fees to museums, swimming pools, etc. at about NOK130 for 24 hrs, (NOK200 for 48 hrs). Taxis are fairly expensive.

Suggested Hotels
Radisson SAS Norge, Ole Bullsplass.
Tel: 55 57 30 00 Fax: 55 57 30 01
Wonderful, atmospheric hotel taken over by the group in 1996. Expensive.
Radisson SAS Royal, Bryggen.
Tel: 55 54 30 00 Fax: 55 32 48 08
Modern addition to the group, set in the midst of ancient Bryggen. Expensive.
First Hotel Marin, Rosenkranzgt.
Tel: 55 30 80 00 Fax: 55 30 80 01
Well-appointed hotel close to Bryggen. Moderate.
Augustin Hotel, C Sundtsgate.
Tel: 55 30 40 00 Fax: 55 30 40 10
Popular hotel on the south side of the Vågen. Moderate.

Suggested Restaurants
Fiskekrogen, Zacchariasbrygge.
Tel: 55 55 96 60
Exclusive waterside restaurant serving international and Norwegian cuisine. Expensive.
Enhjørningen, Bryggen.
Tel: 55 32 79 19
Atmospheric restaurant which recreates the Hanseatic life of the 17th century. Expensive.
Fløien Folkerestaurant, Mount Fløyen.
Tel: 55 32 18 75
Traditional Norwegian restaurant with panoramic views of Bergen. Moderate.

Dawn over the magnificent Oslofjord, the lifeblood of Norway's capital. Its numerous islands are well worth a visit. Natural beauty remains strong in Oslo and lake and forestry cover about half of the city.

Norway's capital city is a real delight. It's very compact and beautifully set, on the edge of a fjord, with broad, airy streets and plenty of greenery. Oslo is an enjoyable place to stroll around, viewing the fine buildings and taking the fresh air in one of the parks, but it also has some wonderful museums that have something to interest everyone. Should you need to venture further afield, the public transport network is excellent. Summer is the time to come, when the evenings are long and the city comfortably warm.

History and Culture

Oslo was known as Christiania until 1925, when it re-adopted its earliest name. The first Oslo stood from the 11th century on the other side of the fjord, but was constantly damaged by fire and was consequently moved in the 17th century by the Danish King Christian IV, after whom it took its new name. The fjord plays a big part in local life. Citizens use its beaches in summer and hop on boats for island excursions.

Sightseeing

The main thoroughfare is Karl Johans gate, leading from the railway station to the royal palace, where security is strangely unobstrusive. You feel you can walk up, knock the door and ask if King Harald is in. A mile or so behind the palace lies Frogner Park. This spacious green area was given over by the Norwegian government to the sculptor Gustav Vigelund, on condition that he fill it with statues. At his death in 1943, he had supplied around 200 amazing pieces of art, including fountains and a bizarre obelisk of writhing human figures, all of which followed the theme of the struggle of human life.

Struggles of a different sort can be unearthed at Norway's most interesting museums, based on the Bygdøy peninsula, a long, healthy stroll, a quick splash on a ferry, or an easy bus ride around the bay from the main city. Set amongst woodland here is Norway's Folk Museum, chronicling life over the centuries and featuring a classic example of a stave church, the

traditional wooden church of Norway. Here, too, is the Viking Ships Museum, displaying three ancient longboats trawled from the mud. The seafaring nature of the Nordic folk is highlighted yet further by a museum dedicated to the expeditions of Thor Heyerdahl. It houses his two flimsy boats, Kon-Tiki and Ra II, which he sailed, against the odds, across the Pacific and the Atlantic respectively. Next door is the Fram Museum, a memorial to the voyages of polar explorer Roald Amundsen. The ship Fram, which he famously took to the Antarctic in 1911, can be toured.

If you're gripped by the haunting pictures of local art hero Edvard Munch, you won't want to neglect the gallery devoted to him, a short ride out from the city centre. He's also featured in the more central National Gallery, along with other European masters. Also in the middle of town, the restored 300-year-old cathedral, the Domkirke, has some fascinatingly macabre crypts, and don't miss a wander around the underground passages of the 13th-century Akershus castle, dominating the eastern edge of the harbour. Converted into a Renaissance palace in the 17th century, it was put to grisly use in World War II as a Nazi prison. It now contains an exhibit about local Resistance activity.

Oslo, like the rest of Norway, must be viewed as an expensive treat. Pounds don't go very far here in restaurants and bars, and you probably won't want to splash out much on the local Scandinavian goods – knitwear, ceramics, wooden crafts – however fine. But plan well and shop around and the city can be more affordable than you think. A good tip is to pick up an Oslo card. This allows you free entrance to the museums and free public transport, for a one-off fee, and can be available for anything from one to three days.

Oslo

Major Events
Oslo Medieval Festival (mid June): celebration of Norse folklore from the Middle Ages.
Oslo Jazz Festival (early August): five days of concerts around the city.
Oslo Chamber Music Festival (late August): summer classical music celebration.
Oslo Sjømatfestival/Trebåtfestival (late August): simultaneous festival celebrating the parts played in Norwegian history by seafood and wooden boats.
Ultima (early October): festival of international contemporary music.

How to get there – and get around
By air: scheduled flights to Oslo-Fornebu Airport (6 miles out) from Heathrow, Gatwick, Stansted and Manchester (longest journey 2 hrs). Frequent buses to the city centre cost around NOK20 and take 25 mins; taxis cost NOK100 and take 15 mins.
Public Transport: Oslo has a good network of buses (costing around NOK18 for 1 hr; NOK40 per day; NOK130 per week) and an efficient metro system. Taxis are fairly expensive.

Suggested Hotels
Grand, Karl Johans gate.
Tel: 22 42 93 90 Fax: 22 42 12 25
Norway's premier hotel, now newly refurbished. Very expensive.
Bastion Hotel, Skippergarten.
Tel: 22 47 77 00 Fax: 22 33 11 80
Luxury hotel which comes highly recommended. Expensive.
Ritz Hotel, Fredrik Stangsgate.
Tel: 22 44 39 60 Fax: 22 44 67 13
Popular hotel fairly close to most amenities. Moderate.

Suggested Restaurants
Bagatelle, Bigdøy Allé.
Tel: 22 44 63 97
Much-vaunted restaurant, famous for its fish and seafood. Very expensive.
Blom, Karl Johans gate. Tel: 22 42 73 00
Restaurant rich in anecdotes and high in quality. Expensive.
Holmenkollen Restaurant, Holmenkollveien. Tel: 22 14 62 26
Popular restaurant specialising in Norwegian fare. Moderate.
Englebret Café, Bankplassen.
Tel: 22 33 66 94
Conservative, but renowned for value-for-money, good regional food. Moderate.

Wawel Castle has its origins in the 10th century, but it is the Renaissance architecture that catches the eye. Inside, there are some particularly fine 16th-century tapestries. The castle has been undergoing major renovations in recent years.

The Polish people may not have have had much to thank the Russians for since World War II, but they can, at least, recognise the importance of the Red Army in saving the beautiful city of Kraków. As the occupying Nazis prepared to leave the city, they planned to destroy the historic centre in their wake. Fortunately, the Russians moved quickly and the Nazis were forced to flee, their destructive plans unimplemented. What they left was a city now numbered in the top 12 historical sights by UNESCO, an immaculate place with some of the finest old buildings in the whole world.

History and Culture

The name Kraków is allegedly derived from a warrior named Krak, who slew a ferocious dragon on the banks of the River Wisla here. He then built himself a fortress and Kraków was born. It became capital of Poland as far back as 1040 but had to be rebuilt following a Tartar invasion. In the 14th century, the city entered a golden age, although it lost capital city status to Warsaw in 1596. Kraków was subsumed into the Austro-Hungarian Empire in the 18th century and, after the horrors of World War II and the lifting of the yoke of Soviet control, it is now a thriving provincial city, with an increasing presence on the world tourist map.

Sightseeing

Kraków's Old Town is frequently referred to as a vast museum, so well-preserved are its Renaissance and baroque buildings. Rynek Glówny is the main market square, and one of the most strikingly beautiful in Europe. It is dominated by the massive bulk of the ancient Cloth Hall and around the outside stand old burgher's houses, churches and cafés. The Cloth Hall is home to one of Kraków's 30-odd museums, the National Museum,

housing Polish paintings and sculptures from over the centuries. For a great view over the city, climb to the top of the City Hall Tower in the square, the last remnant of the proud City Hall sadly destroyed in the 1820s. In the opposite corner is the Romanesque church of St Adalbert's, the oldest and possibly the smallest in the city, while further north, the Gothic Mariacki church, with its cluster of spires, has a magnificent carved wooden altar.

To the west, you won't be able to avoid the venerable buildings of Kraków's University. The second oldest in Europe, it numbers amongst its alumni the astronomer Nicolaus Copernicus and Pope John Paul II, who was later Archbishop of Kraków. Of the many other museums, the pick is the Czartoryski Palace, which exhibits such treasures as works by Leonardo and Rembrandt, which somehow survived the Nazi and Soviet occupations.

On Wawel Hill, near the river, to the south, stand the Gothic cathedral and the fortified Royal Castle. The cathedral dates from the 14th century and has witnessed the coronations and burials of dozens of Polish kings. Don't miss the opulent Sigismund Chapel, a real stunner in the Italian style. Then take a look at the wonderful arcaded courtyard at the Royal Palace. It's considered one of the finest examples of Renaissance architecture.

Across the river, the suburb known as Kazimierz is a place for reflection. This was once home to one of the strongest Jewish communities in Europe – the setting for the film *Schindler's List* – but it is strangely subdued today, Kraków's one-time population of 65,000 being reduced to a mere 1,000 by the end of the war. Many Jews were transported the very short distance to the hideous concentration camps at Auschwitz and Birkenau.

Kraków

Major Events
Shanties: annual festival of sailors' songs!
Organ Music Days (late April): festival of organ music held every year.
International Contemporary Music Festival (late May): annual event for new composers and musicians.
International Gathering of Military Orchestras (mid June): annual get-together of military musical fans.
International Festival of Street Theatres (early July): street entertainers from all over Europe.
Music in Old Kraków (late August): international music festival
Miles Davis Memorial (late September): annual tribute to the great man of jazz.

How to get there – and get around
By air: scheduled flights to Warsaw-Okecie Airport from Heathrow and Manchester, (3¼hrs), then transfer (45 mins) to Kracow-Balice airport (12 miles out). Buses and taxis (taking 30 mins) run to Kraków centre.
Public Transport: Kraków's buses, trams and taxis are reliable and cheap.

Suggested Hotels
Elektor, ul Szpitalna.
Tel: (012) 21 80 25 Fax: (012) 21 86 89
Staid, but comfortable, hotel in the Old Town. Expensive.
Continental, Al Armii Krajowej.
Tel: (012) 37 50 44 Fax: (012) 37 59 38
Well-equipped, modern hotel on the road to the airport, 2 miles from the city centre. Expensive.
Pollera, ul Szpitalna. Tel: (012) 22 10 44
Fax: (012) 22 13 89
The first Polish hotel to return to private hands in 1990, and still with much of its pre-Communist charm. Moderate.

Suggested Restaurants
Elektor, ul Szpitalna. Tel: (012) 21 80 25
Impressive hotel restaurant offering a blend of Polish and French cuisines. Expensive.
Hawelka, Rynek Glówny.
Tel: (012) 22 06 31
Traditional Polish cuisine in grand surroundings. Moderate.
Ratuszowa Café, Rynek Glówny.
Tel: (012) 21 13 26
Café-bar in the dungeons of the old Town Hall Tower (opens till 3pm only). Inexpensive.

Warsaw's monument to composer Frederick Chopin. A museum dedicated to his memory is housed in the city's Ostrogski Palace, while the Chopin Family Salon features a piano he once played. A short ride out is Zelazowa Wola, where Chopin was born in 1810. Concerts are held on its terrace in summer.

Warsaw probably won't win your heart with its looks, but it may earn your respect through the resilience of its people, one of the most trampled upon nations in Europe. Somehow, phoenix-like, they have again risen from the ashes of war. The Nazis managed to virtually level Warsaw, but the city has bounced back in astonishing fashion.

History and Culture

Warsaw, founded in the 13th century, has been Poland's capital since 1596. The Swedes came here in the 17th century, then it fell into Prussian hands before Napoleon created a Grand Duchy around the city. The Russians were next before Poland gained independence in 1918. The invasion by the Nazis in 1939 was the final straw that led to the outbreak of World War II. In the 1980s, dissident workers – remember Solidarity – vigorously contested Soviet control until Poland and its capital received a new, more liberal constitution in 1990.

Sightseeing

The Warsaw you see today is either brutally ugly in the Soviet, functional style, or, in some quarters, a wonderful piece of restoration. The most obvious landmark is the grotesque Palace of Cultures imposed by Stalin. Now containing a casino, theatres and cinemas, it wrecks the city's skyline. Seemingly from another world is the lovely Old Town Square. The original, was flattened by the Nazis, but it has been comprehensively reconstructed. Behind the square is the Gothic cathedral of St John, the city's oldest place of worship. The crypt contains the graves of celebrated Poles.

The city's Royal Castle is essentially early baroque, but with Gothic and rococo elements. It's difficult to believe that the stylised interior is part of a complete reconstruction.

The New Town Market Square is less flamboyant than its older counterpart and accommodates the Church of the Blessed Sacrament, founded in 1688. Near the square is the birthplace of scientist Marie Curie, now a museum dedicated to her life and work.

Pride of place among the city's other museums goes to the National Museum, where impressive Polish and European paintings, successfully tucked away during the war, are now back on display. There's also a Pope John Paul II Museum, with thematically arranged religious artistic treasures Lazienki Park, features a marvellous Palace-on-the-Isle, once the summer residence of Poland's last king.

In the war Warsaw's Jews bravely fought back against their Nazi oppressors, an act that led to the total destruction of the Jewish ghetto. Those that died in this abhorrent crime are remembered in the Heroes of the Warsaw Ghetto monument, while victims of the local concentration camps have their own white marble memorial.

Since the collapse of the Iron Curtain, Poland's tourist trade has increased dramatically, leading to the internationalisation of the hotel and restaurant business. The city also has plenty of little coffee shops. For souvenirs, the obvious specialities are vodka and *sliwki* – plums covered in chocolate.

WARSAW

Major Events

Probaltica (early May): music and arts festival involving Baltic countries.
International Sacred Musical Festival (mid to late May): well-established annual event.
Mozart Festival (June–July): annual celebration of Mozart's music .
Bach International Organ Music Festival (July–August): a self-explanatory gathering.
International Summer Chopin Festival (mid July – late August): Chopin throughout the city.
Warsaw Summer Jazz Days (late July): international jazz acts as an antidote to the plethora of classical activity.
Warsaw Autumn (mid–end September): annual international festival of contemporary music.
Jazz Jamboree (October): Europe's oldest jazz festival, with top international names.

How to get there – and get around

By air: scheduled flights to Warsaw-Okecie Airport (6 miles out) from Heathrow and Manchester (3¼hrs). Buses (taking 30 mins, and costing around PLZ 1.5) run to Warsaw centre; taxis (taking 15 mins) cost around PLZ12.
Public Transport: Warsaw has a comprehensive bus-tram-and growing metro network. Single tickets cost around PLZ1.5 (daily and weekly tickets are also available) and can be bought from ticket huts. Validate the ticket in the vehicle's punch machine. Taxis are reasonably priced. Radio taxis, which can be booked, are more reliable.

Suggested Hotels

Bristol, Krakowskie Przedmiescie. Tel: (022) 625 25 25 Fax: (022) 625 25 77
Well-preserved building housing one of Europe's great hotels. Very expensive.
Sheraton, ul B Prusa.
Tel: (022) 657 61 00 Fax: (022) 657 62 00
Warsaw's newest luxury hotel, with excellent facilities. Expensive.
Orbis Holiday Inn, ul Zlota.
Tel: (022) 620 03 41 Fax: (022) 830 05 69
Excellently-equipped, modern hotel in the city centre. Expensive.
Forum, ul Nowogrodzka.
Tel: (022) 620 03 41 Fax: (022) 830 05 69
Very large, modern hotel in the city centre. Moderate.

Suggested Restaurants

Restauracja Polska. Tel: (022) 826 38 77
Convergence of old and new Poland in atmospheric surroundings. Expensive.
La Bohéme. Plac Teatralny.
Tel: (022) 692 06 81
Stately, cellar-style restaurant, set next to the National Theatre. Moderate.
Montmartre, Nowy Swiat.
Tel: (022) 628 63 15
French-style restaurant with good credentials. Moderate.

If your mental picture of the Algarve is a series of concrete block hotels and raucous nightclubs, think again. While noisy pockets exist, the magnificent south coast of Portugal remains largely as unspoilt as ever.

When you think of the Algarve, it's easy to conjure up images of concrete apartment blocks and tacky souvenir shops . But consider why the Algarve has become such a huge attraction in the first place. Portugal's southern coast is extremely beautiful, with wonderful rocky coves, excellent sandy beaches and particularly friendly locals. Modern developments don't absorb the whole coastline, and this wonderful part of the world seems as appealing as it did before the tourist influx began.

History and Culture

The Algarve owes its name to the Moors who settled here between the 8th and 12th centuries and called the area *Al Gharb,* meaning 'Land to the West'. They left more than a name, however. Traces of Arab influence can still be seen in the square, white houses and on the menus of the region's restaurants. Although Prince Henry the Navigator brought international attention to the Algarve in the 15th century, the region generally slumbered away until the 1960s. Then a new airport was opened at Faro and the holiday boom began. Today, the region relies heavily on tourism and the business of expatriate retirees, but fishing remains important to selected towns and villages.

Sightseeing

Getting around the Algarve is easy, with good roads running along the coastline and regular trains linking the many resorts and small villages. Faro is the central point of the region and, despite its modern developments, still has some of the charm it enjoyed 30 years ago. However, a more authentic base these days is over to the east around the little town of Tavira, so unmoved by tourism that it still has more churches than hotels. The beaches near here are pleasantly underdeveloped and the town itself is a picture: pastel-shaded houses bordering a tranquil river, ornate belltowers, fine waterside gardens, low bridges and an attractive working harbour. The bounty the fishermen bring back goes on sale in the seafront restaurants, with tuna the prize catch.

To the west of Faro is the most built up part of the Algarve, with Lagos the major centre. This is the place to head for if you're looking for pulsating nightlife or want to sunbathe (along with hundreds of other people) in the many sheltered coves. Further along is the region's most important fishing town, Portimão. It has its share of concrete high-rises, but the harbourfront restaurants are still excellent value. Try some char-grilled sardines that didn't find their way to the town's canning factories.

Over to the far west, the land ends at Sagres, or more precisely Cape St Vincent, Europe's most southwesterly point. The area has a rugged beauty, and a desolate, dramatic mood that encourages contemplation. Climb the old town walls at Sagres for a breathtaking view of the powerful ocean.

Away from the sea, inland Algarve remains hardly touched by the new excesses of some of the coastline. Here market towns and hilltop villages centre around attractive little squares, fringed with restaurants serving traditional dishes like spicy piri-piri chicken. Hire a car and take a tour of towns like Silves, with its remains of a Moorish fortress and a 13th-century church.

One reason why so many people retire out here (apart from the marvellous climate, including mild winters) is the excellent sporting provision. The Algarve offer watersports of every kind, tennis clubs and some terrific golf courses. The package holiday image of the Algarve should not put you off a short break here. On the contrary, the sheer number of cheap charter flights should indeed encourage you to take full advantage of this stunning region.

Algarve

Major Events
Easter Processions: the Processions of the Palms and the Burial of the Lord at Tavira and the Procession of the Alleluia and the Contest of the Flowered Torches at nearby São Brás de Alportel.
Algarve International Music Festival (May–July): classical concerts, recitals, chamber music and ballet throughout the region.
Feast of the Popular Saints (June): marches, music and celebrations into the night in commemoration of the Saints Anthony, John and Peter, in Tavira and elsewhere.
Beer Festival (July): annual chance to try Portugal's brews at Silves.
Sardine Festival (August): homage to the town's lifeblood at Portimão.
Conceição de Tavira (August): Portuguese National Folklore Festival, near Tavira.

How to get there – and get around
By air: scheduled flights to Faro Airport from Heathrow, Gatwick, East Midlands and Edinburgh (longest flight 3½ hrs). Buses run to Faro centre (25 mins) and buses or trains then run to Tavira (45–60 mins) and other towns.
Public Transport: Tavira and other towns are easy to explore on foot, but buses and trains ply the Algarve coast. Few buses go into the hinterland, so car hire is recommended.

Suggested Hotels
Casablanca, Rua Sete, Monte Gordo. Tel: (081) 511444 Fax: (081) 511999
Luxury hotel in a well-equipped resort near the Spanish border. Expensive.
Alcazar, Rua de Ceuta, Monte Gordo. Tel: (081) 512184 Fax: (081) 512242
Seaside hotel with good facilities and a distinctly Moorish atmosphere.
Eurotel, Quinta das Oliveiras, Tavira. Tel: (081) 325041 Fax: (081) 325571
Tavira has a shortage of quality accommodation, but this popular aparthotel is well regarded. Moderate.

Suggested Restaurants
The hotel restaurants of the **Casablanca and Alcazar** (see above) have good local reputations for their food. Moderate–expensive.
Restaurante O Pátio, Rua António Cabreira, Tavira. Tel: (081) 23008
One of Tavira's most popular restaurants with some tempting Algarvian fare. Moderate.
Restaurante Imperial, Rua Pires Padinha, Tavira. Tel: (081) 22306
Well-established, riverside hotel, specialising in fish.
Moderate.

The Alfama district of Lisbon is a marvellous place to discover on foot (but taking a map is advised). Its maze of narrow, cobbled streets has hardly changed since the 12th century.

Lisbon is one of the most overlooked cities in Europe, as far as short breaks go. Influenced by Roman and Moorish occupations in the distant past, Lisbon also has a proud maritime heritage, reflected in its various monuments. Built up on the banks of the River Tagus, the city is compact and, in some respects, much like an overgrown small town, characterised by distinctive black and white mosaic pavements, and far from state of the art trams. There are plenty of good hotels and fine restaurants, these are extremely affordable and excellent value, contributing to the overall feel of a city just a little behind the times. Lisbon is none the worse for that and, with its temperate climate, is a treat at any time of the year.

History and Culture

Portugal was a major seafaring nation for some four centuries. Explorers brought back wealth and exciting discoveries. Lisbon benefited from this maritime inheritance and grew into a busy city. However, the 1755 earthquake killed around 40,000 people and destroyed many of the buildings. The rapid rebuilding work left much of the city built on a grid system, which makes certain areas easy to explore. Other areas were not so badly damaged and their tangled maze of ancient streets needs serious concentration to navigate.

Sightseeing

The simplest way to explore this notoriously hilly city is by dividing it into districts. Start near the waterfront, where the Alfama is the old Moorish quarter, is dominated by the Castelo de São Jorge, a medieval fortress set on one of Lisbon's seven hills. Also in the

LISBON

Alfama is the city's cathedral, housing some notable 14th-century tombs and religious artworks. West of the Alfama is the Baixa, the commercial heart of the city, with some fine baroque squares and very good shopping. Traditional crafts flourish here – look for local *azulejos* tiles – and the focal point of life is Rossio Square. At the northern end of Baixa the bars and restaurants pulsate long into the night. Adjoining the Baixa, is the Chiado district, now being refashioned after a fire in 1988 and adopting an affluent, trendy image. You can ride the funicular from here up to the Bairro Alto, the Upper Town. Here is São Roque church, containing some sparkling side chapels. One, dedicated to St John the Baptist, was built in Rome and shipped across. Belém is a riverside suburb out to the west, in the shadow of the modern Monument of the Discoveries, dedicated to the great explorers who set sail from here. Protecting the harbour entrance is the Belém Tower, built in 1512–21. Here, too, is the beautifully elaborate Jerónimos Monastery, originally a modest seaman's chapel, but enlarged and embellished with maritime and colonial profits.

The city's leading cultural centre is the Museu Calouste Gulbenkian. Established by an Armenian oil magnate, it's not just a museum but a collection of concert halls and galleries. Exhibits include ancient treasures and a wealth of modern art. Competing for attention is the separate National Museum of Art, which includes displays of 15th-century works by Portuguese artists.

For outdoor exploring, visit Eduardo VII Park, with its lake, and greenhouses. Wandering here and taking in the views, or browsing the markets and craft workshops, is one of the best ways to appreciate this very individual city.

Lisbon

Major Events

Cycle of the Great Orchestras of the World (early March, late April, early May): appearances by the likes of the Philharmonia, Bavarian Radio Symphony and Metropolitan Opera Orchestras.

Lisbon International Equestrian Jumping Competition (early June): show jumping tournament featuring international stars.

Lisbon Games (late May–June): final events in a six-month long festival of sport, featuring athletics and team games like basketball and street football.

Gulbenkian Festival of Contemporary Music (early–mid June): annual gathering to promote modern-day music.

How to get there – and get around

By air: scheduled flights to Lisbon Airport (5 miles out) from Heathrow, Gatwick, Stansted and Manchester (longest flight 2¼hrs). Taxis to Lisbon centre take 25 mins and cost around PTE1500; buses run every 20 mins, take 30 mins, and cost PTE270.

Public Transport: buses, trams, metro and funicular railways are covered by 4 or 7-day tickets, with some of the cheapest fares in Europe (around PTE1550 and PTE2200). Taxis are also very reasonable.

Suggested Hotels

Da Lapa, Rua do Pau de Bandeira.
Tel: (01) 395 00 55 Fax (01) 395 06 65
Lisbon's premier hotel, overlooking magnificent gardens and close to the Tagus. Very expensive.

Tivoli, Avenida da Liberdade.
Tel: (01) 314 11 01 Fax: (01) 352 42 04
Excellently-appointed city-centre hotel, benefiting from recent refurbishment. Expensive.

Britânia, Rua Rodrigues Sampaio.
Tel: (01) 315 50 16 Fax: (01) 315 50 21
Staid, but comfortable, 1940s city-centre hotel. Moderate.

Príncipe Real, Rua de Algeria.
Tel: (01) 346 01 16 Fax: (01) 342 21 04
Good value-for-money central hotel with superb views of the city. Moderate.

Suggested Restaurants

Gambrinus, Rua das Portas de São Antão. Tel: (01) 342 14 66
Fish restaurant extraordinaire, the most exclusive in the city. Expensive.

Casa de Comida, Travess de Amoireiras. Tel: (01) 388 53 76
A bit of a local secret, hugely popular with locals. Moderate.

Conventual, Praça das Flores.
Tel: (01) 60 91 96
Highly-rated favourite serving primarily Portuguese food. Moderate.

Bachus, Largo da Trinidade.
Tel: (01) 342 28 28
Top-quality international cuisine, if standard in the range of its menu. Moderate.

The majestic natural beauty of Madeira. Rugged volcanic mountains tower over a lush landscape of deep, wooded ravines, wild flowers, palm trees and local agricultural crops - bananas, suger cane, fruit and wine grapes.

Madeira means 'wood' in Portuguese and that's what you'll see plenty of here. Nearer to Morocco than its paternal Portugal, Madeira is warm and bountiful, a volcanic island jutting out of clear blue seas, with ultra-fertile soil that encourages a spectacular range of blossoms. Not surprisingly, the island has become a popular venue for the green-fingered and more sedate holidaymaker, but with a wonderful climate, averaging over 60 degrees even in winter, and hiking, swimming and other sports on hand, there is enough here to keep the energetic happy, too.

History and Culture

Madeira is the largest of a small group of islands discovered by the Portuguese explorer João Gonçalves Zarco in 1419. It is still a Portuguese territory, although strong trading ties exist with Britain. These stem from the marriage of Charles II to the Portuguese princess Catherine of Braganza, and the English king's subsequent concession to local wine-makers, which allowed them to trade with Britain and its colonies. The rich, sweet Madeira wine became a favourite among the British nobility, many of whom settled on the island.

Sightseeing

The island's capital is Funchal, a flower-filled business and political centre. Here, explore as the Old Customs House, now the island's parliament, and the Convent of St Clare, with its

fine ceramic tilework. The Museum of Sacred Art has some notable Flemish artworks, a legacy of the merchants from Bruges who worked here a few centuries ago. Funchal's Botanic Garden has an international reputation. For more heady pleasures, visit one of the wine houses to try the local produce, or chance your arm in a casino at night.

The nearest settlements to Funchal are Monte and Câmara de Lobos. The former is a village four miles northeast, where the big attraction are the wicker sledges. Originally designed to carry produce down to the capital, they now ferry an endless supply of tourists back to Funchal, their lard-greased runners slipping over the smooth old cobbles. There are two drivers to ensure your safety and, whilst it clearly panders to the foreigner, the experience is good fun and rather exciting. Câmara de Lobos is an unspoilt fishing village 11 miles to the west, still looking as it did when famously painted by Winston Churchill, its boats drawn up on the stony beach.

The island is only 35 miles long by 13 miles wide, but, because of the endless hills and valleys, it can take ages to get around. For hiking, head inland to Serra de Agua, a green, rocky area of waterfalls. To see the other side of Madeira, make for Porto Moniz, popular with day-trippers for its pools formed by solidified lava. For an excellent view over the whole island, Pico de Ariero, Madeira's third-highest peak, has an excellent look-out area. These places are fascinating in themselves but it is the drive across the island that provides the real magic – past terraced vines, banana plants and little white houses covered in bougainvillea. The colours and perfumes of Madeira live fondly in the memory.

Madeira

Major Events
Carnival (February): full week of pre-Lent celebrations including floats, colourful processions and dancers.
Flower Festival (April): Madeira in all its glory as the extraordinary range of the island's floral species goes on display
Music Festival (June): classical concerts every weekend.
Madeira Wine Festival (September): the grape harvest and related folklore rituals throughout the island.
Philharmonic Band Festival (October): some 16 bands come together at the summer's end to play a wide range of music.

How to get there – and get around
By air: scheduled flights to Madeira-Funchal Airport (8 miles out of Funchal town) from Heathrow, Gatwick, Glasgow and Manchester (longest flight 4 hrs). Buses and taxis into Funchal are fairly reliable and inexpensive.
Public Transport: buses link Funchal with villages across Madeira, but car hire is recommended.

Suggested Hotels
Reid's Palace, Estrada Monumental, Funchal. Tel: (91) 700 7171
Fax: (91) 700 7177
Idiosyncratic, gracious, cliff-top hotel, long favoured by British aristocrats. Very expensive.
Santa Isabel, Avenida do Infante, Funchal. Tel: (91) 223 111
Fax: (91) 227 959
Excellent hotel with good facilities. Expensive.
Eden Mar, Rua do Gorgulho.
Tel: (91) 762 221 Fax: (91) 761 966
Modern, family complex of suites, shops, pools and restaurants. Moderate.
Madeira, Rua Ivens, Funchal.
Tel: (91) 230 071 Fax: (91) 229 071
Simple, but comfortable, hotel in a quiet street. Inexpensive.

Suggested Restaurants
Casa Dos Reis, Rua Impertriz Amélia, Funchal. Tel: (91) 225 182
Well-regarded, homely restaurant, serving an international menu. Expensive.
Villa Cliff, Estrada Monumental, Funchal.
Tel: (91) 763 725
Centrally-situated and with a good reputation. Expensive.
Red Lion, Rua do Favila, Funchal.
Tel: (91) 63370
International restaurant, popular with tourists. Moderate.

Oporto's well-known Dom Luis I Bridge, a double-decker cross between Sydney Harbour Bridge and the Eiffel Tower. Walk along the upper tier for an unusual perspective of the city.

Oporto is not one of the most relaxed Iberian cities. Instead, it is busy, commercial and industrial. But it does have two particular attractions that never fail to disappoint. The first is port, the second is a stunning train ride up into the rugged, green Douro Valley.

History and Culture

Oporto, also known more simply as Porto, was the city that gave its name to the country. Today, tumbling down the banks of the Douro river, it's the second largest city in Portugal. Its wealth was founded on the wine trade, particularly on port wine, which, ironically, was developed by British wine merchants. They set about fortifying the local wines with brandy, and famous British names still stand out here: Cockburn's, Sandeman and Taylor's.

Sightseeing

Take a hike up the Torre dos Clérigos, the city's trademark tower, for an overall view of the jumble of streets in the old town, with their pastel-painted houses, then make for the Sé, the city's 12th-century cathedral. The rather gloomy interior is more than compensated for by the chapterhouse and the cloisters with their marvellous *azulejos* tilework. Pay a visit also to the São Francisco church, just down the hill from the cathedral. Fourteenth-century Gothic on the outside, it is surprisingly 17th-century baroque on the intricate inside. Near here is the neo-classical Palácio da Bolsa

OPORTO AND DOURO VALLEY

(Stock Exchange), its Arab Room modelled after the Alhambra in Granada. Among the museums, the Soares dos Reis in the Carrancas Palace is big on local decorative arts. For an escape into the open air, visit the Palácio de Cristal park, featuring a domed pavilion concert hall and, in summer months, a giant funfair. Then it's time to head for the port lodges.

The lodges are housed over to the west in the suburb known as Vila Nova de Gaia and are linked to the main city by the double-decker Dom Luis I bridge – Tours of the lodges are often free and include a tasting, but if you want to sample the whole spectrum of port production, pop into the Solar do Vinho do Porto, a comfortable bar on the edge of Palácio de Cristal park. This is run by the port producers themselves and you can try hundreds of varieties at all prices. The best way to appreciate the Douro river and its valley is to let the train take the strain and head out of town. The valley, a twisting, narrow gorge, heads up to the Spanish border. You could pause at the village of Penafiel, to taste the local Vinho Verde, or head on into the river valley proper and on to Peso da Régua, the main port wine depot town, where there are several hotels and restaurants. But the joy of this journey is the view from the train. The track clings to the unspoilt valley, dodging in and out of terraced vineyards. It's an exploration rather than an excursion – the train is often no more than a single carriage – and after the bustle of Oporto is a welcome breath of fresh air. Yet, put the two together, and perhaps also a detour to see the religious architecture of Braga, an hour and half from the city, and you have the makings of a genuinely Classic Short Break.

Oporto and Douro Valley

Major Events
Fanasporto (February): international cinema festival devoted to fantasy movies, promoting new directors.
Inter-Celtic Festival (April–May): celebration of the music and traditions of the region's Celtic roots, and those of other countries.
International Puppet Festival (May): annual festival targeting adults as much as children.
Week of Baroque Music (July): an increasingly popular event in Oporto's cultural year.
Oporto International Music Competition (early October): 11 days of intensive international piano competition.

How to get there – and get around
By air: scheduled flights to Oporto's Francisco Sá Carneiro Airport (13 miles out) from Heathrow, Gatwick and Manchester (longest flight 2¼hrs). Taxis to Oporto centre (20 mins) cost around PTE3000, or take bus no. 56 (30 mins' journey), costing PTE350.
Public Transport: buses and trolley buses are covered by 1-, 4- or 7-day tickets (around PTE350, PTE1700 and PTE2200). Taxis are also quite cheap.

Suggested Hotels
Infante de Sagres, Praça D Filipa de Lencastre.
Tel: (02) 200 81 01 Fax: (02) 31 49 37
Grand hotel in the centre, whose traditions smack of the British influence in the wine trade. Expensive.
Park Atlantic, Avenida da Boavista.
Tel: (02) 600 19 13 Fax: (02) 600 23 031
Upmarket hotel with a good range of facilities. Expensive.
Grande Hotel da Batalha,
Praça da Batalha.
Tel: (02) 200 05 71 Fax: (02) 200 24 68
Stylish, central hotel with links to the past. Moderate.
Hotel São José, Rua de Algeria.
Tel: (02) 208 02 61 Fax: (02) 32 04 46
Centrally-positioned, comfortable hotel. Inexpensive.

Suggested Restaurants
Hotel Jardim de Inferno, Hotel Ipanema Park, Rua de Serralves.
Tel: (02) 610 41 10
Plush hotel restaurant with a reputation for haute cuisine. Expensive.
Aquaráio Marisquiero, Rua Rodrigues Sampaio. Tel: (02) 200 22 31
Well-regarded seafood restaurant. Moderate.
Tripeiro, Rua Passos Manuel.
Tel: (02) 200 58 86
Traditional Portuguese restaurant, which, as the name suggests, specialises in tripe dishes. Moderate.
Típico Mal Cozinhado, Rua Outeirinho. Tel: (02) 208 13 19
'Fado' singing accompanies diners. Moderate.

Moscow is one of those places most people never imagined they'd ever visit. As the seat of the Soviet empire, it looked impregnable to the everyday tourist. While the city is still not the most comfortable for foreigners, it is at least open these days and the chance to see those great Russian icons – Red Square, the Kremlin, St Basil's Cathedral and more – made famous by TV newsreels, should not be ignored.

History and Culture

Moscow was founded in the 12th century but has suffered a turbulent history. Tsar Peter the Great undermined its importance in the 18th century, by transferring the position of Russian capital to St Petersburg, but, when the Bolsheviks rose up in 1917, Moscow soon became the country's power base again. Yet Moscow's troubles never seem to ease, as witnessed by the attempted coups against Gorbachev and Yeltsin. The city has also struggled to come to terms with the free market, and extremes of wealth and poverty are now evident, against a background of a thriving black market. None of this should deter you from making a visit, however, be alert and take care.

Sightseeing

There is only one place to begin in Moscow and that is in Red Square. Flanked on one side by the massive bulk of the Kremlin and on the other by the GUM department store, the square is also distinguished by the colourful confection known as St Basil's cathedral. The elaborate shopping arcade known as GUM (the State Universal Store) is a reminder that Red Square was originally a market place.

St Basil's cathedral is a fabulously ornate construction. Underneath its bright onion domes is now a museum with a labyrinth of dark corridors, twisting staircases and partly restored chapels.

In front of the Kremlin wall you'll find the tombs of Communist worthies like cosmonaut Yuri Gagarin and the macabre mausoleum of the man who started it all, Lenin. His preserved body, complete in polka dot tie, can be viewed. The Kremlin – the name means 'fortress' – is not one building but a collection, including several cathedrals. It was founded in 1156 but the present complex was constructed in the 15th century. The most striking of its cathedrals is the Cathedral of the Assumption, with fabulous 17th century murals, while the Cathedral of the Archangel is the burial place of Russia's earliest rulers, Ivan the Terrible among them. The Kremlin's Patriarch's Palace, including the Church of the Twelve Apostles, is a now a museum featuring the most opulent gifts received by the tsars.

Many visitors will want to pay homage to the Bolshoi, the theatre where Tchaikovsky's *Swan Lake* premiered in 1877. Performances by the world-famous opera and ballet companies take place on most nights and tickets are both obtainable and affordable.

The most bohemian part of the city is Arbat, a 19th-century residential quarter which somehow managed to survive Stalin's urban regeneration in the 1920s and '30s. It is today the haunt of buskers and street artists and the focal point of Moscow's embryonic café culture. Then there are the wonderful parks, especially Gorky Park. It offers views across the Moskva river and has plenty of amusements, like a theatre, an ice-skating rink and two fun fairs.

Eating well in Moscow is not as difficult as you imagine, though you are advised to book restaurants well in advance. Nightclubs tend to be on the expensive side. Save your energy for the days in this bustling, fascinating metropolis.

The Cathedral of the Assumption, one of several cathedrals within the walls of the Kremlin. It serves mostly as a museum these days and, inside Ivan the Terrible's throne is still on display.

Moscow

Major Events

Russian Winter Festival (early January): ballet and opera performances in the Bolshoi and a folklore festival.
Moscow International Film Festival (May): biennial festival of Russian and European cinema.
Festival 'Moscow Stars' (May–June): music and ballet from the Bolshoi and the Moscow Conservatoire.
Golden Autumn (September–mid October): classical concerts in the concert halls, and Bolshoi opera and ballet.
December Evenings (December): concerts of classical music in the White Hall of the Museum of Fine Arts named after Pushkin.

How to get there – and get around

By air: scheduled flights to Moscow-Sheremetyevo Airport (18 miles out) from Heathrow and Gatwick (3 hrs), then by cheap bus (unreliable; 1 hr) or taxi to Moscow (40 mins; costing around US$30 or more, by negotiation).
Public Transport: Moscow's over-worked bus and tram services are more than compensated for by the excellent metro. Taxis are somewhat of a lottery – both in reliability and consistency of fares.

Suggested Hotels

Metropol, Teatralny proezd.
Tel: (095) 927 6000
Tsarist-era grand hotel, with fading grandeur, but still much charm. Expensive.
National, Okhotny ryad.
Tel: (095) 203 6539
Another *fin de siècle* monument to pre-Revolutionary Russia. Expensive.
Ukraina, Kutuzovskt prospekt.
Tel: (095) 243 3030
Featureless, but clean, hotel, situated centrally and overlooking the Moskva river. Moderate.
Belgrad, Smolenskaya ploshchad.
Tel: (095) 248 1643
Functional central hotel. Moderate.

Suggested Restaurants

Silver Age, Teatralny proezd.
Tel: (095) 926 1352
Top-quality European and Russian cuisine, but at a price. Very expensive.
Savoy, Rozhdestvenka.
Tel: (095) 929 8600
Classic Russian restaurant. Expensive.
Russky Zal, Lavrushinsky pereulok.
Tel: (095) 233 1829
Popular restaurant in the centre of Moscow. Moderate.

ST PETERSBURG

There's no gain without pain, the saying goes. It could be used to sum up a short break in Russia. Both Moscow and St Petersburg have their problems these days, but what they have to offer the tourist more than outweighs the negatives. Don't expect a particularly comfortable time, but, with a little planning, an enjoyable, educational experience is assured. St Petersburg has clearly seen better times, but if you can ignore the crumbling facades and peeling paintwork, you can still appreciate the imperial grandeur of this magnificent Baltic port. The brainchild of the westernising tsar, Peter the Great, it is a beautiful city of fine, wide avenues and monumental palaces, built over a series of 'islands' framed by the looping Neva river and its tributaries. You can't ignore the Hermitage art gallery, one of the world's greatest cultural attractions.

History and Culture

St Petersburg was founded by Peter the Great in the early 18th century. He made it the capital of his Russian empire in 1709 and the city prospered through his efforts to align Russia more with Europe, rather than with Asian countries. At the turn of the 20th century, the city became a focus for insurrection, sparking the movement that led to the Russian Revolution of 1917. During World War I, its name was changed to Petrograd and, after it, the Bolsheviks moved the capital back to Moscow. In 1924, Petrograd became Leningrad. During World War II, the city was bombarded by the Nazis and besieged for two and a half years. In 1991, following the collapse of the Soviet Union, the citizens of St Petersburg voted to re-adopt the city's original name.

Sightseeing

The Hermitage Museum is one of the world's finest collections of art. It is housed in the Winter Palace, a splendid royal residence designed by an 18th-century Italian architect. You can tour the royal apartments and see the sumptuous ballroom, the throne room of Peter the Great and the Gallery of 1812, with its portraits of heroes of the Napoleonic Wars. The Hermitage catalogue is a roll-call of old masters. All the great names are here, from Raphael and El Greco to Michelangelo and Leonardo, but the gallery is most famous for its collection of 19th- and 20th-century French paintings.

Adjacent to the Winter Palace is the imperious Admiralty building, graced by a slender, golden spire. Across the river is the beautiful Peter-Paul Fortress.

Extending eastward from the Winter Palace is St Petersburg's elegant main avenue, Nevsky prospekt. The imposing frontages, elaborate bridges, stunning palaces and perfectly proportioned squares combine to make it a fascinating street to wander. Its cemetery is the last resting place of numerous notable Russians, including the composers Rimsky-Korsakov and Tchaikovsky and the novelist Dostoevsky. Dostoevsky also lived in the city and his home has been preserved as a museum. Like all Russian museums, it wonderfully evokes the man and his times.

There is bags more to see in the city but, if you have time to venture outside St Petersburg, there is one place you must take in. The imperial palace at Peterhof was founded, like the city, by Peter the Great. A hydrofoil from St Petersburg (in winter you can take the train) will take you directly to the Grand Cascade, a magnificent sequence of gilded statues and fountains. From here you can go on to visit the equally splendid baroque palace itself.

Eating out in St Petersburg can be expensive, but there are plenty of restaurants to choose from, although not as many 'westernised' places as in Moscow. For alternative evening entertainment, there is, of course, the Mariinsky – or Kirov – opera and ballet company. Nijinsky, Nureyev and Pavlova all danced at Mariinsky, and Tchaikovsky's Nutcracker and Sleeping Beauty both premiered here.

PREVIOUS PAGE: The Hermitage Museum, home to one of the world's greatest collections of art. There are no highlights here; everything is a masterpeice, and the overall effect is overwhelming. There's little point in trying to see it all: be selective, choose one of the four buildings, or even just a part of a building, and take in what you can.

St Petersburg's first ever building, dating from 1703. Its cathedral of Saints Peter and Paul is wholly western in character and houses the tombs of most of Russia's rulers from Peter the Great onwards.

St Petersburg

Major Events
Russian Winter Festival (early January): ballet and opera at the Mariinsky Theatre, and folklore festivals in Pavlovsk Tsarist Estate.
Independence Day (12 June): entertainment indoors and out.
White Nights Festival (mid–late-June): entertainment in all theatres and concert halls of St.Petersburg, plus outdoor events.
Golden Autumn (September–mid October): festival of classical and folk music.

How to get there – and get around
By air: scheduled flights to to Moscow-Sheremetyevo Airport from Heathrow and Gatwick (3 hrs), or Helsinki-Vantaa Airport from Heathrow, Gatwick, Stansted and Manchester (longest journey 2hrs), then transfer to St Petersburg-Pulkovo Airport (1–1/hrs). A cheap bus/metro service runs the 10 miles to St Petersburg centre. Taxis cost around US$30 (but negotiate) and take 15 mins.
Public Transport: St Petersburg has a passable network of buses, trams, trolley-buses, metros, ferries and hydrofoils. Beware of unofficial taxis.

Suggested Hotels
Grand Europe Kempinski, Mikhaylovskaya ulitsa.
Tel: (0812) 119 6000
Very much the top address in St Petersburg, dating from before the Revolution. Very expensive.
Astoria, Bolshaya Morskaya ulitsa.
Tel: (0812) 210 5032
Traditional pre-Bolshevik establishment, still among the city's premier hotels. Expensive.
St Petersburg, Vyborgskaya naberezhnaya. Tel: (0812) 542 9123
Comfortable and well-priced, central hotel. Moderate.
Mir, Gastello ulitsa.
Tel: (0812) 108 5165
Competitively priced and handy for the airport and metro. Moderate.

Suggested Restaurants
Noble Nest, Dekabristov.
Tel: (0812) 312 3205
St Petersburg's much-vaunted top restaurant. Very expensive.
Vienna, M.Morskaya.
Tel: (812) 311 3227
European *haute cuisine* in atmospheric surroundings. Expensive
Senat Bar, Galernaya.
Tel: (812) 314 9253
Brasserie popular with tourists. Moderate.

Barcelona

Barcelona is one of the liveliest cities in Europe, often likened to Paris for its wide avenues and designer shopping. Nearly everyone who visits is immediately impressed, particularly those who appreciate fine art. This is the city of Picasso, Joan Miró and, above all, art nouveau master Antoni Gaudí. Museums and their works vie for attention with the city's wonderful old centre and revitalised areas provided by the 1992 Olympic Games.

History and Culture

Traces of civilisation in the area around Barcelona date back some 7,000 years, but the city itself was founded by the Carthaginians, from Africa, in 218 BC. The Romans took a shine to it and have left some interesting remains. The Franks and the Moors both had their say before Barcelona became a Christian city in the Middle Ages. Its prime position, commanding the Mediterranean, allowed Barcelona to become a nautical power, but its prowess was diminished with the discovery of the New World and the switch of maritime emphasis from the Med to the Atlantic. Barcelona may be part of Spain today, but it is the first city of Catalonia and its Catalan roots are still celebrated in its traditions, local language and annual festivities.

Sightseeing

You could begin in the Barrio Gótico, the marvellous medieval quarter, a web of tiny, dark streets that are home to the magnificent cathedral, started in 1298. Off the cloister opens up the small Romanesque chapel of Santa Llúcia, with its lush, central garden, palm trees and ducks. Nearby is the basilica of Santa Maria del Mar, regarded by many as one of the finest examples of Catalan Gothic architecture, and Plaça de Sant Jaume, the city's political heart.

The Cassa Batlló on Barcelona's Paseo de Gracia boulevard is typical of the distinctive architectural syle Antoni Gaudi brought to his city. His other buildings can be visited with the help of an excellent pamphlet from the tourist board.

Two further Gothic structures are now home to the Picasso Museum, dedicated largely to his early work. The Fundació Miró features pieces by renowned Catalan artist Joan Miró, while there are more varied selections in the Catalan Art Museum and the Modern Art Museum shares its home with the Catalan government.

The city's greatest artistic talent, however, was the Modernist architect and designer Antoni Gaudí. He used the city as his canvas, swirling masterpieces such as the Casa Milà – a highly original apartment block – and the Temple Expiatori de la Sagrada Família, to which he dedicated the last years of his life, and which is still not finished over 70 years later. This is Barcelona's controversial 'Cathedral of the 20th century', a love-it-or-hate-it mélange of architectural styles and religious symbolism. It's an incredible sight. Other buildings in Barcelona by Gaudí can be visited with the help of an excellent pamphlet from the tourist board.

For the best view over the city, take the cable car up to Montjuïc castle, now a military museum. Near here is the Olympic Stadium, while just across the hillside is Spanish Village, a showcase of famous architecture.

Down near the seafront is the series of pulsating streets known as La Rambla. Buskers and dancers work their way around the flower stalls and street cafés to entertain the public, and just off the area is the city's main food market, La Boqueria, a blaze of natural colour and life. Seek out also the magnificent opera house and stroll down to the Columbus Monument on the revitalised harbourfront. An elevator to the explorer's head affords an excellent view back across the city. The harbour area has been cleaned up and is now a very pleasant place to stroll and enjoy a good seafood lunch.

Be careful with Barcelona, it can afflict you with a case of sensory overload. The art and architecture are phenomenal and the vibrant streets never seem to let up. It's a city with something for everyone and yet it's somewhere where, if you prefer, you needn't do anything at all. It's enough to soak up the atmosphere. But give yourself at least three days to do it.

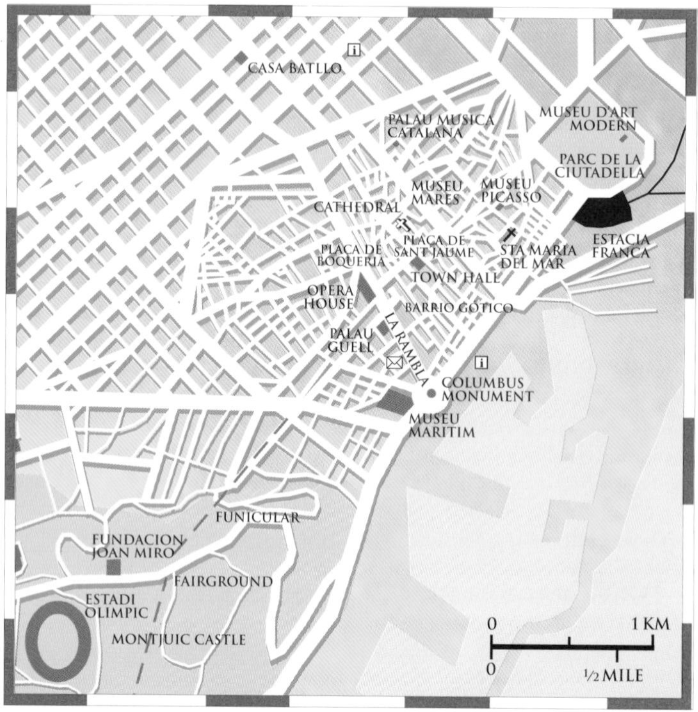

BARCELONA

Major Events

Classical Music (January–May): top-notch concerts by the likes of the London Philharmonic, Vienna Boys Choir and the Berlin Symphony.

Opera (February–June): all the great works.

Festa Major (mid August): different districts compete to stage the best street festival.

La Mercè (late September): Our Lady of Mercy celebrated in a week-long fusion of music, dance and pageantry, culminating in astonishing musical fireworks.

How to get there – and get around

By air: scheduled flights to Barcelona Airport (6 miles out) from Heathrow, Gatwick, Luton, Birmingham and Manchester (longest flight 2⁄ hrs); various buses take between 20 and 40 mins to get to the centre and cost between SP130–450; taxis, taking 20 mins, cost SP2000 and above.

Public Transport: Barcelona's good metro-bus-funicular services cost around SP740 for 10 trips (interchangeable). Taxis are convenient and fairly cheap.

Suggested Hotels

Rey Juan Carlos, Avenida Diagonal. Tel (93) 448 08 08 Fax: (93) 448 06 07 Modern hotel, one of Barcelona's most exclusive. Very expensive.

Ritz-Carlton Arts, Carre de la Marina. Tel: (93) 221 10 00 Fax: (93) 221 10 70 Built for the 1992 Olympics, with dizzying views from the 33rd floor. Expensive.

Le Meridien, Ramblas. Tel: (93) 318 62 00 Fax: (93) 301 77 76 One of Barcelona's most famous hotels, set in the Old Town. Expensive.

Oriente, Ramblas. Tel (93) 302 25 58 Fax: (93) 412 38 19

Popular, traditional Catalan hotel in the Old Town. Moderate.

Suggested Restaurants

Ca l'Isidre, Les Flores. Tel: (93) 441 11 39 Sophisticated bistro, patronised by the rich and famous. Expensive.

Agut d'Avignon, Carrer Trinitat. Tel: (93) 302 60 34 Long-time favourite in the Old Town. Moderate–expensive.

Can Cullerettes, Quintana. Tel: (93) 317 64 85 Popular restaurant with 18th-century origins. Moderate.

Garduña, Mercado La Boquería. Tel: (93) 302 43 23 Famous eating haunt in the covered food market. Inexpensive.

Cáceres. Where? You're not alone if you've only just heard of this Spanish city. But this is such a mesmerising place that it's been declared a World Heritage site. And while the journey from the UK may be a little complicated, you'll be more than amply rewarded with a wonderful short break that doesn't yet feature in the major holiday brochures.

History and Culture

Cáceres was founded by the Romans, although its name is derived from its Arabic title, Cazris. Today, it is the capital of a Spanish province and sits 190 miles west of Madrid in a cattle-farming region. What makes the city so special is its old centre, perched on a hill above the modern town and hemmed in by a ring of remarkably well-preserved medieval walls. The Moors and the Christians fought repeated battles over the settlement, with the strongest period of growth coming after the Christian victory of 1212. The city's wealth was then considerably added to by the conquistadores of the 16th century, who brought back riches plundered from the New World. Today, Cáceres is a good place to look for handicrafts, such as lace, leather, ceramics, and embroidery.

Sightseeing

The heart of Cáceres is tiny, but enough of a maze to confuse even visitors with maps. Its medieval character has been almost perfectly maintained and the streets are filled with delightful little

Amazingly beautiful old city of Cáceres, now declared a World Heritage Site. Although its buildings date from different eras, they are strangely complementary and the overall cityscape is truly harmonious.

CÁCERES

squares, lovely churches and handsome palaces. The numerous tall towers and spires are crowned with stork's nests. The old walls are basically Roman, but have been augmented by the city's various rulers over the centuries.

The cobbled, partially arcaded Plaza Mayor, borders the old town and is the obvious place to begin your explorations. (Wear sensible shoes: the walk is not so easy.) Two Moorish towers stand in the square and the Arco de la Estrella gateway leads on to other areas of interest. The cathedral is Gothic and dominates other fine buildings in the Plaza de Santa Maria. Here, too, is the Episcopal Palace, decorated with engravings of the Old and New World. One intriguing site to visit is the Casa-Museo Yusuf Al Burch, an authentic re-creation of a 12th-century Arabian residence, and make sure you call in at the Provincial Museum. Housed in one of the great mansions and built over the water cistern of the original Moorish castle, it provides an excellent insight into various periods of the city's past. For the same entrance fee you can visit the Fine Arts Museum, where works are mostly religious, but there are items by the likes of Miró and Picasso. At the top of the hill of Caceres, the 16th-century church of San Mateo is a fascinating mixture of architectural styles.

For a good view back over the city, make the short trip out to the 17th-century shrine of the Virgen de la Montaña. It's only two miles to the east and the panoramas are excellent. One of the best day trips is to Trujillo, a 40-minute bus ride out towards Madrid. Although a 10th-century Moorish castle overlooks the town, Trujillo was actually built from the proceeds of the Spanish Peruvian conquests and is known as the 'Cradle of the Conquistadores'. If you have the time and the energy, other towns like Marvão and Abrantes are not short of appeal, while Mérida, 45 miles to the south, has some excellent Roman remains.

Make sure you are back in Cáceres for the evening, however. When darkness falls, you'll really feel you have stepped into another century.

Cáceres

Major Events

Festival of St Sebastian (late January): celebration at Acehuche (30 miles north), featuring the Carantoñas (men dressed in animal skins).

St George's Day (April 23): fiesta for the patron saint of Cáceres – processions, street parties and mock dragons.

Fera Nacional del Queso (late April–early May): week-long gourmet cheese festival at Trujillo.

Classical Theatre Festival (July and August): famous drama festival held at Mérida's stunning Roman theatre.

How to get there – and get around

By air: scheduled flights to Madrid (see p.219), or to Lisbon (see p.193); then train to Cáceres (4–5 hours), with more trains per day from Madrid. Bus or taxi from the station for the 2 miles into the old town.

Public Transport: Cáceres is easy (and best) to explore on foot, but buses and taxis are available. Trains and buses cover most towns in the region.

Suggested Hotels

Meliá Cáceres, Plaza de San Juan.
Tel: (927) 21 58 00 Fax: (927) 21 40 70
Sedate, 16th-century building offering excellent standards of service. Expensive.

Parador de Cáceres, Ancha.
Tel: (927) 21 17 59 Fax: (927) 21 17 29
Modern Parador, which means high levels of comfort. Expensive.

Extremadura, Avenida Virgen de Guadalupe.
Tel: (927) 22 16 00 Fax: (927) 21 10 95
Comfortable hotel close to the old centre. Moderate.

Suggested Restaurants

Atrio, Avenida de España.
Tel: (927) 24 29 28
The city's best-known restaurant, thanks to its imagination and ambience. Expensive.

El Figón de Eustaquio, Plaza de San Juan. Tel: (927) 24 81 94
Traditional Extremaduran cooking in the old part of the town. Moderate.

Bodega Medieval, Calle Orellana.
Popular, traditional bodega serving everything from tapas to à la carte. Inexpensive.

There is nothing more likely to antagonise a Gibraltarian than to be included in a chapter on Spain. Everyone knows that 'the Rock' is a British colony, but, armed with the excuse that this is a guide that uses country names geographically, rather than politically, we shall soldier on.

What's more, it is the very juxtaposition with Spain that makes Gibraltar so interesting. You need to appreciate life on either side of the frontier here in order to understand the contrasts: on one side, southern Andalucia, with its pesetas and paellas; on the other Gibraltar, with its pounds and fish and chips. British traditionalists who are not enthusiastic about 'foreign culture' will instantly feel at home in Gibraltar, but with the benefit of the Spanish sun warming their backs. For years, Spain sealed the border, prohibiting contact with the mainland. These days the crossings are open, but Gibraltar does also have its own airport, so you don't even have to enter Spain at all if you so wish.

History and Culture

As its nickname of 'the Rock' implies, Gibraltar is little more than a giant, rocky promontory, some 2½ miles square, at the point where the Mediterranean meets the Atlantic. It was captured by the British Navy in 1704, in the heydays of maritime conflict, and formally became a British colony in the 1830s. The people who inhabit the Rock are generally not of

One of the attractions of Gibraltar is St Michael's Cave, a cavern so big that it once convinced locals that the entire Rock was hollow. It is lit by green and red lights, with organ music adding fake atmosphere to the natural stalagmite and stalactite show.

GIBRALTAR

British stock at all, but local Spanish or Genoese, descendants of shipwrights who worked for the Royal Navy. But the way of life here remains defiantly British, with Bobbies on the beat, pints in the pubs, red pillar boxes, a Marks & Spencer store on Main Street and the Changing of the Guard at the Governor's residence several times a day.

Sightseeing

At the end of Main Street, near the Alameda Botanical Gardens, a cable car will take you up the mighty massif which, at 1,350 ft, towers over the streets and houses. From the top the views are marvellous: down over the town, across to Algeciras and Spain, or, on a good day, over to the Atlas Mountains in Morocco. (There are also boat services to ferry you across to Africa in one hour.) St Micheals Cave, a cavern so big that it once convinced locals that the entire rock was hollow, is lit by green and red lights, with organ music adding fake atmosphere to the natural stalagmite and stalagtite show.

The most famous inhabitants of the Rock are the tailless Barbary apes. The military presence in Gibraltar – the very reason for its existence in times past – is much more subdued these days, but, at the top of the Rock, you can visit the Upper Galleries – tunnels excavated by the British in the 18th century to create artillery positions. For the energetic, steps lead back down to the town.

On the eastern side of the Rock is the tiny village of Catalan Bay, a fishing settlement founded by the Genoese. Here there's a small but fine beach and a handful of pubs and restaurants.

Gibraltar is not brim-full of attractions: there is only a couple of days' worth of entertainment here, but it's one of those places – a real curiosity – that is great fun for a short break.

GIBRALTAR

Major Events

Annual Flower Show (late April): Gibraltar Horticultural Society's major event, in John Mackintosh Hall.

The Gibraltar Festival Plays (May): Celebration of dramatic arts, as well as dance and the Open Art Exhibition.

Religious and Ceremonial Celebrations (June): Corpus Christi Procession, 21-gun salutes for the Queen's Official Birthday, and the Ceremonial Guard Mount at the Convent, among others.

Gibraltar Regatta (late August): a water sport and social occasion.

Gibraltar Fair (early Sepember): annual crafts and goods fair, with entertainment.

How to get there – and get around

By air: scheduled flights to Gibraltar from Heathrow, Gatwick, Luton and Manchester (longest flight 2½hours). Taxis into town are frequent and reasonable.

Public Transport: Gibraltar being small, with narrow streets and steep gradients, taxis and hire cars are the only way to get about, but are fairly expensive.

Suggested Hotels

The Elliott Hotel, Governor's Parade.
Tel: 70500
Fax: 70243
Elegant hotel with a mix of old colonial ambience and modern facilities. Very expensive.

The Rock Hotel, Europa Road.
Tel: 73000 Fax: 73513
Lovely hotel with the best views in Gibraltar, looking out over the strait to North Africa. Expensive.

Caleta Palace Hotel, Catalan Bay.
Tel: 76501 Fax: 71050
Modern hotel with good facilities, overlooking a sandy beach. Moderate.

Cannon Hotel, Cannon Lane.
Tel: 51711 Fax: 51789
Small, homely hotel in the heart of the town. Inexpensive.

Suggested Restaurants

Both the **Elliott** and **Rock** hotels have high quality restaurants. Expensive.
Other interesting places to eat, all of which feature live music for some of the time, are:

Stakis Casino, Europa Road.
Tel: 76666. Moderate.

Minister's Restaurant, Main Street.
Tel: 41061. Moderate.

Dino's Piazza Grill, Main Street.
47780. Inexpensive.

Granada

The beauty, grandeur and atmosphere of Granada are much hyped, but, no matter how brightly the holiday brochures paint its picture, the city will not disappoint. It stands less than an hour away from the concrete blocks of the Costa del Sol, but belongs in another world. Nestled at the foot of the Sierra Nevada mountain range, this is a city that celebrates two cultures: primarily the Moors who lived here until the end of the 15th century, but also the Christians who replaced them.

History and Culture

Though Granada was founded back in the 8th century, and made capital of an independent kingdom by the Moors in the 13th century, one date stands out above all others in its long history: 1492. That was the year when the Catholic monarchs Ferdinand and Isabella reclaimed the city from the Moors and completed their Christian Reconquest of Arab Spain. Thankfully, they did not ransack the city's palaces, leaving us today a fascinating insight into life at the Moorish court through the unrivalled glory of the Alhambra.

Sightseeing

The Alhambra is not Granada's only attraction, but it might as well be for the thousands of tourists that pour in daily. To avoid the crush and some very long waits, head for the complex early, or leave it until late afternoon. If you can avoid the high summer, even better, but don't give Granada a miss simply because it's likely to be busy. It is too spectacular for that.

It's hard to believe that the Alhambra complex was used as a prison a couple of hundred years ago and was almost blown up by Napoleon's troops. It was established as a citadel in the 11th century but most of the exterior dates from the 13th–14th century. There are three sets of buildings, all ready to enthrall. The first is happily the least spectacular, whetting the appetite for the areas to follow. It is the Alcazaba, a military outpost with a watchtower that commands panoramic views of Granada and the mountains around. Next comes the Alcázar, the main palace. This is the undoubted highlight, so prepare to be impressed. Of particular note are the Sala de las Dos Hermanas, with an incredible honeycomb cupola made up of thousands of small cells, and the Patio de los Liones, so-named for the famous fountain at the centre. Yet the most sumptuous room is still to come. The Salón de Embajadores has walls covered with inscriptions from the Koran, ornamental motifs and brilliantly glazed tiles that glint metallically in the light. After such a show, the 16th-century Palace of Charles V, which houses two fine art museums, can only be a come-down, and deservedly so because Charles, grandson of Ferdinand and Isabella, destroyed a whole wing of the existing structure to build it. Further along is the Generalife, a comparatively simple building, but its fantastic gardens, stunning patios and relaxing pools and fountains are a revelation. Getting the water supply here from the River Darro was a remarkable engineering feet in itself.

In the city below, there are two major sights. The first is the Royal Chapel, which contains the tombs of Ferdinand and Isabella. Next door is the cathedral, mostly 18th-century in construction, but founded on a 16th-century base.

On the hill above Granada are the gypsy cave-dwellings of Sacromonte, where you can pay to hear and see the clatter and flurry of authentic flamenco. If you have a car, make sure you also take a drive up into the mountains. The Sierra Nevada is a major skiing resort in winter, but in summer you can weave your way up for a look at Spain above the clouds and some invigorating walks.

After dark, Granada buzzes into the night. The Alhambra is beautifully illuminated and, if you avoid the obvious tourist traps, there are some super tapas bars to be found, where for the price of a drink, and perhaps a little extra, you also get a small plate of imaginative savouries. Strolling from bar to bar on a balmy evening is an unusual and highly enjoyable way of taking your dinner.

PREVIOUS PAGE: The sumptuous interior of the Alhambra deserves to be one of the wonders of the world. The intricate decoration demands thorough exploration and the picturesque water gardens of the Generalife are a cool oasis on a hot Andalucian afternoon.

The most atmospheric part of Granada is the Albaicín quarter, clinging to the hillside opposite the Alhambra. Here the Moorish influence lingers on in a labyrinth of narrow streets, and there is an air of calm to contrast with the brashness of modern Granada.

Granada

Major Events

Holy Week (week before Easter): religious processions through the streets, with hooded penitents carrying huge crosses.

Música de los Mundos (April): world music event that celebrates the discovery of the New World by Columbus in 1492.

Corpus Christi (early June): pageant and procession to rival the Corpus Christi celebrations of Toledo and Valencia.

Festival Internacional de Música y Danza (mid June–mid July): world-famous festival in which many of the greatest performers play at the Alhambra and elsewhere.

Festival Internacional de Jazz (mid-November): annual jazz get-together.

How to get there – and get around

By air: scheduled flights to Madrid (see p219), then transfer to Granada Airport (50 mins). A shuttle-bus runs to Granada centre (25 mins) or there are cheap taxis. Alternatively, there are flights from even more UK airports to Malaga, where you can hire a car for the 100-mile drive to Granada.

Public Transport: Granada is easily walkable, but buses trundle up the hill to the Alhambra.

Suggested Hotels

Parador de Granada, Calle Real de la Alhambra.
Tel: (958) 22 14 41 Fax: (958) 22 22 64
One of the world's great hotels which has to be booked well in advance. Very expensive.

Alhambra Palace, Calle Peña Partida.
Tel: (958) 22 14 68 Fax: (958) 22 64 04
Mock version of the Alhambra itself: a luxurious hotel with amazing views. Expensive.

América, Calle Real de la Alhambra.
Tel: (958) 22 74 71 Fax: (958) 22 74 70
Very popular hotel, and not just because of its situation. Moderate

Suggested Restaurants

Cunini, Plaza de la Pescadería.
Tel: (958) 25 07 77
Excellent restaurant specialising in seafood. Expensive.

Ruta del Valeta, Carretera Sierra Nevada. Tel: (958) 48 61 34
Highly rated restaurant 3 miles outside the city, on the Sierra Nevada road. Expensive.

Mirador de Morayma, Calle Pianista García Carillo. Tel: (958) 22 82 90
Popular restaurant known for its Andalucian fare. Moderate.

JEREZ

There's an often-neglected corner of Spain that has a rich and proud history and such a pot-pourri of attractions that it makes you wonder why it's not yet on the main tourist trail. Strictly speaking, it is three separate areas – Sherry country, the Costa de la Luz, and the White Towns – but when combined, they conjure up a remarkably fulfilling short break. There are two main centres, Jerez and Cádiz, but this is very much a fly-drive trip, as you will need to get out and about to enjoy the area to the full.

History and Culture

Jerez is, of course, the home of sherry. Its reputation as a wine centre dates back to Roman times, but it is the trade's association with the British that has brought much of its kudos. British merchants showed an interest as early as the 12th century and, by the 19th century, had bought into the business, setting up the famous name bodegas that still operate here today. Cádiz, 15 miles to the south, on the coast, is famous for a quite different reason. Its roots go way, way back, probably well over 3000 years, but it was in the 15th-century that the city began to prosper, as an important port for trade arriving from the New World. It was here, in 1587, that Sir Francis Drake set fire to the Spanish fleet to prevent the Armada setting sail. Cádiz remains a naval port today.

Sightseeing

Though the city does have an 11th-century Arab castle and the remnants of ancient town walls, the most obvious reason for visiting Jerez is to explore the sherry bodegas. They are usually only open in the morning, and many close down in August. You should try to book your visit first.

West of Jerez is another sherry town, but on a much smaller scale. This is Sanlúcar de Barrameda, home of manzanilla sherry. Being out on a limb, it no longer attracts the crowds but it is a pleasant little town, with some decent beaches and, across the estuary, the marvellous Doñana National Park. Whilst in Sanlucár, try a chilled glass of manzanilla with some local seafood.

Cádiz has the air of a slightly run-down seaside town, but one that still has plenty of salty atmosphere. It is built on a narrow peninsula, at the gateway to a natural bay-harbour. The warren of narrow streets is a pleasure to explore, the two cathedrals both worth a peek, and don't miss the climb to the top of the Torre Tavira.

South east from Cádiz lies the so-called Costa de la Luz, a still remarkably unspoilt coastline, dotted with small tuna-fishing towns and fabulous sandy beaches. There are one or two modern developments springing up along the way, but the area is nothing like as commercialised as the Mediterranean *costas*. It was off the coast of Cape Trafalgar, along here, that Admiral Nelson was fatally wounded in 1805.

The little roads heading inland take you into the terrain of the Pueblos Blancos, the 'White Towns' which cling to many of the hilltops. In the scorching sunlight and against the clear blue sky, these untarnished settlements dazzle you with their brilliance. The roads linking them are spectacular, too, leading you up through wooded hills and down across hidden valleys, along rivers and past glinting lakes. One of the best-known of the Pueblos Blancos is Arcos de la Frontera, perched like the prow of a ship on a rocky pinnacle. Its strategic importance during the Moorish era, when it was one of the Muslim kingdom's frontier towns is still obvious. El Bosque is equally pretty, filled with flower boxes, while the best known small town in the area is Ronda, tucked away in the mountains above the Costa del Sol. A sheer gorge cuts right through the middle of this ancient market town, and the 18th-century bridge that spans it is a fine feat of engineering. Here, too, is a still-active bullring (said to be the birthplace of the purest form of bullfighting), and a well-preserved set of Arab baths. The remains of the original Roman settlement, including a theatre, can be seen 12 miles away.

The Gonzalez Byass bodega at Jerez, were the air hangs heavy with the aroma of evaporating wine. As in all local bodegas, don't expect to be led through dark cellars. Sherry needs to be exposed to the air to mature and so the wine casks, stacked three or four high, are stored in warehouses, instead.

The dramatic bridge the gorge at Ronda, one of Spain's major bull fighting centres. Actor and film-maker Orson Welles loved this old Andelucian settlement so much, that he requested that his ashes be buried at the home of his friend, matador Antonio Ordónez, on the outskirts of town.

JEREZ

Major Events
Carnaval (February): the biggest carnival in mainland Spain at Cádiz, to celebrate the end of winter and the coming of Lent.
Feria del Caballo (early May): Jerez's famous horse fair with prancing palaminos and colouful flamenco dancers
Manuel de Falla Classical Music Festival (June): special Cádiz festival in honour of the Andalucian composer who was born in the city.
Classical Music Festival (August): annual classic concerts held in Sanlúcar de Barrameda.
Exaltación al Río Guadalquivir (mid August): horse racing on the Guadalquivir estuary beach at Sanlúcar.
Fiesta de la Vendimia (early September): homage to the grape crops that help make sherry wine unique, at Jerez and Sanlúcar.

How to get there – and get around
By air: scheduled flights to Jerez de la Frontera International Airport (5 miles out) from Gatwick only (2 hrs 40 mins), then bus to Jerez (15 mins). Buses and trains link to Cádiz (45 mins), and buses run to Sanlúcar de Barrameda (1 hr).
Public Transport: Jerez, Cádiz and the other towns are easy to explore on foot. Reasonable bus and train services link Cádiz and Jerez, and the rest of Andalucia, but car hire is recommended.

Suggested Hotels
Parador Atlantico, Avenida Duque de Nájera, Cádiz.
Tel: (56) 226905 Fax: (56) 214582
Another classic Parador, gracing the old town of Cádiz. Expensive.
Royal Sherry Park, Avenido Alvaro Domecq, Jerez de la Frontera.
Tel: (56) 300600 Fax: (56) 305001
Evocative address on top of several bodegas, but no lack of class for all that. Expensive.
Los Helechos, Calle Madre de Dios, Sanlúcar de Barrameda.
Tel: (56) 361349 Fax: (56) 369650
Very popular hotel in the home of manzanilla sherry. Moderate.

Suggested Restaurants
El Faro, Calle San Félix, Cádiz.
Tel: (56) 211068
Atmospheric restaurant, specialising in seafood and regional cooking. Expensive.
La Mesa Redonda, Calle Manuel de la Quintara, Jerez de la Frontera.
Tel: (56) 340069
Pleasant little restaurant of high quality. Moderate.
Casa Bigote, Bajo de Guía, Sanlúcar de Barrameda. Tel: (56) 362696
Fresh fish and other seafood straight from the harbour. Moderate.

MADRID

SPAIN

If you're an art lover, or a party animal, Madrid is the place for you. The vibrant capital of Spain does not sell the holidaymaker short. There are at least half a dozen wonderful museums and galleries, and the nightlife is so lively that the midday siesta serves not so much to ward off the blazing sun, but to catch up on some desperately needed shuteye. Spend the days absorbed in the creative genius of the world's greatest artists, then join the locals for a round of tapas bars, restaurants and night clubs that pulsate until dawn.

History and Culture

Starting life as a Moorish city named Magerit, Madrid was still not much more than a modest provincial town when King Philip II made it his national capital in 1561. From its central position, he could rule all parts of the country. Occupied by Napoleon, Madrid rebelled, as it did for as long as possible against the Nationalist forces of Franco in the Spanish Civil War. Today, all roads lead to Madrid (they even have kilometre posts stating how far you are from the capital) and along these roads have come people from all parts of Spain, creating a fun-loving Spanish omelette of a city, ready to embrace novelty and adventure.

Sightseeing

Your daylight hours in Madrid should not be wasted. Every hour lost is an artistic masterpiece shunned. The of all the cultural attractions is the Prado Museum. Here the collection can only be truly appreciated if seen, but names like El Greco, Goya, Velázquez, Rubens, Bosch, Titian, Botticelli and Mantegna will surely whet the appetite. Cheekily positioned across the road from the Prado is the one-time private collection of a Swiss steel family at the Museo Thyssen-Bornemisza. It focuses primarily on German and modern art, and its stars are Paul Klee, Max Ernst and Hans Holbein, supported by a few Van Goghs, a Duccio or two and Caravaggios. For an even greater contrast to the majesty of the Prado, visit the Centro de Arte Reina Sofia, a former convent now a state-of-the-art gallery, where a bewilderment of pieces by the great surrealists assails the eye. Miró and Dali feature prominently, but the pièce de résistance is Picasso's shocking *Guernica*, his portrait of the Fascist destruction of that town during the Civil War. At this point, art fatigue may well be setting in, but there's more to come and it cannot be ignored. The Royal Academy of Fine Arts features classic items by Italian masters like Tintoretto, Veronese and Caravaggio, plus canvases by Rubens, El Greco and, especially, Goya, and there are yet more great works in the marvellously grand Royal Palace. After this, you can, at last, begin to think of other pleasures, but don't ignore the excellent City Museum, which chronicles the life and traditions of Madrid in attention-grabbing high-tech fashion.

For a restorative, head for the beautifully arcaded Plaza Mayor. They used to fight bulls here and, but today it is the home of café society, where rows upon rows of pavement tables demand that you take a seat, although less expensive refreshment stops can be found just around the corner. Those in dire need of open spaces will welcome Retiro Park. This is where the locals chill out, particularly on Sunday, when the whole family takes the air. Also on Sunday, pop along to the Rastro flea market to see the locals fighting for bargains. On other days, go to the opposite extreme and window shop at the chic boutiques of Calle Serano.

When the sun eventually goes down (the days are thankfully long here), those with enough energy can prepare for the nocturnal marathon. Restaurants serve late, so it's a question of joining the locals rather than beating them. The dining experience is excellent. Few cities can match Madrid for the diversity or quality of its restaurants, and the home of tapas serves up the tasty little snacks all day long. After dinner, if you want to act like a true Madridleno, visit a nightclub or – taking due care – just wander around for a few hours. No one seems to sleep in this town, not until lunchtime at least.

Horseguards at Madrid's splendid 18th-century Royal palace. Among its highlights are a music museum, containing Stadivarius violins, and the Royal Armoury. However it is wonderful artworks by the likes of Goya, El Grecco and Rubens that really place it on the tourist map.

Tapas bars, such as the one indicated in this mosaic sign, are fundamental to the Spanish way of life. The locals even have a name for the process of wandering from tapas bar to tapas bar in the evening: they call it *el tapeo.*

MADRID

Major Events
Cumbre Flamenca (April): top dancers from all over Spain indulge themselves at this festival.
Dos de Mayo (May 2): four-day celebration of an 1808 revolt against Napoleon's army of occupation.
Festival de San Isidro (mid May): open-air entertainment, costumes and bullfights (Spain's greatest) in honour of the saint.
Madrid Jazz Festival (October): one of Europe's best conventions.
New Year's Eve (December 31): ritual grape swallowing to the chimes of the clock in the Puerto del Sol.

How to get there – and get around
By air: scheduled flights to Madrid-Barajas Airport (8 miles out) from Heathrow, Gatwick, Luton, Glasgow and Manchester (longest flight 2 hrs 40 mins), then bus (30 mins; costing around SP360) or taxi (20 mins; SP1500) to the city centre.
Public Transport: Madrid has a good metro and bus network (single ticket SP 130; 10 tickets SP660 for both services, but the tickets are not interchangeable).

Suggested Hotels
Ritz, Plaza de la Lealtad.
Tel: (91) 521 28 57 Fax: (91) 532 87 76
Spain's most famous hotel, now returned to its pre-Civil War grandeur. Very expensive.
Palace, Plaza de Cortes.
Tel: (91) 360 80 00 Fax: (91) 360 81 00
Facing the Prado and pushing the Ritz very hard for exclusivity. Very expensive.
Reina Victoria, Plaza Santa Ana.
Tel: (91) 531 45 00 Fax: (91) 522 03 07
Famous hotel now associated with the world of bullfighting. Expensive.
Mercátor, Calle Atocha.
Tel: (91) 429 05 00 Fax: (91) 369 12 52
Comfortable hotel in the heart of old Madrid. Moderate.

Suggested Restaurants
Lhardy, Carrera de San Jerónimo.
Tel: (91) 521 33 85
Famous restaurant for over 150 years. Expensive.
Jockey, Amador de los Ríos.
Tel: (91) 319 24 35
Still one of the best restaurants in Madrid with a loyal clientele. Expensive.
Botín, Calle de Cuchilleros.
Tel: (91) 521 33 85
This claims to be the oldest restaurant in the world (dating from 1725). Moderate.
Teatriz, Calle Hermosilla.
Tel: (91) 577 53 79
Italian-style restaurant in interesting, theatrical surroundings. Inexpensive.

Palma's majestic cathedral illuminates at night. It is surrounded by a maze of small lanes and alleyways, which are fun to explore. Two chapter houses now serve as the cathedral's museum.

Palma de Mallorca

It's truly amazing, when you consider how many thousands of British holidaymakers wing their way to the island of Mallorca each year, just how few take the time to acquaint themselves with its capital city. Lost in a headlong rush for sun, sea, sand and everything else that begins with 's', they skip this lovely old city and head off down the coast. For a weekend break, however, Palma is the place to visit, thanks to its stylish shops, plethora of good restaurants and bars, and its historic architecture.

History and Culture

Palma was established by the Romans in the 1st century BC. Its wealth increased over the centuries till it was taken over by the Moors around the year 900 and then fell to Christians in 1229. The years that followed were prosperous and Palma merchants traded far and wide. It is still an important port city, even if the most obvious vessels are of the pleasure variety these days. Despite the package holiday boom of the past 30 years, which has turned the coastline around Palma into a concrete playground, the city itself remains thankfully unfazed and unscathed.

Sightseeing

The undoubted highlight of the city is the magnificent limestone cathedral, standing proud and pinnacled over a forest of palm trees at the water's edge. Surrounded by a maze of small lanes and alleyways, its origins lie in the 13th century, but it has been adapted over the centuries, including in the 20th century, when the Modernist architect Antonio Gaudí renovated one or two features and added his own distinctive touch. The church of San Francisco is another reminder of the city's Gothic past, while, in contrast, the Arab Baths offer an excellent chance to witness the once prevalent Moorish architecture. There are plenty of other historic buildings in the city centre, some of which, with their magnificent courtyards, can be visited, but just a mile or two to the west stands the even more impressive medieval Bellver Castle. Unusually circular in shape, from its towers to its turrets, the beautifully preserved, orange-gold-coloured fortress was once a royal palace, then a prison. The name means 'lovely view', self-explanatory when you stand on its terrace and look over the bay and city below. The fact

that such a fortified structure has existed in Palma reveals the strategic importance the Spanish have traditionally placed on the Balearic islands.

If you feel the urge to laze in the sun, there are a number of decent beaches on the fringe of the city. El Arenal is probably the favourite, but, if you prefer less commercial sands, jump on a bus and head for one of the quieter stretches of coast – there are still plenty to be found. From Palma, you can tour the entire island. To get as far away from the raucous tourist centres as possible, make for the north of the island, where mountains and forests shelter peaceful little coves and beaches, and orange and lemon groves fringe neat, unspoiled villages.

Back in the city, the nightlife is good – but you can have it loud or you can have it calm. As evidence of the latter, one of the most popular pastimes is the *paseo*, the evening stroll around the old streets. Locals pause for a chat; visitors stop for a drink or an ice-cream. The port area is particularly popular, a palm-shaded promenade alongside a sea of bobbing boats. In addition, there are plenty of good restaurants, in all price brackets, and, unlike in the popular resorts, not all of them are geared exclusively to tourists. To its great benefit, Palma is still a working city: the 300,000 people who live here need to relax, too, so there's much less commercialism to the catering.

Indeed, the city's individual, human face is one of its most endearing qualities, when you consider how other parts of this beautiful island have been fabricated and homogenised. And, if you come in the close season, when there are hardly any foreign tourists to be spotted, despite temperatures rarely dipping below 60 degrees, you'll see the locals come out to play and you'll find Palma becomes even more enjoyable.

Palma de Mallorca

Major Events

Fiesta de San Sebastián (January 20): classical music, drama and street theatre.
Palma Carnival (mid–late February): entertainment, processions and fireworks
Spring Opera Series (March–June): up to four different works are performed each year.
Summer Serenades (August): classical concerts at Bellver Castle.
The King's International Cup (early August): international sailing week, with King Juan Carlos usually participating.

How to get there – and get around

By air: scheduled flights to Palma de Mallorca Airport (7 miles out) from Heathrow, Gatwick, Luton and East Midlands (longest journey 2¼hrs), then by cheap bus or taxi to Palma (15–20 mins). There are also charter flights from other UK airports in summer.
Public Transport: Palma is best negotiated on foot, but adequate buses link the centre to suburban resorts like Magalluf and El Arenal, and to other parts of the island. However, for greater flexibility, car hire is advised.

Suggested Hotels

Arabella Golf Hotel, Vinagrella.
Tel: (971) 799999 Fax: (971) 799997
Exclusive, sporty hotel with golf, tennis and swimming. Very expensive.
Son Vida, Urb Son Vida.
Tel: (971) 790000 Fax: (971) 790017
Plush resort hotel in a rebuilt castle, 2 miles out of town. Very expensive.
Palas Atenea, Puerto Ingeniero Gabriel Roca.
Tel: (971) 281400 Fax: (971) 451989
Popular marina-side hotel on Palma's seafront. Expensive.
Saratoga, Paseo Mallorca.
Tel: (971) 727240
Air-conditioned rooms in a central hotel. Moderate.

Suggested Restaurants

Son Vida, Urb Son Vida.
Tel: (971) 790000
Hotel restaurant with an exceptional reputation. Expensive.
Porto Pí, Calle Garita. Tel: (971) 400087
Mediterranean cuisine at a popular restaurant. Moderate.
Ca'n Carlos, Calle del Agua.
Tel: (971) 713869
Well-priced Balearic menu. Inexpensive.

SAN SEBASTIÁN

San Sebastián's beaches are excellent, making it a huge draw in summer. However, despite its many efforts to attract the South of France jet set, San Sebastián remains much less snooty and noticeably more relaxed.

San Sebastián is prosperous, rather exclusive, but utterly beautiful, set around a picturesque, semi-circular bay, no more than a dozen miles from the French border. The city known as Donostia to the Basques is quite unlike many Spanish cities.

History and Culture

Once a confined old town, dedicated to whaling, deep-sea fishing and the tourist trade developed by the pilgrim route to Santiago de Compostela, San Sebastián really came into its own in the mid-19th-century, when someone recommended sea-bathing as a cure for the Queen of Spain's herpes. Whether it was successful remains in doubt, but the very fact that she graced the city with her presence gave San Sebastián new status among coastal cities. During the regime of General Franco, most of the government packed their bags in summer and left baking hot Madrid for the bracing breezes and golden sands of this Bay of Biscay resort.

Sightseeing

Take time to wander the streets of the old town. It is mainly 19th-century, but was rebuilt along older lines, after a devastating fire during a siege by the British, and it contrasts markedly with the wide, leafy avenues of modern San Sebastián. In this maze of small lanes, tiny darkened shops, arcaded plazas, and atmospheric bars can be found at every turn, and providing a tapas circuit for the locals every evening. Down at the port, market stalls tout seafood straight from local waters. The old town also features such fine churches as the 16th-century San Vicente and the beautiful, baroque basilica of Santa María del Coro. Behind San Vicente is the absorbing Museum of San Telmo, housed in a

former Dominican monastery, which exhibits archaeological finds and miscellaneous artworks.

At the far end of the quay are the Aquarium, with a tunnel for undersea viewing, and the Naval Museum. Above all this looms the wooded Monte Urgull. It is well worth the climb to see the rebuilt fort and to take in the magnificent views that are enjoyed by the giant statue of Jesus, which watches over the city. You could also make the greater effort to scale Monte Igüeldo, at the other end of the mile-and-a-half-long bay, past the best of the city's three beaches, the Concha, and the palace once used by Spanish royalty. The views are even better and, if the hike seems too daunting, there is always the funicular to grind you to the top. For a picnic, take one of the many boats which cross to the little island of Santa Chiara, standing proud in the middle of the bay.

Several venues host daily competitions of pelota – a sort of frantic squash involving wicker hand baskets. these help reinforce the concept that this is not Spain at all, but Basque Country, with a culture, language and heritage all of its own.

San Sebastián's restaurant scene is acknowledged as one of the best in Spain. Appetites whetted by the fresh sea air can be assuaged by some truly gourmet cooking.

For an excursion from San Sebastián, Bilbao is 50 miles east, along the coast. Although traditionally seen as an industrial port, the city has now brightened up considerably, through sparkling new buildings and parklands. It has an intriguing old centre and is one of the friendliest cities you are likely to encounter. One of the latest attractions is the excellent Guggenheim Museum.

San Sebastián

Major Events

St Sebastian's Day (January 20): noisy, 24-hr celebration featuring parades, music and feasting.

International Festival of New Music (March): celebration of contemporary sounds.

Jazz Festival (mid July): two weeks of all that's best in jazz

Semanas Grandes (early August): cultural and sporting events and Basque folklore

International Film Festival (mid September): one of the great European film festivals

Baroque Music Festival (November): music of the 17th and 18th century in concerts around the city

How to get there – and get around

By air: scheduled flights to Madrid (see p.219), then transfer to Bilbao (50 mins), and bus to San Sebastián (1 hr, costing around SP1000).

By car: ferries to Santander from Plymouth and Bilbao from Portsmouth (30–36 hrs), then by tolled motorway to San Sebastián (1–2 hrs).

Public Transport: San Sebastián has good buses and taxis' but most sights are within walking distance.

Suggested Hotels

Mariá Cristina, Paseo República Argentina.
Tel: (943) 42 49 00 Fax: (943) 42 67 70
San Sebastián's most exclusive address; the home of the International Film Festival. Expensive.

De Londres y de Inglaterra, Calle Zubieta. Tel: (943) 42 69 89
Fax: (943) 42 00 31
Famous, traditional hotel on La Concha beach. Moderate.

Monte Igüeldo, Paseo de Faro.
Tel: (943) 21 02 11 Fax: (943) 21 50 28
Overlooking the bay, with the best view in San Sebastián. Moderate.

Suggested Restaurants

Arzak, Calle Alto del Miracruz.
Tel: (943) 27 84 65
High on the gourmet's list of Spanish restaurants – although the specialities are Basque. Expensive.

Akelaré, Paseo Padre Orcolaga.
Tel: (943) 21 50 52
The combination of gastronomic and panoramic delights is irresistible. Expensive.

Cristina, Paseo República Argentina.
Tel: (943) 42 49 00
Elegant and impressive hotel restaurant. Moderate.

Santiago de Compostela has drawn pilgrims for over a thousend years. A statue of St James, flanked by two ornate towers, stands over the cathedral's 18th-century brocade facade.

Santiago de Compostela

Santiago may only now be finding its way into the tourist brochures, but foreigners have been flocking here for centuries. The city has been described as the third most sacred site in the Christian world, after Jerusalem and Rome, and yet, at times, it could be argued that it has meant more to the countless pilgrims who have made their way here than the two more famous Holy Cities. It's not been an easy place to reach (some might say that it still isn't). The pilgrim route has entailed crossing the Pyrenees and trudging through the dusty north of Spain to green Galicia on the Atlantic coast, but this has never daunted the devout, who have traditionally worn the seashell emblem of the city. With the benefits of modern transport, it certainly should not deter today's pilgrims, be they religious or otherwise.

History and Culture

Santiago translates as 'St James' and it is the apostle, or at least his remains, who has placed this city on the map. In the year 813, legend has it, a bright light led a local hermit to discover the body of the disciple in the countryside. The ground shone like a field of stars *(campus stellae* in Latin, hence 'Compostela'). Thirty years later, the saint rose up, mounted a white charger and led the Spanish Catholics into battle against the Moors. The news of such miracles quickly spread through the clerical world and Santiago became *the* place to visit. A cathedral was built in the 11th century to house the remains of the

saint, and monasteries flourished along the route to house the estimated half a million pilgrims Santiago was receiving every year. Today, Santiago is a university city, which guarantees a lively nightlife, and is the capital of the lovely province of Galicia.

Sightseeing

The cathedral must be, your first port of call. The apostle's crypt sits beneath the high altar. Whatever you do, don't miss the spectacular masses at noon on Friday and Saturday, when the massive incense burner – so big it needs eight priests to manoeuvre it – is dramatically swung above the heads of the congregation.

Outside, the square in front of the cathedral, the Plaza de Obradoiro, is a real stunner, but wonderful architecture abounds throughout this city. Just on the outskirts sits the fascinating little 12th-century church of Santa María del Sar, where the walls bizarrely taper in at the base.

Wonderful beaches can be found at Noia, an attractive small fishing village just one hour away by bus, while, in the other direction, La Coruña is a bustling old port. You may also wish to seek out the country's westernmost headland, Cape Finisterre. Its name translates as 'end of the earth'.

The proximity of the sea manifests itself in the seafood menus of Santiago's restaurants and the tapas in the bars of the old town, where the local wine is the order of the day.

Finally, although the city is likely to be at its busiest, try to squeeze in to witness the festivities staged for St James's Day on July 25. They are really something.

Santiago de Compostela

Major Events
Galician Folklore Festival (mid–late July): regional celebrations with music, dance, cinema, fairs and processions.
Fuego del Apóstle (late July): firework extravaganza preceding the festival of the patron saint and the Day of the Galician Homeland.
St James's Day (July 25): the cultural highlight, with the anticipation building for three weeks before; whenever 25 July falls on a Sunday (as in 1999), extra special celebrations mark the day.
International Music Festival (mid August–mid September): annual festival of concerts and recitals.
European Rendezvous on the Pilgrims Way to Santiago (mid–late October): celebration each autumn of the pilgrims' devotion.

How to get there – and get around
By air: scheduled flights to Santiago Airport (10 miles out) from Heathrow and, via Bilbao, from Manchester (2–2½ hrs). Alternatively, there are seasonal flights from Gatwick to La Coruña Airport (30 miles out). Reasonably-priced taxis are available to take you into Santiago from both airports.
By car: ferry from Plymouth to Santander, or Portsmouth to Bilbao (30–36 hrs) then by road (little motorway).

Public Transport: Santiago is easy to walk around, but buses and trains link the city with other major towns in the region. Car hire is recommended for greater flexibility.

Suggested Hotels
Reyes Católicos, Praza de Obradoiro.
Tel: (981) 58 22 00 Fax: (981) 56 30 94
One of the world's greatest hotels, this former hostel for poor pilgrims shares the square with the great cathedral.
Very expensive.
Los Tilos, Montouto. Tel: (981) 59 77 00
Comfortable, modern hotel just outside the city. Expensive.
Hostel San Francisco,
Campillo de San Francisco.
Tel: (981) 57 24 63 Fax: (981) 57 19 16
Former school for Franciscan monks near the cathedral. Moderate.

Suggested Restaurants
Reyes Católicos, Praza de Obradoiro.
Tel: (981) 58 22 00
The splendid hotel's restaurant does not disappoint. Expensive.
Toñi Vicente, Avenida Rosalia de Castro.
Tel: (981) 59 41 00
Highly thought of gastronomic experience.
Expensive.

SEVILLE

Seville is the classic southern Spanish city – colourful, historic and scorching hot in summer. For a short break, it is unbeatable: you really feel you have embraced another culture – in some ways another era – whilst only being a couple of hours away from the UK.

History and Culture

Seville owes its appearance and atmosphere to its chequered past. The Romans laid down the infrastructure that other civilisations built upon. The Moors came here from Africa in the 8th century and left an indelible mark that the Christians who followed in the 13th century could not wash off. There were New World influences, too. It was from Seville that Magellan set sail on his voyages of discovery, and to Seville that Columbus brought back treasures previously unknown. In later centuries, Seville fared less well. The decline of Spain as a world power was reflected in the city, and Seville also suffered an earthquake and some terrible floods. It has revived in the 20th century, however, and become a showpiece for the best southern Spain has to offer.

Sightseeing

The undoubted highlights of Seville are the enormous 15th-century cathedral and its graceful Giralda belltower. Inside the cathedral – one of the three largest in the world – are a massive carved wooden alterpiece, masterpieces by Goya and Murillo, and the tomb of Christopher Columbus. Alongside stands the Giralda, once a Moorish minaret, dating from the 12th century. If you have the energy, you must climb the belltower, not just for the views over the city, but also to see the broad, gentle ramps which take you to the top – wide enough to carry two men on horseback.

Opposite the religious centre is the Alcázar, or royal palace, inspired by Granada's Alhambra. It was here that Ferdinand and Isabella received Columbus after his expedition. While the exterior may look rather daunting, the interior rooms are surprisingly ornate, and the rambling gardens, are a pleasant retreat. A short stroll from the Alcázar takes you to the María Luisa Park and its Plaza de España, a semi-circular exhibition terrace. Wander around the intricate arcades, over the delicate bridges and feast your eyes on the busy blue and orange tilework.

Back in the centre, seek out the Hospital de la Caridad, a 17th-century structure with a series of arcaded courtyards and a fine collection of artworks. This was built by a repentant rake who, it is alleged, was the real-life inspiration for Don Juan, whose fictional story was set, like the operas *Carmen* and *The Marriage of Figaro,* in Seville.

After Madrid, Seville is Spain's biggest bullfighting centre. You may not want to witness the carnage, but a tour of the bull ring is an educational experience. The more artistically inclined will be keen to visit the Museo de Bellas Artes, which contains the next best collection of Spanish paintings after the Prado in Madrid, while the young at heart will want to seek out the new theme park, based on the discovery of the Americas.

When night falls, and the heat still refuses to subside, take a gentle stroll along the Guadalquivir river to view the famous Golden Tower, or among the narrow twisting streets of the flower-bedecked Santa Cruz quarter is one way of cooling down, especially if you stop at a bar for a drink and some tapas. The city bustles along late into the night, so don't expect a quiet evening, or an early dinner.

The Alcázar has been the seat of Seville's rulers since Roman times. The current structure, built on parts of the former Moorish palace, was constructed in the 14th century. Further extensions were added in Renaissance style.

The narrow, twisting streets of the old Santa Cruz quarter, close to the cathedral, are filled with flowers and the scent of orange blossom. It's a particularly atmospheric area to wander through in the evening, with some great tapas bars.

SEVILLE

Major Events
Semana Santa (late March to Early April): Easter celebrations with parades of religious images.
Feria de Sevilla (April): lavish and colourful processions carrying on from the Easter festivities – music, flamenco dancing, bullfights and fireworks.
Festival Internacional de Danza Sevilla (May): the annual festival of dance, set in the Roman ruins of Itálica, the birthplace of both Trajan and Hadrian.
Festival Internacional de Jazz (November): popular festival of all that's good in jazz from around the world.
How to get there – and get around
By air: scheduled flights to Seville San Pablo Airport (7 miles out) from Heathrow only (flight 2½ hrs). There are also flights to to Madrid (see p.219); then several flights daily to Seville (55 mins). Taxis to Seville centre take 12 mins; buses are frequent and take 20 mins.
Public Transport: the reliable buses cost around PTA120 per ticket, or PTA550 for 10. Taxis are quite cheap.

Suggested Hotels
Alfonso XIII, San Fernando.
Tel: (95) 422 28 50 Fax: (95) 421 60 33
Highly-regarded hotel of great tradition and style. Very expensive.
Colón, Canalejas.
Tel: (95) 422 29 00 Fax: (95) 422 09 38
Superbly situated and appointed hotel close to the Guadalquivir. Expensive.
Emperado Trajano, José Laguillo.
Tel: (95) 441 11 11 Fax: (95) 453 57 02
Hotel of some charm and quality near the central railway station. Moderate.
Doña Mariá, Don Remondo.
Tel: (95) 422 49 90 Fax: (95) 421 95 46
Modern, comfortable city-centre hotel. Moderate.

Suggested Restaurants
Egaña Oriza, San Fernando.
Tel: (95) 422 72 11
Andalucian meats and game feature here. Expensive.
El Burladero, Canalejas.
Tel : (95) 422 29 00
High class food in the elegant restaurant of the Hotel Colón. Expensive.
La Raza, Avenido Isabel la Católica.
Tel: (95) 423 38 30
Long-established restaurant specialising in seafood and local produce. Moderate.
El 3 de Oros, Santa Maria la Blanca.
Tel: (95) 442 27 59
Bar-restaurant serving traditional Andalucian cooking. Inexpensive.

TOLEDO

Toledo has changed little since the 16th century, the old town still surrounded by the moat-like River Tagus. Muslim, Christian and Jewish cultures have merged here over the centuries, leaving an array of architectural styles.

It is a sad fact of travelling life that you often have to scrape beneath the tacky commercial veneer of tourism to unearth the genuine beauty of a city. So it is to a degree with Toledo. There is an abundance of kitsch to be pushed aside to get to the soul of the place, yet enough of the real Toledo somehow immediately shines through. This is the city that the great El Greco chose to make his home in the 16th century. That says much about the character of the place. After all, what self-respecting Renaissance genius would want to live somewhere with nothing intriguing to paint?

History and Culture

Toledo has its roots in Roman times. In the 5th century, the Visigoths made it their capital, then the Moors took control in 712. However, it was under the Christians, who arrived in the 11th century, that Toledo enjoyed its golden era. As capital of Christian Spain until 1561, it grew prosperous and was revered throughout the country. Toledo has gradually declined in importance ever since.

Sightseeing

The moody Alcázar fortress, which towers over the city, has been rebuilt many times, most recently following the Civil War, when it was besieged and destroyed by Republican forces. It now houses a military museum, recalling the drama of those days in 1936. The magnificent cathedral is a wonder, 250 years in the making and an eye-grabbing collection of stained-glass, elaborate decorations and countless works of art. The highlight is the *Transparente*, around the back of the high altar, an extravagant baroque creation of paintings and marble sculptures. In the sacristy hang paintings by El Greco,Van Dyck, Goya and Velásquez, whilst in the treasury is a stunning 16th-century show of gold and silver, which is still paraded through the streets for Corpus Christi.

To the south is the old Jewish quarter, with two surviving synagogues. El Tránsito dates from the 14th century and houses a museum of Spanish Jewish culture. The other expresses the religious mix of Toledo's past. Dating from the 12th century, it looks like a mosque and has the seemingly paradoxical name of the Synagogue of Santa María la Blanca. All is explained by the fact that it was later converted to a Christian church, but with its historic layout largely untouched.

You must take in more of El Greco's work while in Toledo. His highly charged religious portraits and striking splashes of colour say much about the mood and spirit of the city he loved and the time in which he lived. The Greek artist's masterpiece *The Burial of Count Orgaz* can be found in the church of St Thomas, and other items can be viewed in the Casa del Greco, which was never actually his home but is now a museum dedicated to his life and work. In Santa Cruz, a 16th-century church-turned-hospital and now museum, there's another excellent selection of his canvases, along with notable artworks by other masters.

Although Toledo is only just over one hour from Madrid, and seems an obvious place to visit on an 'away day', don't skimp on your stay here.

One reason that it is included in this book as a short break in its own right is the pleasure that staying overnight here brings. Not only will it give you the vital time you need to explore all the city's secrets, but the evenings, free of tour buses, are a delight and allow you to fully savour the Toledo atmosphere. To see the baking sun rise and set over the rocky outcrop that the city calls its home, the skyline spires casting shadows over the warren of ancient streets, is a rare pleasure. El Greco lived here nearly 40 years; surely you can spare two or three nights?

Toledo

Major Events

Semana Santa (late March–early April): elaborate and colourful celebration of Easter, with a procession winding its way through the narrow streets.

Virgen del Valle (early May): local carnival, pageant and parades.

Semana Grande del Corpus (late June): one of Spain's most famous religious festivals, an amazing experience for all involved.

Fiestas Patronales (mid–late August): a week of celebrations in honour of the Virgen del Sagrario, with entertainments, bulls and fireworks.

How to get there – and get around

By air: scheduled flights to Madrid, then bus via Madrid centre (15 mins; costing around SP325), changing for Toledo (1 hr 20 mins; SP575). Alternatively, trains from Madrid to Toledo take 1½ hrs and cost SP615.

Public Transport: Toledo is a walking city, but buses link the old town to the rail and bus stations (about SP100). Taxis are scarce and expensive.

Suggested Hotels

Parador del Toledo, Cerro del Emperador. Tel: (925) 22 18 50 Fax: (925) 22 51 66
Wonderful hotel with unrivalled views of the city. Very expensive.

Alfonso VI, General Moscardó. Tel: (925) 22 26 00 Fax: (925) 21 44 58
Excellent, upmarket hotel in the old town. Expensive.

Hostal del Cardenal, Paseo de Recaredo. Tel: (925) 22 49 00 Fax: (925) 22 29 91
Atmospheric hotel, home to Toledo's archbishops of the past. Moderate.

Suggested Restaurants

Adolfo, Calle de Granada. Tel: (925) 22 73 21
Tagus trout and other local specialities are on offer in this authentic medieval setting. Expensive.

Hostal del Cardenal, Paseo de Recaredo. Tel: (925) 22 49 00
Good food from the archbishops' kitchen. Moderate.

Rincón de Eloy, Juan Labrador. Tel: (925) 22 93 99
Popular restaurant serving Castilian and international dishes.

VALENCIA

Valencia is a mostly modern city, and not, it must be said, particularly well planned – a legacy of negligent officials and wartime bombing. But this is the place to come if you like lush gardens, juicy oranges fresh from the tree, or a glimpse of the emotional works of Goya. Valencia is a city of contrasts. The ancient blue domes of churches fight for attention with ugly block developments, and baroque architecture in the old town is at odds with the functional structures of the newer quarters. It's also big, Spain's third largest city, and with size comes plenty of choice. As a weekend break, it offers a flavour of real Spain without a heavy tourist presence.

History and Culture

Valencia, like many Spanish cities, grew up under the Moors. These African Muslims dominated the city for 400 years, with the exception of the short period when El Cid recaptured it in the 11th century. The Moors set down the area's strong agricultural roots, and they can be thanked for the rice fields, which inspired the city's great contribution to the culinary world – paella. The Christians fought back and regained the city in the 13th century and Valencia has been one of Spain's most prosperous cities since.

Sightseeing

Valencia's old town is where the main sights lie, and it's compact and easy to explore on foot. The central square, Plaza de la Reina, is dominated by two towers: the baroque spire of the church

Valencia is the place to look in small stores for ceramics and authentic hand-painted fans, finely carved from bone or wood. However, there are also numerous high-class boutiques, for the fashion-conscious, and, at the other end of the scale, a daily flea market at Plaza Alfonso el Magnánimo.

of Santa Catalina and the octagonal Miguelete, which is the belltower of the cathedral – take a hike up the spiral staircase for the best city views. The cathedral itself is the cities most interesting building, a mixture of styles from Romanesque to baroque. Its museum houses a jewel-encrusted gold tabernacle, which is borne through the street for Corpus Christi, plus a prized ancient chalice, declared to be the Holy Grail, the cup used by Christ at the Last Supper. There are plenty of other fine buildings in the old town, including the Lonja de la Seda, which recalls the importance the silk trade once had in Valencia.

The city's most striking feature, however, are the amazing parklands that occupy the site once filled by the River Turia, which was largely diverted to prevent flooding. Here, the old river bridges cross over amusement areas and dense, copses of trees. The other garden you must see in the city is the Botanic Garden, home to more than 40,000 plants from all over the globe.

Across the 'river' is the Museum of Fine Arts, housing the works of Spanish masters. The IVAM modern art museum is also worth a visit, as is the Ceramics Museum, chronicling the history of the local craft.

Valencia's markets are as colourful as you would expect from an Iberian city and the shops reflect the city's status as Spain's design capital. After dark, the nightlife is as busy as you want it to be. There are plenty of quiet corners, if you need to relax after a heavy day, or you can join the locals who have a reputation for partying. The ultimate Valencian experience is to come for the Fallas celebrations in March, when bonfires and fireworks aren't the only things lit up.

Valencia

Major Events

Las Fallas (mid March): famous week-long festivities with parades, bonfires, fireworks, music and dancing – all celebrating the end of winter.

Corpus Christi (June): street processions with huge floats symbolising Biblical mysteries.

Feria de Julio (July): a month of open-air concerts, bullfights, dramatic presentations, parades, fireworks and a 'battle of the flowers'.

La Mostra de Valencia Cinema del Mediterrani (October): annual Mediterranean Film Festival.

How to get there – and get around

By air: scheduled flights to Valencia Airport (8 miles out) from Heathrow and Gatwick (longest flight 2¼hrs). Taxis to Valencia centre take 15 mins; cheaper buses are fairly infrequent and take 20 mins.

Public Transport: reliable buses within the town cost around PTA80 per ticket, or PTA550 for 10. Taxis are also quite cheap.

Suggested Hotels

Meliá Valencia Palace, Paseo de la Alameda.
Tel: (96) 337 50 37 Fax: (96) 337 55 32
Valencia's top hotel, overlooking the Rio Turia across from the old town. Very expensive.

Astoria Palace, Plaza Rodrigo Botet.
Tel: (96) 352 67 37 Fax: (96) 352 80 78
Luxury hotel in the heart of the old town. Expensive.

Reine Victoria, Calle de Barcas.
Tel/Fax: (96) 352 04 87
Good quality, central hotel with many facilities. Moderate.

Excelsior, Calle Barcelonina.
Tel: (96) 352 46 12 Fax: (96) 352 34 78
Comfortable, well-priced hotel in the old town. Moderate.

Suggested Restaurants

Meliá Valencia Palace, Paseo de la Alameda.
Tel: (96) 337 50 37
The most exclusive eating place in Valencia is at the best hotel. Expensive.

La Hacienda, Calle Navarro Reverter.
Tel: (96) 373 18 59
High standard Spanish and international cuisine. Expensive.

Les Graelles, Arquitecto Mora.
Tel: (96) 360 47 00
Quality international dishes. Expensive.

Rias Gallegas, Cirilo Amorós.
Tel: (96) 351 21 25
Comfortable restaurant with private dining rooms. Moderate.

GOTHENBURG

It is generally accepted Gothenburg is Sweden's prettiest and friendliest city. These are not its only attractions. Add in one of the biggest indoor shopping centres in Europe, the largest amusement park in Scandinavia and a fascinating maritime history, and the essential elements for a successful short break are in place.

History and Culture

Gothenburg, or Göteburg, as the locals know it, is the country's second city and was founded in 1619, using expertise from Dutch canal builders to overcome its marshy setting at the mouth of the River Göte. Linked to the capital, Stockholm, by the Göte Canal since 1832, it has become Sweden's gateway to mainland Europe. This southern part of the country originally belonged to Denmark, and other Swedes reckon you can still hear traces of Danish in the local dialect.

Sightseeing

Gothenburg isn't one of those hurry-up-or-you-won't-pack-it-all-in places. It is very compact, the public transport system is excellent and its attractions are extensive enough without being overwhelming. The excellent Art Museum, offers work by Impressionists, modern artists and Sweden's own greats. Equally enjoyable is the Röhsska Museum, depicting Sweden's lifestyle down the ages. More historic finds are displayed in the Stadsmuseum,

Gothenburg's harbour is full of interest, not least in its Maritime Museum, where you could easily spend a whole day looking over the 14 ships, boats and submarines – a combination of merchant and military vessels – which are moored up.

now housed in a building which was once the base of the powerful East India Company, which shipped goods in and out of the port.

Outside, Gothenburg appeals through its leafy streets, fine buildings and pleasant little squares. The main strip is the Avenyn, its pavements filled with bars and restaurants. Another popular place to eat and drink is Linnégatan, to the west of the city centre. The cobbled streets here are filled with crafts and antiques shops. In this neighbourhood stands Liseberg amusement park, offering entertainment for all in summer months, from white-knuckle rides to pleasant gardens.

For shopping, and Gothenburg has some excellent designer outlets, head for the boutiques of the Avenyn, or the giant Nordstan mall, an indoor retailing complex. Just off the Avenyn is Trädgårdsföreningen park, full of fragrance and birdsong.

Be sure to take a trip around the harbour. You can either pay for a tourist ride or simply jump aboard one of the public ferries. The views are terrific and you pass the 17th-century Nya Elfsborg fortress, guarding the entrance to the port.

Gothenburg is also a fine launching pad to other parts of southern Sweden. This end of the country is remarkably unspoilt. The city of Malmö is worth a pause, with a fine history museum and a moated 16th-century castle. Just a short hop over the water is the Danish capital of Copenhagen.

When it comes to nightlife, Gothenburg has plenty going on. For the culturally minded, there is the glorious waterside opera house, cleverly designed to resemble a ship, plus a concert hall and a theatre well worth visiting. The city's restaurants offer ethnic eateries dotted around the typical Swedish establishments. Here you can eat Dutch, Czech or Polish, if you prefer. It's just one of the reasons why Gothenburg is a major tourist centre.

GOTHENBURG

Major Events

Gothenburg Film Festival (end January–early February): celebration of Sweden's cinematic heritage.
International Science Festival (early May): spotlight on technology and inventions.
The Gothenburg Party (early–mid August): music, fireworks and general mayhem in the city centre.
Gothenburg Jazz Festival (late August): jazz jamboree with an emphasis on Trad.

How to get there – and get around

By air: scheduled flights to Gothenburg-Landvetter Airport (13 miles out) from Heathrow and Gatwick (2 hrs). Buses (taking 30 mins and costing around SKR75) run to Gothenburg centre. There are also taxis.
By car: ferries from Harwich (24 hrs) and Newcastle (23 hrs) to Gothenburg.
Public Transport: Gothenburg has an efficient tram, bus and local ferry network with interchangeable tickets (SKR16 single; SKR100 for 10).

Suggested Hotels

Sheraton, Södra Hamngatan.
Tel: (031) 80 60 00 Fax: (031) 15 98 88
Big and opulent: one of Sweden's finest hotels. Very expensive.
Mornington, Kungsportsavenyn.
Tel: (031) 17 65 40 Fax: (031) 711 34 39
Upmarket, popular hotel. Expensive.
Panorama, Eklandagatan. Tel: (031) 767 00 00 Fax: (031) 767 70 70
Well-appointed hotel, close to the city centre. Moderate.
Hotel Lorensberg, Berzelig.
Tel: (031) 81 06 00
Friendly place with unusual murals. Moderate.

Suggested Restaurants

Le Village, Tredje Långg.
Tel: (031) 24 20 03
Quality restaurant serving international cuisine. Expensive.
Kometen, Vasag. Tel: (031) 13 79 88
Traditional Swedish fare. Moderate.
GG12, Kungsportsavenyn.
Tel: (031) 10 58 26
Well-respected fish restaurant. Moderate.

Stockholm has a reputation for being the world's prettiest capital city, and it doesn't let you down. Built on a network of small islands, on the edge of the Baltic, it is also one of the world's most ecologically-conscious cities. If museums turn you on, Stockholm will keep you happy for weeks and in these, as in almost every aspect of Swedish life, quality shines through.

History and Culture

Stockholm owes its being to a certain Birger Jarl, who, in 1255, set up a fortress on one of the 14 islands that dot the coastline in these parts. By the 16th century, Stockholm was a growing power and eventually became capital of the Swedish Baltic empire, dominating trade throughout Scandinavia. The industrial revolution woke the city from a temporary doze and Stockholm has been the boiler house of Swedish prosperity ever since.

Sightseeing

Follow the natural geographic divisions – the various islands – to find the best sightseeing route. Gamla Stan is the old town, spread over three islands and combining medieval streets, Renaissance mansions and wealthy merchants' houses. The colourful façades and gabled roofs of Stortoget, the main square, provide an atmospheric introduction to the old town. In the streets around it is the city's prime church, the Storkyrkan, dating from the 13th century and fabulously ornate on the inside. Dominating the area is the old royal residence of Kungliga Slottet. Its baroque internal décor is an eye-opener, and it includes several museums.

Bear in mind that many museums are

Stockholm lives up to its reputation as the prettiest capital city in Europe. It is also one of the most environmentally-aware, with very clean waters around its bay and plenty of protected wilderness in and around the city.

STOCKHOLM

closed on Mondays, but don't miss the highlights like the Moderna Muséet, with a fabulous collection of modern art, and the National Museum, where Renoir, Rembrandt and others share the limelight. North of the centre, is the excellent Natural History Museum, and the Botanical Gardens are also worth a peek.

The island of Djurgården is the city's pleasure area, with a specially designated Eco Park. Development above or below the ground is already banned here for posterity. From the island's TV tower, the views help put the great buildings into perspective, while on the western side of Djurgården are yet more fascinating museums. Swedish life since the 16th century is chronicled in the Nordic Museum, and don't miss the Vasa Museum, featuring a 17th-century warship dredged from the mud in 1961. The nearby Water Museum is a high-tech complex that enables you to spend 24 hours in a rain forest and get close to marine creatures, while Skansen open-air museum consists of 150 historic buildings from all over the country, plus a large zoo, specialising in Nordic fauna. Pay the extra to visit the Aquarium, where macaws fly free.

The city also has a major opera house, made famous by the shooting here, during a masked ball in 1792, of King Gustav III, an act which inspired Verdi's opera *Un Ballo in Maschera*. More culture can be found over on the artsy island of Södermalm, just south of the old centre, where the atmosphere is particularly relaxed and galleries and cafés underline the unusual sophistication that this remarkable city calls its own. Relax here, then head back in town for a smorgasbord supper.

STOCKHOLM

Major Events
Stockholm Art Fair (mid March): post-1945 exhibits from galleries all over the world.
Popcorn Film Festival (late May–early June): film festival devoted to young film-makers.
Archipelago Fair (late May): floating boat market and a parade of sail
Restaurant Festival (early June): local restaurateurs provide food and entertainment in the park.
Stockholm Water Festival (early August): festival afloat, with restaurant marquees, music and dance, crafts and sport.
Advent in Stockholm (December): Christmas Market, Nobel Prize Day (the awards are announced here) and the Lucia Day processions and concerts.

How to get there – and get around
By air: scheduled flights to Stockholm-Arlanda Airport (28 miles out) from Heathrow, Gatwick, Stansted, London City and Manchester (longest flight 2 hrs 10 mins).Buses (taking 40 mins and costing around SKR60) and taxis (35 mins; SKR350) run to the city centre.
Public Transport: Stockholm's metro and bus services complement one another (single tickets SKR14; 72-hour tickets SKR120), and frequent, cheap ferries link the major islands in the archipelago. Taxis are expensive.

Suggested Hotels
Grand, Södra Blaiseholmshamnen.
Tel: (08) 637 35 00 Fax: (08) 611 86 86
Stockholm's premier hotel, with views of the water and royal palace.
Very expensive.
Scandic Hotel Slussen, Guldgränd.
Tel: (08) 51 73 53 00
Fax: (08) 71 73 53 11
Excellent hotel overlooking the water.
Expensive.
Reisen, Skeppsbron.
Tel: (08) 22 32 60 Fax: (08) 20 15 59
Long-time favourite on the waterfront in the old town, serving excellent breakfasts.
Expensive.
City Hotel Kungsgatan, Kungsgatan.
Tel: (08) 723 72 20 Fax: (08) 723 72 99
Comfortable, well-regarded hotel.
Moderate.

Suggested Restaurants
Den Gyldene Freden, Osterlänggatan.
Tel: (08) 24 97 60
Founded in 1722 and famous for its ambience and excellent Swedish dishes.
Expensive.
Ocean, Norr Mälarstrand.
Tel: (08) 652 40 90
Fashionable restaurant serving the best of new Swedish cuisine. Moderate.
Per Olssons, Grev Turegatan.
Tel: (08) 660 06 14
Acclaimed restaurant specialising in Swedish country cooking. Moderate.

The stunning scenery of the Bernese Oberland is typified by the view down this alpine valley from the Jungfraujoch railway. It's not a cheap thrill (the round trip from Interlaken will set you back around £70), and you have to change trains, but the experience is truly memorable.

BERNESE OBERLAND

The Bernese Oberland is the playground of the Alps. Getting out and about is the name of the game here – to hike along mountain trails, to ride cable cars to some of Europe's highest peaks, to take boats out onto stunning lakeland waters. The towns in the region mostly provide just the basics: hotels, restaurants and perhaps one or two modest attractions. Even Interlaken, the acknowledged capital of the area, has little to keep you anchored to base. But, with so much to see and do on its doorstep, that matters not in the slightest.

History and Culture

The Bernese Oberland, an area squeezed between the Aare and the Rhône rivers, has become a holidaymaker's mountain paradise. The major town, Interlaken, is situated on a bridge of land between two major lakes, Lake Thun and Lake Brienz, hence its rather blunt, descriptive name. It began life in 1130, as a village surrounding a monastery. The monastery has long gone, but the 35-acre meadow that once formed part of its grounds has been left undeveloped so as not to obscure the magnificent view of the mighty Jungfrau and its neighbouring peaks.

Sightseeing

Interlaken's own attractions can be summed up in one short list: a cheese farm, an elegant casino-cum-concert hall and some neat old buildings. The adventure begins when you leave Interlaken for your day trips.

By far the most popular excursion is the two-and-a-half hour train journey to Jungfraujoch, the highest railway station in Europe, at well over 11,000 feet. Closer to Interlaken, the alpine air can be taken via the funiculars

which winch you up to Harderkulm (4,300 feet) and Heimwehfluh (2,200 feet). Alternatively, catch a train to Wilderswil for the rack railway to Schynige Platte. There's an excellent alpine garden at the 7,000-foot summit.

For a more relaxed afternoon, take one of the steamers onto the lakes. They have restaurants, bars and sun decks, so you can grab a bite to eat, sip a drink and catch a few rays while ogling the unrivalled mountain scenery. The boats will also ferry you to the dramatic cliff caves at Beatushöhlen, where St Beatus's ancient cell can be found, and to the castles at the towns of Spiez and Thun.

Make sure you take the bus ride to the town of Lauterbrunnen, nestled in a U-shaped valley, to see the amazing Trümmelbach waterfalls, which deafeningly cut their way through the inside of a mountain face. Follow the galleries and take the underground funicular to see the water at its most majestic. The falls are at their most powerful when the snow above melts in May or June.

Whichever way you turn from Interlaken, you will be spoilt for scenery, but the young at heart can step on the adrenaline and try some wilder activities. Everything from mountain biking, paragliding and bungee jumping to river rafting, windsurfing and ice climbing can be attempted in the Interlaken area, plus some of the world's best skiing in winter.

After an exhilarating day, the modest pleasures of the little town seem very appropriate, as you wind down over a drink on a café terrace or a warming meal in one of the little restaurants.

Bernese Oberland

Major Events (all Interlaken)
Folklore Music Days (April): celebration of alpine folklore each spring.
William Tell Open-Air Theatre (June–September): traditional *al fresco* rendering of Schiller's classic play, performed regularly since 1912.
Interlaken Music Festival (mid August): high-class guest performers grace this annual festival of orchestral concerts.
Federal Folklore Festival (September): Swiss national festival of folklore.

How to get there – and get around
By air: scheduled flights to Berne-Belp Airport from London City Airport only (2 hrs), then bus to Interlaken (40 mins). Alternatively, there are scheduled flights to Zürich-Kloten Airport (see p.247). Trains from Zurich Airport to Interlaken take 2½ hrs (but the scenery is wonderful).
By rail: Eurostar to Paris Gare du Nord then change to Gare de Lyon for the TGV to Berne. Change at Berne for Interlaken East station (total journey 9 hrs).
Public Transport: Interlaken is easy to get around on foot. Buses and taxis are available for outlying areas whilst trains, cable cars, funiculars, coaches and lake ferries link other centres in the Bernese Oberland, and car hire is a sensible option.

Suggested Hotels (all Interlaken)
Victoria-Jungfrau, Höhewig.
Tel: (033) 828 28 28 Fax: (033) 828 28 80
Plush Victorian-style grandeur, with an excellent indoor pool/spa and views of the famous peak. Very expensive.
Beau Rivage, Höhewig.
Tel: (033) 821 62 72 Fax: (033) 823 28 47
Traditional Grand Hotel with an indoor pool and sauna. Expensive.
Interlaken, Höhewig.
Tel: (033) 826 68 68 Fax: (033) 826 68 69
Fifteenth-century hotel, now carefully restored, near the 'East' railway station. Moderate.

Suggested Restaurants (all Interlaken)
Stellambiente (Hotel Stella), General Guisanstrasse. Tel: (033) 822 88 71
International gourmet cuisine with surprise menus. Expensive.
Neuhaus, Seestrasse.
Tel: (033) 822 82 82
Situated on Lake Thun and famous for its big fish buffet. Moderate.
Brasserie 17, Rosenstrasse.
Tel: (033) 822 32 25
International dishes, plus live music Thursday evenings, September–June. Inexpensive.

GENEVA

It may not be the capital city, but Geneva is the place most outsiders associate with Switzerland. No doubt the high international profile it has adopted is largely responsible. Here the Red Cross was founded and the League of Nations had its headquarters. This 'internationalism' provides the focus for the city's tourist trade, combined with Swiss staples like clock- and watchmaking and the legacy of the Reformation. The stunning beauty of Lac Léman seems almost an afterthought.

History and Culture

Geneva was a late-comer to the Swiss Confederation, having been previously part of France and only signing up in 1815, following the demise of Napoleon. Previously, Geneva had enjoyed a schizophrenic past. For centuries, it was a focal point for liberalism, then, in the mid 16th century, the tide turned and the Reformists took hold. The fiery John Calvin took control, imposing religious rectitude on the citizens. In the 18th century, Geneva became an intellectual centre, with thinkers like Rousseau and Voltaire making the city their home.

Sightseeing

To get a feel for this beautiful city, let the River Rhône do its job and split the centre into two. On the right bank (the north) can be found the great international institutions. In 1863, Henri Dunant, sickened by the brutality handed out to war prisoners and the wounded, founded the Red Cross in Geneva. Its museum contains a deeply moving exhibition of the organisation's sterling humanitarian work. Not far

Lac Léman (Lake Geneva) and the spectacular Jet d'Eau fountain, which shoots 130 gallons of water into the sky every second, to a height of 470 feet. On hot days, you can cool off under its gentle spray.

away is the Palais des Nations, built in the 1930s to house the League of Nations, the forerunner of the United Nations, which has its European headquarters in the building today. Guided toursare available.

On the left bank, south of the river, is the Jardin Anglais, noted for its clever floral clock with, at the end of a nearby pier, the spectacular Jet d'Eau fountain. Moving inland from the glorious lakeside, you encounter the old heart of Geneva, the medieval town of rising, cobbled streets and pretty squares. In the 15th-century Hôtel de Ville, the first Geneva Convention was signed in 1864. Adjacent are the old arsenal and the 12th-century Maison Tavel, an excellent museum covering local life in the 14th–19th centuries.

The mark of the Reformists can be seen in the Gothic cathedral, which was stripped of its finest adornments. The 157-step spiral staircase leads up to one of the best views over the old town, while down below, catwalks allow you to wander above some interesting early excavations. The Art and History Museum's prize exhibits are masterpieces by Hodler and Witz. Look in the Petit Palais to see works by Cézanne, Renoir and the Surrealists. The Watch and Clock Museum traces the history of chronological craftsmanship.

Before you leave, walk past the Reformation Monument, and the gaze of Calvin, Knox, Bèze and Farel, the four most zealous preachers from this sombre phase of Geneva's history. Then return to enjoy the bars and cafés of the old town, as well as the many multi-cultural restaurants that prove that delightful Geneva has no intention of losing its reputation as a truly international city.

Geneva

Major Events
International Motor Show (mid March): famous annual exhibition.
Fêtes de Genève (early August): shows, concerts, parades, fairs and fireworks along the lakeshore.
La Batie Festival of Genèva (September): concerts, theatre and dance.
International Music Competition (mid September – early October): annual contest for vocalists, cellists and flautists.
Feast of the Escalade (December): processions and dancing to commemorate the unsuccessful storming of the ramparts by the Savoy army in 1602.

How to get there – and get around
By air: scheduled flights to Geneva International Airport (3 miles out) from Heathrow, Gatwick, Luton, London City and Manchester (longest flight 2 hrs 10 mins). Buses (10 mins; around CHF 2.20), trains (7 mins; CHF4.50) and taxis (10 mins; CHF30) run to the city centre.
By rail: Eurostar to Paris Gare du Nord. Cross to Gare de Lyon for TGV to Lyon and then change for Geneva (total journey 8–9 hours).
Public Transport: Efficient trams and buses (but complicated ticketing, costing from CHF 1.50 for 30 mins to CHF 8.50 per day for unlimited travel in all zones). Taxis are good but expensive.

Suggested Hotels
Le Richemond, Jardin Brunswick.
Tel: (022) 731 14 00 Fax: (022) 731 67 09
In a city of classy hotels, this is just about the tops. Very expensive.
Beau Rivage, quai du Mont Blanc.
Tel: (022) 716 66 66 Fax: (022) 716 60 60
Also on the Right Bank, this pushes the Richemond all the way for exclusivity and luxury. Very expensive.
Du Midi, place Chevelin. Tel: (022) 731 78 00 Fax: (022) 731 00 20
Popular hotel in the city centre. Expensive.
Strasbourg-Geneva, rue J-J. Pradier.
Tel: (022) 906 58 00 Fax: (022) 738 42 08
Comfortable and accessible hotel, close to the railway station. Moderate.

Suggested Restaurants
The two 5-star hotels listed above have wonderful, but very expensive restaurants. Other suggestions:
Le Béarn, quai de la Poste.
Tel: (022) 321 00 28
Exquisite, yet tiny, restaurant on the Left Bank. Expensive.
Les Armures, rue du Puits-St-Pierre.
Tel: (022) 310 34 42
Good Swiss specialities, indoors or out in the neat alleyway near the cathedral. Inexpensive.

The Château St-Maire, near the cathedral in Lausanne. It was once a fortified bishop's residence (15th–16th century) and is now the seat of the local government. Parts are open to the public.

Lausanne

Lausanne is far from being the obvious place in Switzerland to choose for a short break. But that's why it's so appealing. For a taste of real Switzerland, Lausanne has it all – a medieval old town, plenty of examples of efficient Swiss modernity and, above all, stunning views of lake and moutain.

History and Culture

Lausanne is built on two levels on the banks of Lac Léman (Lake Geneva). The old town is perched on the higher part; the lower lakeside area, today called Ouchy, was initially just a fisherman's hamlet. Religion has shaped this city in big ways. Initially Catholic, Lausanne was completely absorbed by the Reformation, which led to the loss of many of its earliest places of worship. In the 18th and 19th centuries, it became a centre for enlightenment, attracting a literary circle which reads like a *Who's Who* of great scribes: Voltaire, Byron, Rousseau and Victor Hugo. Lausanne has become the home town of the International Olympic Committee.

Sightseeing

Parts of the old town were lost in the 1940s and 1950s, as the city authorities sought to improve and sanitise the most run-down areas. However, enough remarkable medieval streets remain to convince the visitor he has stepped back to another time. The traffic-free narrow lanes, red rooftops and bulging flower boxes set the scene for an atmospheric

stroll. Here, in the old sector, is Switzerland's prize cathedral, the 12th-century Notre Dame. It's the best-preserved Gothic building in the country but, thanks to the reforming Protestants, the interior is not as sumptuous as it used to be. Some terrific features do remain, though, such as the harmonious rose window. The cathedral's steeple not only offers magnificent views, but is also still used for the medieval tradition of calling out the hours during the night-time 'watch', performed between 10pm and 2am.

The Historical Museum, housed in the old bishop's palace in Cathedral Square, includes a scale model of the old city. Adjoining the same square is the cobbled place de la Palud, surrounded by an arcaded Renaissance town hall and other fine old structures, including a clock with moving figures that spring to life every hour.

One of the city's more unusual exhibits is the gallery founded by artist Jean Dubuffet, which he devoted to the works of unprofessional, untrained painters, criminals and even the mentally insane.

To descend to Ouchy and the lakeside, take what is known here as the Metro. It's actually a funicular and it saves a demanding hike. Down at the shore, the usual water-based activities can be enjoyed, although there's pleasure enough in wandering along the Mediterranean-style quays. Down here, too, is the modern Olympic Museum. Along with a history of the Olympic movement and the games themselves, it houses audio-visual displays, robotics and a wealth of Olympic memorabilia.

Just across the water of Lac Léman sits the city of Montreux, famed for its television festival and annual jazz event. You'll struggle to find a room in Montreux when the jazz is in full flow (July), so Lausanne, just an hour and a half's cruise away, is the perfect alternative.

LAUSANNE

Major Events
Cully Jazz Festival (late March): annual event staged in the wine cellars and other village venues six miles from the city.
Fête du Soleil (late April): Lausanne's Carnival.
Fête à Lausanne (late June): colourful celebrations in the heart of the city.
Festival de la Cité (early July): Lausanne's major festival with 250 free events held over a week.

How to get there – and get around
By air: scheduled flights to Geneva International Airport (26 miles west);see p.240. Trains run every 30 mins to Lausanne (taking 50 mins) and cost around CHF20.
Public Transport: Lausanne has a good network of buses, trams and the funicular 'Metro'. Tickets, from slot machines, cost upwards of CH1.30 per journey. Taxis are fairly expensive.

Suggested Hotels
Beau-Rivage Palace, place du Port. Tel: (021) 613 33 33 Fax: (021) 613 33 34
Wonderfully luxurious hotel on the edge of the lake. Very expensive.
Royal-Savoy, Avenue Ouchy.
Tel: (021) 614 88 88 Fax: (021) 614 88 78
Distinguished hotel halfway between the old town and the lake. Expensive.
Victoria, Avenue de la Gare.
Tel: (021) 320 57 71 Fax: (021) 320 57 74
Good quality hotel close to the station. Expensive.
Régina, Grand-St-Jean.
Tel: (021) 320 24 41 Fax: (021) 320 25 29
Comfortable, centrally-situated hotel. Moderate.

Suggested Restaurants
Beau Rivage Palace, place du Port.
Tel: (021) 613 33 33
The renowned hotel is equally noted for its food. Very expensive.
La Résidence, place du Port.
Tel: (021) 613 34 34
Gourmet restaurant in lavish surroundings. Expensive.
Auberge du Lac de Sauvabelin, Pinte à Fromage. Tel: (021) 647 39 29
Haven of calm on a small forest lake, 5 min from the centre. Moderate.
Au Couscous, Rue Enning.
Tel: (021) 312 20 17
North African, vegetarian and international fare. Moderate.

SEPTEMBRIS
SACRAMENTI FIDEM
CECIDERUNT
SOLERTI AMICORUM CURA
XVI.
DUCES
XVI.
ERLACH.SALIS-ZIZERS.
VVILD.CASTELBERG
ERNEST.FORESTIER
WALTNER.I.MAILLARDOZ.MULLER.
CAPREZ.ALLEMANN.
CIRCITER DCCLX.
H.SALIS-ZIZERS.DURLER
E.ZIMMERMANN.REPOND
DELUZE.A.ZIMMERMANN.
LACORBIERE.
FORESTIER
MILITES CIRCITER

Lucerne

Lucerne – or Luzern, as its native German speakers prefer to call it – is no great secret. Cosily snuggled in the middle of Switzerland, it has become something of a crossroads for tour buses. But there is more to Lucerne than its geographical convenience: it is an historically intriguing city in one of the most glorious settings you could hope to find. With time at your disposal, the city will leave a rather more favourable memory than the of Swiss folk artificial culture with which most travellers depart.

History and Culture

Lucerne may a tourist hub today, but it's always been a rendezvous for travellers and merchants. For centuries, it has been the main commercial centre in Central Switzerland, dominating the route north from the Gotthard Pass, a vital trading route through the Alps. It hugs the north-western shore of a stunningly blue stretch of water known popularly as Lake Lucerne, but locally as the Vierwaldstättersee, or 'lake of the four forest cantons'. The name refers to the four historic cantons of Switzerland that surround it, and which formed the heart of the Swiss Confederation. The city has always prospered from this strategic position, as can be seen on a walking tour of the centre, where many fine medieval structures still exist.

Sightseeing

A wander around the old town (Altstadt), inevitably focuses on the rushing River Reuss, which cuts through the heart of the city on its way to the lake. A number of old bridges pass over the river, most famously the 14th-century Kappellbrücke, or chapel bridge. At the southern end of the bridge is the Jesuit Church, with a cheerily ornate baroque interior in pink and white. East of the river, near the lakeshore, stands the city's landmark church, the Hofkirche, its graceful twin spires stretching high above the old city skyline. It is home to a world-famous, 4,950-pipe organ. Close by, tucked away in some unpromising backstreets, is the city's Löwendenkmal, or Lion Monument, an enormous rock carving depicting a weeping, dying lion, symbolising the Swiss soldiers who were killed protecting Marie Antoinette in Revolutionary Paris. Also near here is the Panorama, an impressive 360-degree battle scene from the 19th century.

On the cultural side, Lucerne has several good museums, among them the Wagner Museum. It was here that the German composer wrote *Siegfried* and *Die Meistersänger*. For those interested in the renowned technological expertise of the Swiss, a visit to the Verkehrshaus is essential. This transport museum – described as a 'theme park' by the tourist office – has fascinating exhibits, from steam trains to space travel.

As if the town itself was not appealing enough, the greatest joy of a visit to Lucerne is to take advantage of its position, at the gateway to the Swiss Alps. A relaxing cruise on the lake brings home the power of the surrounding mountains, at least one of which must be climbed to make the visit complete. Not that there's a great deal of climbing involved: cable cars and cog railways take most of the strain. Most popular is Mount Pilatus, reputedly haunted by the ghost of Pontius Pilate. Taking the boat over to Alpnachstad, and joining the cog railway, allows you to savour the stunning views from the summit. Another option is Mount Rigi, the 'Queen of the Mountains', while a third is Mount Titlis. An hour's train ride from Lucerne takes you up into the beautiful monastery village of Engelberg, from where a series of cable cars lifts you 10,000 feet to the snowy summit of Mount Titlis, the last car revolving as it is rises to ensure everyone sees the unfolding alpine panorama. On a clear day, you can make out the Matterhorn and the Jungfrau peaks. At the top, take a chilly walk inside a glacier, or pop outside for a quick snowball fight or a spot of inner-tube tobogganing. Inevitably, the tourist buses will also be there, but as in Lucerne, they don't hang around too long and you should soon have the place more to yourself.

PREVIOUS PAGE. Lucerne's Lion Monument is a giant rock carving of a weeping, dying lion. It symbolises the Swiss soldiers who were killed trying to protect Marie Antoinette in Paris during the French Revolution.

The famous covered wooden bridge, the Kappellbrücke, in Lucerne was, sadly, devastated by fire in 1993 but has been sensitively, if not quite invisibly, restored. To its left can be seen the octagonal old city Water Tower.

Lucerne

Major Events
Luzerner Fasnacht (mid February): Mardi gras-type carnival with street processions and entertainment to celebrate the onset of Lent.
Osterfestspiele (late March): Easter festival of music and processions.
International Festival of Music (mid August–mid Sepember): famous since 1938 and the days of Toscanini, and for its Wagnerian undertones.
Lucerne Blues Festival (mid November): annual gathering of the best in jazz-blues-soul.

How to get there – and get around
By air: scheduled flights to Zürich Airport (see p.247). Trains from Zürich Airport, changing at Zürich central station, for Lucerne take 1hr 20 mins.
Public Transport: Cheap bus/tram services radiate out from and along the lakeshore. Daily tickets cost CHF10; 3-day tickets (hotel guests only) cost CHF8.

Suggested Hotels
Grand Hotel National, Haldenstrasse.
Tel: (041) 419 09 09
Fax: (041) 419 09 10
Stately hotel offering the greatest comforts, overlooking the lake and adjacent to the casino. Very expensive.
Des Balances, Weinmarkt. Tel: (041) 410 30 10 Fax: (041) 410 64 51
Popular lakeside hotel, formerly the Town Hall, near the Kapellbrücke. Expensive.
Anker, Pilatusplatz. Tel: (041) 210 30 76 Fax: (041) 210 24 55
Comfortable, quiet hotel near the railway station. Moderate.

Suggested Restaurants
Des Balances, Weimarkt.
Tel: (041) 410 30 10
Hotel restaurant, specialising in Swiss cuisine, in atmospheric surroundings. Expensive.
Schiffrestaurant Wilhelm Tel, Landungssteg (pier Schweizerhof).
Tel: (041) 410 23 30
Restaurant afloat, with lovely lake and mountain views, blending Swiss and oriental styles. Moderate.
Restaurant Reussbad, Brüggligasse.
Tel: (041) 240 54 23
Traditional fish restaurant in a quiet setting near the river. Moderate.
Han, Carlton-Tivoli Hotel, Haldenstrasse. Tel: (041) 410 77 00
Mongolian barbecue in the Carlton-Tivoli hotel. Moderate.

The quaysides of lovely Lake Zürich are super places to stroll around and cool off. Fine old guild-houses and well-tended gardens line one side, while small boats bob around at their moorings on the other.

Zürich comes as a surprise. Despite its stern reputation as one of the world's major financial centres, it has all the attributes needed to charm visitors – a setting on the shores of Lake Zürich surrounded by mountains, some delightful old squares and buildings, and plenty of chic shops and restaurants. One of its greatest assets may be that it seems so untouristy, and perhaps the cost of living here helps explain why. But there are reasonably priced places to stay and eat and, if you shop wisely, it needn't break your bank.

History and Culture

Zürich has developed mostly in the last 200 years. In the early 1800s, its population numbered less than 20,000; today, a third of a million inhabitants make it the largest city in Switzerland. Its wealth has been built on machinery, electrical goods and banking. It may not be the capital any longer, but it is certainly the financial heart of this prosperous country.

Sightseeing

For evidence of the money that floats around in these parts, take a stroll down leafy Bahnhofstrasse, the stateliest street in town. The prices may prevent you from crossing any thresholds, but the window shopping is great. Cheaper pleasures can be found along the quaysides, and on the Quaibrücke, the river bridge closest to the lake. A wander through the pedestrianised streets and intimate squares of the medieval old town is equally enjoyable, especially in the evening, when the many bars and cafés come to life.

Among the main attractions are the fine Fraumünster church, with a neat copper spire and five outstanding

Zürich

stained-glass windows by Marc Chagall, the Romanesque cathedral whose stark twin towers offer splendid city views, and the 13th-century Peterskirche. You can't miss it's 16th-century clock, the largest in Europe, at 28 feet across.

The city has a very decent Fine Arts Museum, including works by such luminaries as Picasso and the Impressionists, and also worth a look is the Swiss National Museum. This traces local life from the year dot to present day. A short walk away is the city's highest spot, Linderhof. This wide terrace of lime trees overlooks the River Limmat, which splits Zürich in two. It's popular with locals who come to grapple with the three giant chess sets. One attraction not to be missed, is the Lindt Chocolate Factory. It's only open Wednesday–Friday, but there are free samples at the end.

Boat trips will take you out onto Lake Zürich and to the little villages hugging its shoreline. The more energetic can take the Uetliberg Railway up to Uto-Kulm (2860 feet), from where there's a memorable view of the city, lake and – in the distance – Alps, and then begin a mountain walk.

You can also take the train to the independent principality of Liechtenstein, sandwiched between Switzerland and Austria, less than two hours to the east. A local bus completes the journey over the border. The two-street main town of Vaduz is a tourist trap in every sense, but, if you want your passport franked with another new country, or wish to add a few exotic stamps to your collection, the trip will be well worthwhile.

Zürich is not short of excellent restaurants. You can try the rather hackneyed local fondues, if you wish, or indulge yourself with more substantial Swiss favourites. Fast food outlets also abound, so you needn't starve even in this well-to-do city.

Zürich

Major Events

Sechseläuten (mid April): Zürich spring festival, with processions and the burning of the *Böögg* (mock snowman).
Techno Parade (August): annual street parade of the latest in high-tech.
TheaterSpektakel (August and September): festival of avant-garde drama.
Knabenschiessen Festival (mid September): three-day market, funfair and shooting competitions.

How to get there – and get around

By air: scheduled flights to Zürich-Kloten Airport (8 miles out) from Heathrow, Gatwick, London City, Birmingham, Edinburgh, Manchester, Newcastle and Southampton (longest journey 3 hrs). Buses (taking 20 mins) and trains (12 mins) run to the city centre (both costing CHF5.10); taxis cost CHF40.
Public Transport: Zürich has efficient trams and buses (singles cost CHF2.10; 24-hr CHF720; 72-hr CHF20). Taxis are good and reasonable.

Suggested Hotels

Dolder Grand, Kurhausstrasse.
Tel: (01) 269 30 00 Fax: (01) 269 30 01
Super-luxury hotel in a residential area close to the centre. Very expensive.
Eden du Lac, Utoquai.
Tel: (01) 266 25 25 Fax: (01) 266 25 00
Fine hotel with wonderful lake views, but just 5 mins from the centre. Expensive.
Helmhaus, Schiffländeplatz.
Tel: (01) 251 88 10 Fax: (01) 251 04 30
Charming hotel in the centre of the old town. Moderate.
Astor, Weinbergstrasse.
Tel: (01) 251 35 60 Fax: (01) 251 49 15
Comfortable hotel, close to the station. Moderate.

Suggested Restaurants

Restaurant Diff, Stampfenbachstrasse.
Tel: (01) 360 60 60
One of the Zürich Sofitel's restaurants, but now known in its own right. Expensive.
Walliser Keller, Zähringerstrasse.
Tel: (01) 269 44 44
Popular cellar restaurant specialising in fondue dishes. Moderate.
Kropf, In Gassen. Tel: (01) 221 18 05.
Long-established favourite in the city centre. Moderate.

جل جلاله

ISTANBUL

As the gateway between Europe and Asia, Istanbul occupies a remarkable position. But this frontier is not only geographic, for here the West meets the East in more ways than one: the city has been a melting pot of Christianity and Islam for centuries. The often anarchic streets and fierce traffic will not appeal to everyone, yet the city's treasures more than make up for the lack of calm.

History and Culture

Istanbul – or Byzantium as it then was – was founded by the Greeks five centuries before Christ. It reached its peak early, in the 4th century AD, when Constantine transferred the seat of the Roman Empire here from Rome. With Constantine's conversion to Christianity, the newly-renamed Constantinople, became the heart of the Christian world. The city fell to the Muslim Ottomans in 1453 and became an Islamic city. New mosques and minarets were constructed to rival the splendour of the early Christian churches. The great empire the Ottomans extended from the Danube to the Red Sea gradually crumbled away, and Constantinople's influence was diminished yet further in 1923 when it was re-dubbed Istanbul and lost the position of Turkish capital to Ankara.

The interior of the amazing Aya Sofia. The Muslims turned this Christian church into a mosque and plastered over the wonderful mosaics, but, now it has been deconsecrated as a museum, the original images are once again on show. The dome is remarkable, and was innovative in its time, stretching 106 feet across.

Sightseeing

Istanbul stands on the Bosphorus, where the Black Sea meets the Sea of Marmara, and is split in two by the Golden Horn waterway. Most sights are huddled together south of the Golden Horn. Begin with the remarkable Aya Sofya, the spiritual heart of the Christian world when constructed in the year 532. To outdo Christian Aya Sofya, the Muslims constructed the Blue Mosque in the 17th century. It takes its name from the magnificent tilework on the interior. The influence of Aya Sofya is again apparent in the Suleymaniye Mosque, whose designers used the old church as their model.

Istanbul's greatest monument is the Topkapi Palace. Once the residence of the Ottoman rulers, it is now a museum, with some stunning courtyards and a treasury displaying jewels beyond belief. Don't miss the Harem (book a tour as soon as you arrive). The sumptuous furnishings and fabulous decor reveal how richly the emperor's mother, wives and children lived.

The Archaeology Museum claims to have the tomb of Alexander the Great. But you need to be outdoors, too, exploring the Turkish streets and markets – the Grand Bazaar and the Egyptian Bazaar specialise in crafts and spices, respectively.

For the best city views, you can either take to the water or head on up. The ferries crossing the bays provide unforgettable cityscapes, particularly at dawn or dusk, showing thrusting spires, mellow domes and a jumble of other buildings new and old, while the 14th-century Galata Tower, across the ugly new Galata Bridge, has an unrivalled panorama of the city.

To freshen up, you could allow yourself to be scraped, slapped and steamed in an authentic Turkish bath, before heading out to sample the city's distinctive cuisine – kebabs, excellent fresh fish, wonderful vegetables, baklava and other pastries, and, of course, Turkish Delight, all rounded off with a strong cup of Turkish tea or gritty Turkish coffee: a fragrant yet robust combination with a powerful, lingering finish – just like Istanbul itself.

The Grand, or Covered, Bazaar in Istanbul is almost a town in itself: three miles of lanes, streets and alleyways, selling everything from gold and silver to Turkish carpets. Keep on the move if you don't want to be haggled into a purchase.

Istanbul

Major Events

International Film Festival (March–April): Turkey's own developing film industry with a sprinkling of foreign films, too.

International Theatre Festival (May): celebration of regional and national theatre.

International Arts Festival (June–July): traditional, classical and modern dance, as well as an eclectic range of music.

International Jazz Festival (July): annual gathering of jazz lovers from all over Europe and beyond.

How to get there – and get around

By air: scheduled flights to Istanbul Atatürk Airport (15 miles out) from Heathrow and Gatwick (3¼hrs). Buses take 30 minutes to get to central Istanbul (costing around TRL15,000); taxis take 25 mins (TRL45,000).

Public Transport: Istanbul has a chaotic mélange of bus, dolmus (minibus), old tram, new tram, old metro and new metro services, plus ferries criss-crossing the waterways. Taxis are less hassle and relatively cheap, but make sure the meter is started when you get in.

Suggested Hotels

Ceylan Intercontinental, Asker Ocagi Caddesi. Tel: (212) 231 21 21 Fax: (212) 231 21 80
Impressive facilities and high standards of luxury next to Taksim Park and close to the Galata Bridge. Expensive.

Swissotel, Bayildim Caddesi. Tel: (212) 259 01 01 Fax: (212) 259 01 05
Excellent hotel, close to the business and shopping districts. Expensive.

Ayasofia Pansiyonlari, Sogukcesme. Tel: (212) 513 36 60 Fax: (212) 513 36 69
Curious, yet charming, wooden structure near the Topkapi Palace. Moderate.

Suggested Restaurants

Paper Moon, Ulus Caddesi. Tel: (212) 282 16 15
Upmarket and well-respected restaurant serving international cuisine. Expensive.

Komyali, Topkapi Sarayi. Tel: (212) 526 25 27
Classic Turkish establishment in the surprisingly restaurant-free district near the main sights. Moderate.

Hanbaba, Istüklai Caddesi. Tel: (212) 244 18 86
Smart, but value-for-money restaurant in the Taksim district.

INDEX

The publishers wish to thank the following photographers, picture libraries and organisations for supplying the photographs reproduced in this book, and to whom copyright in the photograph belongs:

COLORIFIC!: pages 16, 37, 39, 43, 52, 67, 74, 143, 144, 150, 164, 250 and 222.
ETHEL DAVIES: pages 44, 83, 85, 91, 93, 95, 98, 100, 102, 104, 105, 106, 108, 110, 182, 233, 235, 237, 241 and 246.
PAUL DAWSON: page 8.
LARRY DUNMIRE: pages 125 and 127.
CHRIS FAIRCLOUGH COLOUR LIBRARY: pages 50, 60, 124, and 211.
JOHN HESELTINE: pages 3, 69, 75, 163, 166 and 169.
IMAGE SELECT INTERNATIONAL: pages 114 and 168.
INNSBRUCK TOURISM: page 15.
J ALLAN CASH: pages 64, 78, 80, 123, 139, 149, 188 and 203.
DAVID MOSSMAN: Inside back flap.
PHOTONICA: Front cover (bottom), page 4.
EDDY POSTHUMA DE BOER: pages 176, 178 and 180.
NEIL SETCHFIELD: pages 81, 119 and 219.
SPECTRUM: pages 23, 25, 29, 48, 54, 62, 66, 96, 114, 115, 117, 121, 129, 133, 135, 141, 146, 147, 155, 157, 171, 190, 192, 194, 196, 201, 204, 207, 214, 216, 217, 224, 226, 228, 229, 231, 239, 243 and 245.
SUPERSTOCK: pages 1, 18 and 70.
TELEGRAPH COLOUR LIBRARY: pages 11, 13, 27, 31, 32, 34, 41, 46, 56, 58, 59, 72, 86, 88, 90, 131, 136, 137, 152, 159, 161, 173, 184, 186, 198, 200, 209, 216, 220, 248 and front cover (middle left:J.P.Fruchet).
MARK WADLOW: page 21.